T0213625

Lecture Notes in Computer Science 9966

Commenced Publication in 1973
Founding and Former Series Editors:
Gerhard Goos, Juris Hartmanis, and Jan van Leeuwen

More information about this series at http://www.springer.com/series/7407

Guang R. Gao · Depei Qian
Xinbo Gao · Barbara Chapman
Wenguang Chen (Eds.)

Network and Parallel Computing

13th IFIP WG 10.3 International Conference, NPC 2016
Xi'an, China, October 28–29, 2016
Proceedings

 Springer

Editors
Guang R. Gao
University of Delaware
Newark, DE
USA

Depei Qian
Beihang University
Beijing
China

Xinbo Gao
Xidian University
Xi'an
China

Barbara Chapman
Stony Brook University
Stony Brook, NY
USA

Wenguang Chen
Tsinghua University
Beijing
China

ISSN 0302-9743   ISSN 1611-3349 (electronic)
Lecture Notes in Computer Science
ISBN 978-3-319-47098-6   ISBN 978-3-319-47099-3   (eBook)
DOI 10.1007/978-3-319-47099-3

Library of Congress Control Number: 2016952885

LNCS Sublibrary: SL1 – Theoretical Computer Science and General Issues

Printed on acid-free paper

This Springer imprint is published by Springer Nature
The registered company is Springer International Publishing AG
The registered company address is: Gewerbestrasse 11, 6330 Cham, Switzerland

Preface

These proceedings contain the papers presented at the 2016 IFIP International Conference on Network and Parallel Computing (NPC 2016), held in Xi'An, China, during October 28–29, 2016. The goal of the conference was to establish an international forum for engineers and scientists to present their ideas and experiences in network and parallel computing.

A total of 99 submissions were received in response to our Call for Papers. These papers originate from Australia, Asia (China, Japan), and North America (USA). Each submission was sent to at least three reviewers. Each paper was judged according to its originality, innovation, readability, and relevance to the expected audience. Based on the reviews received, a total of 19 papers were retained for inclusion in the proceedings. Among the 19 papers, 12 were accepted as full papers for presentation at the conference. We also accepted seven papers as short papers for a possible brief presentation at the conference. We accepted another ten papers for a poster session (but without proceedings). Thus, only 19 % of the total submissions could be included in the final program, and 29 % of the submitted work was proposed to be presented at the conference.

The topics tackled at this year's conference include resource management, in particular solid-state drives and other non volatile memory systems; resiliency and reliability; job and task scheduling for batch systems and big data frameworks; heterogeneous systems based on accelerators; data processing, in particular in the context of big data; and more fundamental algorithms and abstractions for parallel computing.

We wish to thank the contributions of the other members of the Organizing Committee. We thank the publicity chairs, Xiaofei Liao, Cho-Li Want, and Koji Inoue, for their hard work to publicize NPC 2016 under a very tight schedule. We are deeply grateful to the Program Committee members. The large number of submissions received and the diversified topics made this review process a particularly challenging one.

August 2016

Guang R. Gao
Depei Qian
Xinbo Gao
Barbara Chapman
Wenguang Chen

Organization

General Co-chairs

Guang Rong Gao	University of Delaware, USA
Xinbo Gao	Xidian University, China
Depei Qian	Beihang University, China

Organization Chair

Quan Wang	Xidian University, China

Program Co-chairs

Barbara Chapman	Stony Brook University, USA
Wenguang Chen	Tsinghua University, China

Publication Chair

Stephane Zuckerman	University of Delaware, USA

Local Arrangements Co-chair

Qiguang Miao	Xidian University, China

Publicity Chairs

Koji Inoue	Kyushu University, Japan
Xiaofei Liao	Huanzhong University of Science and Technology, China
Cho-Li Wang	University of Hong Kong, SAR China

Web Chair

Yining Quan	Xidian University, China

Steering Committee

Cheng Ding	University of Rochester, USA
Jack Dongarra	University of Tennessee, USA
Kemal Ebcioglu (Chair)	Global Supercomputing, USA
Guang Rong Gao	University of Delaware, USA

Jean-Luc Gaudiot	University of California, Irvine, USA
Tony Hey	Microsoft, USA
Hai Jin	Huanzhong University of Science and Technology, China
Guojie Li	Institute of Computing Technology, China
Yoichi Muraoka	Waseda University, Japan
Viktor Prasanna	University of Southern California, USA
Daniel Reed	University of Iowa, USA
Weisong Shi	Wayne State University, USA
Zhiwei Xu	Institute of Computing Technology, China

Program Committee

Abramson	University of Queensland, Australia
Hong An	University of Science and Technology of China, China
Pavan Balaji	Argonne National Lab, USA
Taisuke Boku	University of Tsukuba, Japan
Sunita Chandrasekaran	University of Delaware, USA
Barbara Chapman	Stony Brook University, USA
Wenguang Chen	Tsinghua University, China
Yurong Chen	Intel, China
Yeching Chung	National Tsinghua University, Taiwan
Yuefan Deng	Stony Brook University, USA
Zhihui Du	Tsinghua University, China
Robert Harrison	Stony Brook University, USA
Torsten Hoefler	ETH, Switzerland
Kise Kenji	Tokyo Institute of Technology, Japan
Keiji Kimura	Waseda University, Japan
Chao Li	Shanghai Jiao Tong University, China
Miron Livny	University of Wisconsin at Madison, USA
Yi Liu	Beihang University, China
Kai Lu	National University of Defense Technology, China
Yutong Lu	National University of Defense Technology, China
Yingwei Luo	Peking University, China
Xiaosong Ma	Qatar Computing Research Institute, Qatar
Philip Papadopoulos	University of California, San Diego, USA
Xuanhua Shi	Huazhong University of Science and Technology, China
Weiguo Wu	Xi'An Haotong University, China
Jingling Xue	University of New South Wales, Australia
Chao Yang	Institute of Software, Chinese Academy of Sciences, China
Jun Yao	Huawei, China
Li Zha	ICT, Chinese Academy of Sciences, China
Weihua Zhang	Fudan University, China
Yunquan Zhang	ICT, Chinese Academy of Sciences, China

Contents

Memory: Non-Volatile, Solid State Drives, Hybrid Systems

VIOS: A Variation-Aware I/O Scheduler for Flash-Based Storage Systems

Jinhua Cui[1], Weiguo Wu[1(✉)], Shiqiang Nie[1], Jianhang Huang[1], Zhuang Hu[1], Nianjun Zou[1], and Yinfeng Wang[2]

[1] School of Electronic and Information Engineering,
Xi'an Jiaotong University, Shaanxi 710049, China
cjhnicole@gmail.com, wgwu@xjtu.edu.cn
[2] Department of Software Engineering,
ShenZhen Institute of Information Technology, Guangdong 518172, China

Abstract. NAND flash memory has gained widespread acceptance in storage systems because of its superior write/read performance, shock-resistance and low-power consumption. I/O scheduling for Solid State Drives (SSDs) has received much attention in recent years for its ability to take advantage of the rich parallelism within SSDs. However, most state-of-the-art I/O scheduling algorithms are oblivious to the increasingly significant inter-block variation introduced by the advanced technology scaling. This paper proposes a variation-aware I/O scheduler by exploiting the speed variation among blocks to minimize the access conflict latency of I/O requests. The proposed VIOS schedules I/O requests into a hierarchical-batch structured queue to preferentially exploit channel-level parallelism, followed by chip-level parallelism. Moreover, conflict write requests are allocated to faster blocks to reduce access conflict of waiting requests. Experimental results shows that VIOS reduces write latency significantly compared to state-of-the-art I/O schedulers while attaining high read efficiency.

Keywords: Process variation · Solid state drive · I/O scheduling · Flash memory · Parallelism

1   Introduction

As NAND flash storage capacity becomes cheaper, NAND flash-based SSDs are being regarded as powerful alternatives to traditional Hard Disk Drives (HDDs) in a wide variety of storage systems [1]. However, SSDs introduce an out-of-place update mechanism and exhibit asymmetric I/O properties. In addition, a typical SSD usually offers rich parallelism by consisting of a number of channels with each channel connecting to multiple NAND flash chips [2,3]. Most of conventional I/O schedulers including NOOP, CFQ and Anticipatory are designed to mitigate the high seek and rotational costs in mechanical disks, leading to many barriers to take full advantage of SSDs. Thus, I/O scheduling for SSDs has received much

© IFIP International Federation for Information Processing 2016
Published by Springer International Publishing AG 2016. All Rights Reserved
G.R. Gao et al. (Eds.): NPC 2016, LNCS 9966, pp. 3–16, 2016.
DOI: 10.1007/978-3-319-47099-3_1

attention for its ability to take advantage of the unique properties within SSDs to maximize read and write performance.

Most of existing I/O scheduling algorithms for SSDs, such as PAQ [4], PIQ [5] and AOS [6], focus on avoiding resource contention resultant from shared SSD resources, while others take special consideration of Flash-Translation-Layer (FTL) [7] and garbage collection [8]. These works have demonstrated the importance of I/O scheduling for SSDs to reduce the number of read and write requests enrolled in conflict, which are the major contributors to access latency. However, little attention has been paid to dynamically optimize the data transfer latency, which could naturally reduce the access conflict latency when conflicts are unavoidable anymore.

The capacity of NAND flash memory is increasing continuously, as a result of technology scaling from 65 nm to the latest 10 nm technology and the bit density improvement from 1 bit per cell to the latest 6 bits per cell [9,10,20]. Unfortunately, for newer technology nodes, the memory block P/E cycling endurance has significantly dropped and process variation has become relatively much more significant. Recently many works have been proposed to exploit the process variation from different perspectives. Pan et al. [11] presented a dynamic BER-based greedy wear-leveling algorithm that uses BER statistics as the measurement of memory block wear-out pace by taking into account of inter-block P/E cycling endurance variation. Woo et al. [12] introduced a new measure that predicts the remaining lifetime of a flash block more accurately than the erase count based on the findings that all the flash blocks could survive much longer than the guaranteed numbers and the number of P/E cycles varies significantly among blocks. Shi et al. [13] further exploited the process variation by detecting supported write speeds during the lifetime of each flash block and allocating blocks in a way that hotter data are matched with faster blocks, but they did not reorder the requests in the I/O scheduling layer. Therefore, none of these works focuses on incorporating the awareness of inter-block variation into I/O scheduling to minimize the access conflict latency of I/O requests.

This paper proposes a variation-aware I/O scheduler to exploit the speed variation among blocks for write performance improvement without degrading read performance. The key insight behind the design of VIOS is that a variation-aware scheduler can organize the blocks of each chip in a red-black tree according to their detected write speeds and maintain a global chip-state vector, where the current number of requests for each chip is recorded, so as to identify conflict requests. By scheduling arrived requests into hierarchical-batch structured queues to give channel-level parallelism a higher priority than chip-level parallelism and allocating conflict write requests to faster blocks to exploit inter-block speed variation, access conflict latency of waiting requests is reduced significantly. Trace-based simulations are carried out to demonstrate the effectiveness of the proposed variation-aware I/O scheduling algorithm.

The rest of the paper presents the background and related works in Sect. 2. Section 3 describes the design techniques and implementation issues of our VIOS for flash storage devices. In Sect. 4, experimental evaluation and comparison with several alternative I/O schedulers are illustrated. Section 5 concludes this paper.

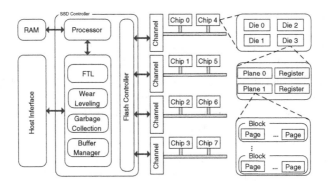

Fig. 1. SSD hardware diagram

2   Background and Related Work

2.1   SSD Organization

Flash memory chips are organized in channels and ways, as shown in Fig. 1. Within each flash memory chip are one or more dies, each further consisting of multiple planes, which are the smallest unit to be accessed independently and concurrently. Each plane is composed of a number of erase units, called blocks, and a block is usually comprised of multiple pages, which are the smallest unit to read/write. There are four main levels of parallelism which can be exploited to accelerate the read/write bandwidth of SSDs. Actually, the importance of exploiting parallelism on read/write performance improvement has been testified by numerous research works from different perspectives. For example, Roh et al. [14] explored to enhance B+-tree's insert and point-search performance by integrating a new I/O request concept (psync I/O) into the B+-tree which can exploit the internal parallelism of SSDs in a single process, Hu et al. [2] argued that the utilization of parallelism, primarily determined by different advanced commands, allocation schemes, and the priority order of exploiting the four levels of parallelism, will directly and significantly impact the performance and endurance of SSDs.

Since the advance command support required by the die and plane level parallelism is not widely supported by most of SSDs, the degree of parallelism is usually governed by the number of channels multiplied by the number of flash memory chips in a channel, without taking the die and plane level parallelism into consideration. In this paper, our VIOS also exploit both channel-level parallelism and chip-level parallelism by scheduling arrived requests into hierarchical-batch structured queues.

2.2   Process Variation of Flash Memory

Along with the bit density developments and technology scaling of NAND flash memory, the aggravating process variation (PV) among blocks has been magnified, which results in largely different P/E cycling endurance within different memory blocks when given the same ECC. PV is caused by the naturally occurring variation in the attributes of transistors, such as gate length, width and oxide thickness, when integrated circuits are fabricated. The distribution of the Bit Error Rates (BER) of flash blocks is characterized as the log Gaussian distribution by measuring 1000 blocks of a MLC NAND Flash memory chip manufactured in 35-nm technology at the same 15K P/E cycles [11].

Besides, there is a close relationship between BER and the speed of write operations. Typically, when program operations are carried out to write data into flash memory cells, the incremental step pulse programming (ISPP) scheme is introduced to appropriately optimize program voltage with the certain step size ΔV_p that triggers a trade-off between write speed and BER. Using larger ΔV_p, fewer steps are used to the desired level, thus the write latency is shorter. As the promising effect of reducing the write latency of write requests, however, the margin for tolerating retention errors is also reduced, resulting in higher BER. Therefore, with the awareness of both process variation and the BER-speed relationship, write speed for lower-BER blocks can be increased at the cost of reduced noise margins, while that for higher-BER blocks should be carefully optimized without exceeding the capability of the deployed ECC. The challenge to detect the proper write speed for each block at its current worn out state is also solved by periodically reading out the written data to find out the number of faulty bits, and the analysis indicates that overhead is negligible [13]. In this paper, the blocks of each chip are sorted according to their detected write speeds and conflict write requests are allocated to faster blocks to reduce access conflict of waiting requests.

2.3 I/O Scheduler for Flash-Based SSDs

An increasing number of I/O scheduling algorithms have been proposed to improve flash memory storage system performance from different perspectives. The first two algorithms for Flash-Based SSDs called IRBW-FIFO and IRBW-FIFO-RP were designed by Kim et al. [15]. The basic idea is to arrange write requests into bundles of an appropriate size while read requests are independently scheduled by taking the read/write interference into consideration. Numerous research works enhanced the IRBW-FIFO and IRBW-FIFO-RP by exploiting rich parallelism in I/O scheduling, such as PAQ [4] and PIQ [5]. In addition, there is also recognition on the importance of fairness in multi-programmed computer systems and multi-tenant cloud systems, such as FIOS [16] and FlashFQ [17].

However, little attention has been paid to optimize the data transfer latency dynamically, which could naturally reduce the access conflict latency when conflicts can not be avoided anymore. Our VIOS focuses on incorporating the awareness of inter-block variation into I/O scheduling to minimize the access conflict latency of I/O requests. Fortunately, all these existing algorithms are somewhat orthogonal to our work, and can be used concurrently with the proposed VIOS to optimize the efficiency of flash-based I/O scheduling.

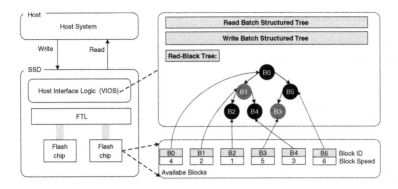

Fig. 2. Organizational view of the VIOS scheduler

3   Details of VIOS

Motivated by the increasingly significant inter-block variation introduced by the advanced technology scaling, a variation-aware I/O scheduler is proposed to minimize the access conflict latency of I/O requests. The proposed VIOS scheduler is implemented in the host interface logic (HIL), where the knowledge of both the interface protocols and SSD specific characteristics contributes to better device-specific scheduling decisions for I/O requests. The main idea behind the design of VIOS is to allocate conflict write requests to faster blocks so as to reduce access conflict latency of waiting requests. To achieve this, our scheduler organizes the blocks of each chip in a red-black tree according to their detected write speeds and maintains a global chip-state vector, where the current number of requests for each chip is recorded, so as to identify conflict requests.

3.1   Block Management

After detecting the proper write speed for each block at its current worn out state by periodically reading out the written data to find out the number of faulty bits, it is important to manage blocks with different write speeds for VIOS to easily schedule requests to appropriate blocks. In VIOS, the red-black tree structure is adopted as the main data structure to sort its blocks in detected speed order. Since the advance command support required by the die and plane level parallelism is not widely supported by most of SSDs and the relatively higher chip-level conflicts are the major contributors to access latency, the blocks of each chip are associated with a red-black tree respectively. Figure 2 shows the main data structures associated with VIOS. Once all the pages of a block have been programmed, it will be set as an invalid node in the red-black tree. When the prepared empty blocks are used up, a time-consuming task called Garbage Collection (GC) is triggered to reclaim stale pages for free write space and then the states of erased blocks become valid again. The blocks are evicted and inserted into another place of the red-black tree only when the write speed detection process is triggered and its ΔV_p is decreased, corresponding to reduced write speed.

3.2   Global Chip-State Vector

To build a scheduling algorithm that can identify conflicts and exploit the speed variation based on the degree of conflicts, we propose a global chip-state vector to track the current number of requests for each chip. The global chip-state vector mainly depends on the location of data, which is determined by different data allocation schemes and the logical sector number (LSN) of I/O requests. Let's take an SSD where the number of chips is *ChipNum* and the size of each page is *PageSize* as an example. For a given static allocation scheme where the priority order of parallelism is channel-level parallelism first, followed by the chip-level parallelism [18], the assemblage of chips accessed by request r can be defined as:

$$A_r = \left\{ \mu | \mu = \left(\frac{(lsn(r) + \lambda) * SectorSize}{PageSize} \right) \% ChipNum \right\}$$
$$where \quad 0 \le \lambda < len(r) \tag{1}$$

where *lsn(r)* and *len(r)* are the accessed logical sector number and data size in sectors of request r respectively, while *SectorSize* is the sector size in bytes. For a global chip-state vector defined as $(NR_0, NR_1, \ldots, NR_i)$ where NR_i is the current number of requests for chip i, when pushing arrived requests into the queue or issuing chosen requests to SSDs, the NR of each chip accessed by requests is updated as follows:

$$NR_i = \begin{cases} NR_i + 1 & arriving \\ NR_i - 1 & issued \end{cases}, i \in A_r \tag{2}$$

3.3   Conflict Optimized Scheduling Mechanism

Next, we propose the conflict optimized scheduling technique, which aims to reduce access conflict latency by exploiting the rich parallelism within SSDs and the speed variation among blocks. It consists of two components: (1) a hierarchical-batch structured queue to avoid conflicts from chip to channel. (2) A variation-aware block allocation technique that assigns conflict write requests to faster blocks to reduce access conflict of waiting requests.

Hierarchical-Batch Structured Queue. Since there are four main levels of parallelism which can be exploited to accelerate the read/write bandwidth of SSDs, the conflicts can also be classified into four types based on the physical resources contended by arrived requests. Among them, channel conflicts and chip conflicts are taken into account for the reason that the advance command support required by the die and plane level parallelism is not widely supported by most of SSDs. In the hierarchical-batch structured queue, the requests are grouped into batches from bottom up based on the chip-level and channel-level conflict detection respectively. Requests in the same chip batch can be serviced in chip-level parallel, while requests belong to the same channel batch can be executed in completely independent channel-level parallel. Each chip batch and channel batch use A_{chip} and $A_{channel}$ respectively to track the assemblage of chips and

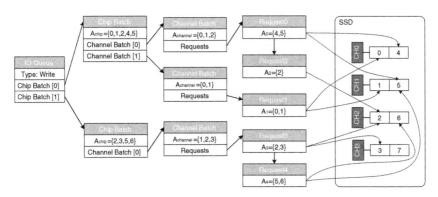

Fig. 3. An example that shows VIOS conflict reduction with the hierarchical-batch structured queue

channels accessed by all its requests. Each time when a new request r arrives, the detection of chip-level conflicts is enabled by repeated intersection operations of A_{chip} with A_r, whose resulting assemblage of conflict chips ($A_{conflict}$) can be modeled as:

$$A_{conflict} = A_{chip} \cap A_r \qquad (3)$$

Once a chip batch that has no conflict with r is found, which means $A_{conflict}$ is empty, the request is added to the chip batch and A_{chip} is updated. Otherwise, a new chip batch is created for the new request. After that, the detection of channel-level conflicts is performed in the same manner to further exploit channel-level parallelism of requests within the same chip batch. For example, after scheduling the first five requests into the hierarchical-batch structured queue shown in Fig. 3, if one more request accessing chips {6, 7} arrives, it is found that there is no chip-level conflict between the new request and the first chip batch, where the new request is thus added and A_{chip} is updated to {0, 1, 2, 4, 5, 6, 7}. Then each channel batch of the first chip batch is checked and the second channel batch where the new request has no channel-level conflict is chosen with $A_{channel}$ being updated to {0, 1, 2, 3}.

Variation-Aware Block Allocation. Motivated by the findings that speed variation among blocks can be easily detected, we propose a variation-aware block allocation algorithm to optimize the data transfer latency dynamically, which could naturally reduce the access conflict latency when conflicts cannot be avoided anymore. Each time when a request is issued, the NR of each chip accessed by the request is checked and then updated. Since a request processing may access multiple chips in NAND flash memory, we scatter the request into separate sub-requests. Each sub-request is only able to gain access to one chip. The sub-request accessing the chip whose NR is more than 1 will be allocated to a faster block from the red-black tree of the chip. Otherwise, a slower block is chosen for the sub-request. Figure 4 shows the process of scheduling three

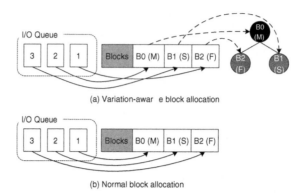

Fig. 4. Block allocation process. Program speed represented by Slow (S), Medium (M) and Fast (F).

conflict sub-requests when only three pages in three blocks with different speeds are empty. As Fig. 4(a) shows, the variation-aware block allocation algorithm assigns the first two sub-requests to currently faster blocks for the reason that one or more sub-requests are still waiting in the queue. The last sub-request is allocated to a slower block because no conflict sub-request is waiting at this moment. Assuming that the write latency of fast, medium and slow blocks are $150\,\mu s$, $180\,\mu s$, and $210\,\mu s$ respectively, the average request response time of the proposed algorithm is $(150 + 330 + 540)/3 = 340\,\mu s$, while that of the normal algorithm (Fig. 4(b)) which distributes blocks in order is $(180 + 390 + 540)/3 = 370\,\mu s$. Therefore, by incorporating the awareness of inter-block variation into I/O scheduling, the access conflict latency of I/O requests is reduced significantly.

Overhead Analysis. The overheads of the proposed I/O scheduler are analyzed as follows. According to the detailed descriptions of components above, the implementation of VIOS needs to maintain hierarchical-batch structured queues in the I/O queue. Since the number of channels and chips in NAND flash memory is limited, all sets can be stored as binary words and the set-intersection/set-union operation can be performed as an O(1)-time bitwise-AND/OR operation. This storage overhead is negligible for an I/O queue. Furthermore, the complexity of adding an incoming I/O request into the hierarchical-batch structured queues is proportional to the sum of the number of chip batches and the number of channel batches, and it is less than the queue length of I/O scheduler, which also has negligible cost.

4   Experimental Results

To evaluate our proposed variation-aware I/O scheduler, we perform a series of trace driven simulations and analysis. We implement VIOS as well as baseline NOOP scheduling and state-of-the-art PIQ scheduling within an event-driven simulator named as SSDSim [18], which provides the detailed and accurate simulation of each level of parallelism. Note that write speed detection technique is implemented with all of the schedulers. We simulate a 128 GB SSD with 8 channels, each of which is connected to 8 chips. For the flash micro-architecture configuration, each flash chip employs 2 dies, where each die contains 4 planes and each plane consists of 2048 blocks. Each flash block contains 64 pages with a page size of 2 KB. All these settings are consistent with previous works [5]. Page mapping FTL is configured to maintain a full map of logical pages to physical ones and greedy garbage collection scheme is implemented.

The BER growth rate that follows Bounded Gaussian distribution is used to simulate the process variation of flash memory, where the mean μ and the standard deviation σ are set as 3.7×10^{-4} and 9×10^{-5} respectively [11]. The maximal possible write step size is set to 0.6 and the step of decreasing ΔV_p is set to 0.03. We use 600 μs as the 2 bit/cell NAND flash memory program latency when ΔV_p is 0.3, 20 μs as memory sensing latency and 1.5 ms as erase time. Four different wear-out stages corresponding to 15K, 12K, 9K and 6K P/E cycles are evaluated. We evaluate our design using real world workloads from MSR Cambridge traces [19] and the write-dominated Financial1 trace [20], where 500000 I/Os of each trace are used in accordance with previous work.

4.1   Performance Analysis of VIOS

Our experiments evaluate scheduling performance with read and write latency. Figure 5 shows the average read latency for NOOP, PIQ and VIOS tested under the P/E cycling of 12K. As can be observed, VIOS improves the average read latency by about 17.66 % compared to NOOP, indicating that the hierarchical-batch structured read queue helps VIOS exploit multilevel parallelism inside SSDs by resolving resource conflicts. However, the improvements in average read latency brought by VIOS are not significantly higher than those obtained when using PIQ. This is because the variation-aware block allocation technique of VIOS mainly serves write request, and read requests are always preferentially scheduled in both PIQ and VIOS without being affected by write performance improvement.

Figure 6 plots the simulation results on average write latency when different scheduling algorithms are used in the variation-induced SSDs. To facilitate the comparison, the average write latency is normalized against the case of using NOOP algorithm. The first thing to observe is that VIOS outperforms NOOP and PIQ with write latency reduction by 22.93 % and by 7.71 % on average, respectively. This is because both the hierarchical-batch structured write queue and the variation-aware block allocation algorithm reduce access conflict of write requests. However, the write performance improvements under different traces vary greatly. For example, compared to PIQ, the greatest improvement made in the *src* trace is 17.17 %, but the slightest improvement made in the *mds* trace is only 2.73 %. This is due to the different percentages of requests enrolled in conflict – VIOS works for I/O intensive applications where more requests can be processed in parallel and optimized. Table 1 shows the percentages of conflicts

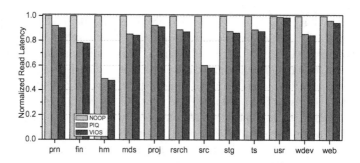

Fig. 5. Average read latencies for three different types of schedulers (normalized to the NOOP scheduler)

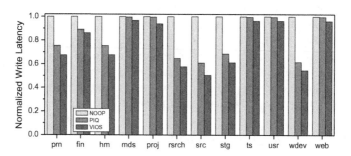

Fig. 6. Average write latencies for three different types of schedulers (normalized to the NOOP scheduler)

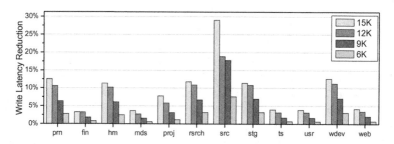

Fig. 7. A comparison of the write latency reduction relative to PIQ among four different wear-out stages

collected under the P/E cycling of 12K with NOOP scheduler. One can also observe that the percentage of conflicts in *src* is 77.74 %, which has an impact on improving efficiency of VIOS. In contrast, that of *mds* is 4.70 %, indicating that fewer conflicts lead to slighter write performance improvement.

Figure 7 gives a comparison of the write latency reduction relative to PIQ among four different wear-out stages. One can observe from these results that the write latency reduction is positive all the time, which means VIOS always outperforms PIQ under four different wear-out stages. Furthermore, VIOS improves

Table 1. Characteristics of used workloads

Traces	Read I/O	Write I/O	ReadConflicts	WriteConflicts	ConflictsRatio
prn	61422	438578	37678	261787	59.89
fin	129342	370658	12135	129379	28.30
hm	139527	360473	54387	168864	44.65
mds	26301	473699	10947	12570	4.70
proj	151549	348451	38615	32852	14.29
rsrch	43803	456197	19413	217828	47.45
src	81377	418623	28146	360549	77.74
stg	43818	456182	21657	210355	46.40
ts	76687	423313	27566	7161	6.95
usr	206983	293017	91391	9068	20.09
wdev	102663	397337	48986	170202	43.84
web	239458	260542	89753	19184	21.79

write performance by 2.25 %, 5.25 %, 7.71 % and 9.63 % on average under the
P/E cycling of 6K, 9K, 12K and 15K respectively. As can be observed, with the
increased number of P/E cycling, the write performance improvement brought
by VIOS gets greater. This is a very reasonable result since BER spread grows
as flash memory cells gradually wear out with the P/E cycling, corresponding
to more significant variation among blocks, which improves the efficiency of the
variation-aware block allocation strategy in VIOS. Overall, these results clearly
demonstrate the effectiveness of VIOS in reducing the write latency during the
entire flash memory lifetime.

4.2 Sensitivity Analysis of VIOS

To measure the sensitivity of VIOS to the I/O intensity, we repeated our experiments by varying the number of chips and the baseline program latency. Either
fewer chips or slower program speeds increase the probability of access conflict.
Figure 8 plots the normalized average write latency for each trace under 64,
56, 48, 40 and 32 chips when using VIOS. From the plots, it can be seen that
the write latency increases as the number of chips decreases. For most traces,
varying the number of chips from 64 to 32 increases the write latency by less
than 25 %. However, for traces src and wdev, the increase in write latency is
59.48 % and 36.09 % respectively. By comparing the results with the percentages of write conflicts shown in Table 1, it can be observed that the increment
in average write latency is greater when the number of write conflicts is larger.
For example, the write latency of src that has most write conflicts (360549) is
increased with maximum rate (59.48 %), while these of mds, ts and usr which
have fewer write conflicts (12570, 7161 and 9068) are increased with minimum rate (6.05 %, 5.29 % and 4.91 %). On one hand, the number of conflicts is

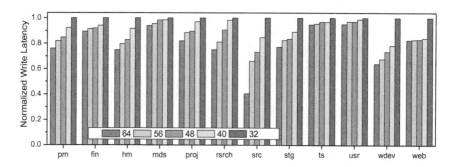

Fig. 8. Average write latencies for five different numbers of chips when using VIOS (normalized to 32 chips)

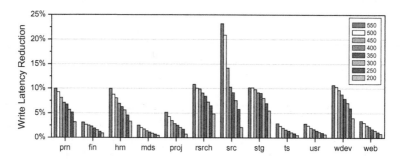

Fig. 9. A comparison of the write latency reduction relative to PIQ among eight different baseline program latencies

proportional to the quotient of access density and the number of chips, which means that more conflicts occur when reducing chips for traces with more intensive I/O. On the other hand, the average write latency is proportional to the square of the number of write conflicts, amplifying the effect of each new conflict.

Figure 9 plots the impact of the baseline program latency on the write latency reduction relative to PIQ. The x-axis is the baseline program latency for $\Delta V_p = 0.3$, varying from $200\,\mu s$ to $550\,\mu s$. The number of conflict requests increases as the program latency is delayed, thus improving the benefit from hierarchical-batch structured queues and variation-aware block allocation technique. However, the effect of program latency delay is greater than that of reduction in the number of chips. For example, from $200\,\mu s$ to $550\,\mu s$, the write latency reduction for *rsrch* varies from $4.83\,\%$ to $10.85\,\%$, compared to a slighter variation from $10.92\,\%$ to $13.63\,\%$ as the number of chips varies from 64 to 32. The major reason is that delaying program latency not only increases the number of conflict requests, but also amplifies the access conflict latency, which is the dominant factor for slow write operations.

5   Conclusion

In this paper, we propose a variation-aware I/O scheduler (VIOS) for NAND flash-based storage systems. The process variation is exploited to reduce the access conflict latency of SSDs when conflicts are unavoidable anymore. VIOS organizes the blocks of each chip in a red-black tree according to their detected write speeds and allocate conflict write requests to faster blocks to exploit inter-block speed variation. In addition, the hierarchical-batch structured queue that focuses on the exploration of the parallelism of SSDs is presented. Furthermore, with diverse system configurations such as wear-out stages, the number of chips and the baseline program latency, VIOS reduces write latency significantly compared to the state-of-the-art NOOP and PIQ while attaining high read efficiency.

Acknowledgment. The authors would like to thank the anonymous reviewers for their detailed and thoughtful feedback which improved the quality of this paper significantly. This work was supported in part by the National Natural Science Foundation of China under grant No. 91330117, the National High-tech R&D Program of China (863 Program) under grant No. 2014AA01A302, the Shaanxi Social Development of Science and Technology Research Project under grant No. 2016SF-428, the Shenzhen Scientific Plan under grant No. JCYJ20130401095947230 and No. JSGG20140519141854753.

References

1. Min, C., Kim, K., Cho, H., Lee, S.W., Eom, Y.I.: SFS: random write considered harmful in solid state drives. In: USENIX Conference on File and Storage Technologies, p. 12, February 2012
2. Hu, Y., Jiang, H., Feng, D., Tian, L., Luo, H., Ren, C.: Exploring and exploiting the multilevel parallelism inside SSDs for improved performance and endurance. IEEE Trans. Comput. **62**(6), 1141–1155 (2013)
3. Chen, F., Lee, R., Zhang, X.: Essential roles of exploiting internal parallelism of flash memory based solid state drives in high-speed data processing. In: IEEE 17th International Symposium on High Performance Computer Architecture, pp. 266–277, February 2011
4. Jung, M., Wilson III, E.H., Kandemir, M.: Physically addressed queueing (PAQ): improving parallelism in solid state disks. ACM SIGARCH Comput. Architect. News **40**(3), 404–415 (2012)
5. Gao, C., Shi, L., Zhao, M., Xue, C.J., Wu, K., Sha, E.H.: Exploiting parallelism in i/o scheduling for access conflict minimization in flash-based solid state drives. In: 30th Symposium on Mass Storage Systems and Technologies, pp. 1–11, June 2014
6. Li, P., Wu, F., Zhou, Y., Xie, C., Yu, J.: AOS: adaptive out-of-order scheduling for write-caused interference reduction in solid state disks. In: Proceedings of the International MultiConference of Engineers and Computer Scientists, vol. 1 (2015)
7. Wang, M., Hu, Y.: An I/O scheduler based on fine-grained access patterns to improve SSD performance and lifespan. In: Proceedings of the 29th Annual ACM Symposium on Applied Computing, pp. 1511–1516, March 2014
8. Jung, M., Choi, W., Srikantaiah, S., Yoo, J., Kandemir, M.T.: HIOS: a host interface I/O scheduler for solid state disks. ACM SIGARCH Comput. Architect. News **42**, 289–300 (2014)

9. Ho, K.C., Fang, P.C., Li, H.P., Wang, C.Y.M., Chang, H.C.: A 45 nm 6b/cell charge-trapping flash memory using LDPC-based ECC and drift-immune soft-sensing engine. In: IEEE International Solid-State Circuits Conference Digest of Technical Papers, pp. 222–223, February 2013

10. Zuloaga, S., Liu, R., Chen, P.Y., Yu, S.: Scaling 2-layer RRAM cross-point array towards 10 nm node: a device-circuit co-design. In: IEEE International Symposium on Circuits and Systems, pp. 193–196, May 2015

11. Pan, Y., Dong, G., Zhang, T.: Error rate-based wear-leveling for NAND flash memory at highly scaled technology nodes. IEEE Trans. Very Large Scale Integration (VLSI) Syst. **21**(7), 1350–1354 (2013)

12. Woo, Y.J., Kim, J.S.: Diversifying wear index for MLC NAND flash memory to extend the lifetime of SSDs. In: Proceedings of the Eleventh ACM International Conference on Embedded Software, p. 6, September 2013

13. Shi, L.H., Di, Y., Zhao, M., Xue, C.J., Wu, K., Sha, E.H.M.: Exploiting process variation for write performance improvement on NAND flash memory storage systems. IEEE Trans. Very Large Scale Integr. (VLSI) Syst. **99**, 1–4 (2015)

14. Roh, H., Park, S., Kim, S., Shin, M., Lee, S.W.: B+-tree index optimization by exploiting internal parallelism of flash-based solid state drives. In: Proceedings of the VLDB Endowment, pp. 286–297 (2011)

15. Kim, J., Oh, Y., Kim, E., Choi, J., Lee, D., Noh, S.H.: Disk schedulers for solid state drivers. In: Proceedings of the Seventh ACM International Conference on Embedded Software, pp. 295–304, October 2009

16. Park, S., Shen, K.: FIOS: a fair, efficient flash I/O scheduler. In: USENIX Conference on File and Storage Technologies, p. 13, February 2012

17. Shen, K., Park, S.: FlashFQ: a fair queueing I/O scheduler for flash-based SSDs. In: USENIX Annual Technical Conference, pp. 67–78, June 2013

18. Hu, Y., Jiang, H., Feng, D., Tian, L., Luo, H., Zhang, S.: Performance impact and interplay of SSD parallelism through advanced commands, allocation strategy and data granularity. In: Proceedings of the International Conference on Supercomputing, pp. 96–107, May 2011

19. Narayanan, D., Thereska, E., Donnelly, A., Elnikety, S., Rowstron, A.: Migrating server storage to SSDs: analysis of tradeoffs. In: The European Conference on Computer Systems, pp. 145–158, April 2009

20. UMass Trace Repository. http://traces.cs.umass.edu

21. Cui, J., Wu, W., Zhang, X., Huang, J., Wang, Y.: Exploiting process variation for read and write performance improvement of flash memory. In: 32th International Conference on Massive Storage Systems and Technology, May 2016

Exploiting Cross-Layer Hotness Identification to Improve Flash Memory System Performance

Jinhua Cui[1], Weiguo Wu[1]([✉]), Shiqiang Nie[1], Jianhang Huang[1], Zhuang Hu[1],
Nianjun Zou[1], and Yinfeng Wang[2]

[1] School of Electronic and Information Engineering,
Xi'an Jiaotong University, Shaanxi 710049, China
cjhnicole@gmail.com, wgwu@xjtu.edu.cn
[2] Department of Software Engineering,
ShenZhen Institute of Information Technology, Guangdong 518172, China

Abstract. Flash memory has been widely deployed in modern storage systems. However, the density improvement and technology scaling would decrease its endurance and I/O performance, which motivates the search to improve flash performance and reduce cell wearing. Wearing reduction can be achieved by lowering the threshold voltages, but at the cost of slower reads. In this paper, the access hotness characteristics are exploited for read performance and endurance improvement. First, with the understanding of the reliability characteristics of flash memory, the relationship among flash cell wearing, read latency and bit error rate is introduced. Then, based on the hotness information provided by buffer management, the threshold voltages of a cell for *write-hot* data are decreased for wearing reduction, while these for *read-hot* data are increased for read latency reduction. We demonstrate analytically through simulation that the proposed technique achieves significant endurance and read performance improvements without sacrificing the write throughput performance.

Keywords: NAND flash memory · Endurance · Raw bit error rate · Threshold voltage · Cross-layer

1 Introduction

In recent years, storage devices equipped with NAND flash memory have become widely used for a multitude of applications. Due to its high density, low power consumption, excellent IOPs performance, shock-resistance and noiselessness, NAND flash-based solid state drive (SSD) is considered as an alternative to hard disk drive (HDD) as the second storage device [1]. With semiconductor process technology scaling and cell density improvement, the capacity of NAND flash memory has been increasing continuously and the price keeps dropping. However, technology scaling inevitably brings the continuous degradation of flash memory endurance and I/O performance, which motivates the search for methods to improve flash memory performance and lifetime [2,3].

© IFIP International Federation for Information Processing 2016
Published by Springer International Publishing AG 2016. All Rights Reserved
G.R. Gao et al. (Eds.): NPC 2016, LNCS 9966, pp. 17–28, 2016.
DOI: 10.1007/978-3-319-47099-3_2

Flash lifetime, measured as the number of erasures a block can endure, is highly correlated with the raw bit error rate (RBER), which is defined as the number of corrupted bits per number of total bits read [4]. As the endurance of flash cells is limited, RBER is expected to grow with the number of program/erase (P/E) cycles, and a page is deemed to reach its lifetime if the combined errors are not correctable by error correction code (ECC). Many methods have been proposed to maximize the number of P/E cycles in flash memory. They include enhancing the error correction capability of ECC [5–7], distributing erasure costs evenly across the drives blocks [8–10], and reducing the threshold voltages for less wearing incurred by each P/E cycling [11–13].

Flash read latency is also highly correlated with RBER. The higher the RBER, the stronger the required ECC capability, as well as the higher the complexity of ECC scheme and the slower the read speed. Recently, several works have been proposed to reduce read latency by regulating the memory sensing precision. Zhao et al. [5] proposed the progressive soft-decision sensing strategy, which uses just-enough sensing precision for ECC decoding through a trial-and-error manner, to obviate unnecessary extra sensing latency. Cui et al. [3] sorted the read requests according to the retention age of the data, and performed fast read for data with low retention ages by decreasing the number of sensing levels.

In this paper, the relationship among flash cell wearing, read latency and RBER is introduced. On one hand, flash cell wearing is reduced by lowering the threshold voltages but at the cost of less noise margins between the states of a flash cell, which in turn increase RBER and delay read operations. On the other hand, read latency can be decreased by improving the threshold voltages for lower RBER, which, however, results in more cell wearing. Based on the above relationship, we propose a comprehensive approach (HIRE) to exploit the access hotness information for improving read performance and endurance of flash memory storage systems. The basic idea is that we design a cross-layer hotness identifier in the buffer replacement management model of NAND flash memory, hence data pages in the buffer list can be classified into the following three groups, namely *read-hot*, *write-hot* and *mixed-hot*, respectively. Moreover, the fine-grained voltage controller is designed to supervise and control the appropriate threshold voltages of flash cells. In particular, the threshold voltages of a cell for *write-hot* data are decreased for wearing reduction, while these for *read-hot* data are increased for read latency reduction.

Trace-based simulations are carried out to demonstrate the effectiveness of our proposed approach. The results show that the proposed HIRE approach reduces the read response time by up to 43.49 % on average and decreases the wearing of flash memory by up to 16.87 % on average. In addition, HIRE does not have a negative write performance effect. Besides, the overhead of the proposed technique is negligible. In summary, this paper makes the following contributions.

- We proposed a cross-layer hotness identifier in the buffer replacement management model of NAND flash memory to guide flash read performance and endurance improvement.

- We proposed a voltage controller in the flash controller to improve flash-based system performance metrics with the guidance of the proposed hotness identifier, which manages the appropriate threshold voltages for three types of data (*read-hot*, *write-hot*, *mixed-hot*) evicted by the buffer replacement algorithm.
- We carried out comprehensive experiments to demonstrate its effectiveness on both the wearing and read latency reduction without sacrificing write performance.

The rest of this paper is organized as follows. Section 2 presents the background and related work. Section 3 describes the design techniques and implementation issues of our hotness-guided access management for flash storage devices. Experiments and result analysis are presented in Sect. 4. Section 5 concludes this paper with a summary of our findings.

2 Background and Related Work

In this section, we first present the tradeoff between flash cell wearing and read latency, which is due to two relationships. The first one is the relationship between threshold voltage, wearing and RBER. The second one is the relationship between error correction capability, read latency and the number of sensing levels when adopting LDPC as the default ECC scheme, which brings superior error correction capability as well as read response time degradation at the same time. Finally, previous studies related to this work are introduced for further work in this area.

2.1 Tradeoff Between Flash Cell Wearing and Read Latency

Firstly, the tradeoff between flash cell wearing and read latency is due to the relationship between threshold voltage, wearing and RBER. A flash chip is built from floating-gate cells whose state depends on the amount of charge they retain. Multi-level cell (MLC) flash memory uses cells with 4 or 8 states (2 or 3 bits per cell, respectively), as opposed to single-level cell (SLC) flash memory, which has 2 states (1 bit per cell). Every state is characterized by a threshold voltage (V_{th}), which can be changed by injecting different amounts of charge onto the floating-gate. Recently, several works have showed that flash cell wearing is proportional to the threshold voltages [11,12,14]. The stress-induced damage in the tunnel oxide of a NAND flash memory cell can be reduced by decreasing the threshold voltages, and vice versa. Besides, the threshold voltages affect RBER significantly. When the threshold voltages are decreased, the noise margins among flash cell states are reduced, which reduces the capability for tolerating retention errors and increases RBER. Therefore, the tradeoff between wearing and RBER can be explored by controlling the threshold voltages with a wide range of settings. The less threshold voltages of a flash state, the less flash cell wearing, meanwhile, the higher RBER.

Fig. 1. Relationship between flash cell wearing and read latency.

Secondly, the tradeoff is due to the significant relationship between error correction capability, read latency and the number of sensing levels when adopting LDPC scheme. The flash controller reads data from each cell by recursively applying several read reference voltages to the cell in a level-by-level manner to identify its threshold voltage. Therefore, sensing latency is linearly proportional to the number of sensing levels. In addition, when N sensing levels quantize the threshold voltage of each memory cell into $N+1$ regions, a unique $\lceil \log_2 (N + 1) \rceil$-bit number is used to represent each region, indicating that transferring latency is proportional to the logarithm of $N+1$. Although read requests are delayed by slower sensing and transferring when using more sensing levels, more accurate input probability information of each bit for LDPC code decoding can be obtained, thus improving error correction capability (CBER).

Based on the precondition that RBER should be within CBER of the deployed LDPC code, the tradeoff between flash cell wearing and read latency can be concluded from above two relationships. As shown in Fig. 1, flash cell wearing can be reduced by lowering the threshold voltages but at the cost of less noise margins between the states of a flash cell, which in turn increase RBER and delay read operations.

2.2 Related Work

Several methods for improving NAND flash memory I/O performance and endurance have been suggested by exploiting either of the two described relationships. By tasking advantage of the relationship between threshold voltage, wearing and RBER, Peleato et al. [12] proposed to optimize the target voltage levels to achieve a trade-off between lifetime and reliability, which tried to maximize lifetime subject to reliability constraints, and vice versa. Jeong et al. [11] presented a new system-level approach called dynamic program and erase scaling to improve the NAND endurance, by exploiting idle times between consecutive write requests to shorten the width of threshold voltage distributions so that blocks can be slowly erased with a lower erase voltage. However, both of them would induce the negative effects such as increased error and decreased write throughput.

Another set of approaches takes the relationship between error correction capability, read latency and the number of sensing levels into account. For example, Zhao et al. [5] proposed the progressive sensing level strategy to achieve latency reduction, which uses soft-decision sensing only triggered after the hard-decision decoding failure. Cai et al. [4] presented a retention optimized reading (ROR) method that periodically learns a tight upper bound and applies the optimal read reference voltage for each ash memory block online. Cui et al. [3] sorted the read requests according to the retention age of the data, and performed fast read for data with low retention ages by decreasing the number of sensing levels. These state-of-the-art retention-aware methods improve the read performance significantly, and fortunately they are orthogonal to our work.

These studies demonstrate that wearing reduction by adjusting voltage and read performance improvement by soft-decision memory sensing are useful. However, none of these works consider the tradeoff between read latency and wearing when exploiting both of the two described relationships. In this paper, we focus on reducing both the read latency and wearing by controlling the threshold voltages based on the hotness information of each request, which can be easily acquired from the buffer manager.

3   Exploiting Cross-Layer Hotness Identification to Improve Read and Endurance Performance (HIRE)

In this section, we propose HIRE, a wearing and read reduction approach, which includes two new management strategies: *Hotness Identifier (HI)* captures the access hotness characteristics at the flash buffer management level and *Voltage Controller (VC)* modulates the appropriate threshold voltages of a flash cell. We first present the cross-layer study on the access hotness characteristics of each data page in several workloads based on the buffer replacement policy. Then, on the basis of the observations of this cross-layer study, we propose a hotness-guided voltage controller to reduce the wearing and read latency. Finally, we present the overhead analysis.

3.1   Cross-Layer Study for Hotness Identifier

In order to guide wearing and read latency reduction, the access hotness characteristics of each data page are needed. The hotness in this work means the frequency of read or write operations on each data page for a given period of time. We find that the hotness characteristics can be archived by the buffer manager. Buffer replacement policy can optimize the I/O sequence and reduce storage accesses, thus improving the overall efficiency of the storage system. In this study, we use the simple and efficient Least Recently Used (LRU) policy to acquire these information. Note that other buffer replacement algorithms for NAND flash-based storage systems, e.g., PT-LRU [15] or HA-LRU [16], are completely orthogonal to our work, and can be also used with the proposed HIRE approach to improve flash-based system performance metrics.

We implement the *Hotness Identifier (HI)* strategy in the buffer manager. LRU uses a linked list to manage all cached data page, and when data page is evicted out of the buffer, the historical statistical information about the read/write hit can be used to identify the access hotness characteristics because the read/write hit statistical information reflect the access history. In order to collect the access hotness characteristics, each data page in the buffer list adds

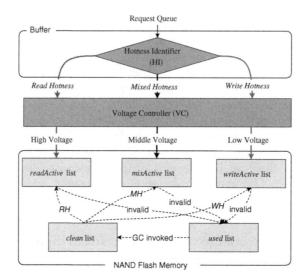

Fig. 2. Flow in the wearing and read latency reduction approach.

two attributes: buffer read hit count C_r and buffer write hit count C_w. If one data page is first referenced, it will be added into the MRU position of the buffer linked list, besides, its corresponding buffer read/write hit count value will plus one according to its read/write operation, respectively. When the data page in the buffer is referenced again, LRU adjusts the position of the data page to the MRU position of the linked list, meanwhile, its corresponding buffer read/write hit count value will also plus one according to its read/write operation.

During the eviction procedure, we classify the data access characteristics in the buffer into three types, as shown in Fig. 2. When the buffer does not have a free page slot for the new access data, LRU preferentially evicts the data page in the LRU position of the linked list, which is the least recently accessed data page. At this time, when the read hit ratio grows to a high watermark $\frac{C_r}{C_r+C_w}$ $> w$ (in this work $w = 95\%$), the most hit statistical information of a data page are read, and we determine it as *read-hot (RH)*. For instance, the request data pages in the *WebSearch* trace from a popular search engine [17] are all read only, therefore, all data pages in this trace will be identified as *RH*. When the write hit ratio grows to a high watermark $\frac{C_w}{C_r+C_w} > w$, the most hit statistical information of a data page are write, and we determine it as *write-hot (WH)*. Hence, other pages mixed with read and write hit are identified as *mixed-hot (MH)*. As a result, data page are classified into three groups according to their access hotness characteristics.

3.2 Voltage Controller in HIRE

Based on the access hotness characteristics of each data page, the *Voltage Controller (VC)* strategy, aiming to the wearing and read latency reduction, is proposed, as shown in Fig. 2. Furthermore, blocks transition between five states are used in this work to cooperate with the fine-grained voltage controller strategy, namely *clean, readActive, writeActive, mixActive* and *used. Clean* state is an initial state of a block which receives none program operation, or is erased.

To improve the read performance, VC implemented in the flash controller boosts the threshold voltages of flash cells that store *RH* data, and hence the noise margins between the states of a flash cell increase, increasing the wearing of flash memory, but it leads to lower raw bit error rates so that its read performance is further improved. Note that *RH* data defines the resources stored in *RH* data page. Moreover, VC performs this *RH* data on a block with *readActive* state. If there is no *readActive* block, a block with *clean* state will be chosen as the current *readActive* block. When all pages on the *readActive* block have been written, it moves to the *used* state, and a new *readActive* block will be produced by the above method. Note that although the wearing is estimated to somewhat higher than that of the horizontal voltage line, fewer P/E (Program/Erase) operations in this *read-hot* data compensates for the wearing increment. Thus, this relatively small increment of wearing is acceptable to achieve the read performance improvement in the *read-hot* data.

If one data is classified as *WH*, the threshold voltages of corresponding flash cells are reduced, which reduces the wearing of flash memory. Simultaneously, VC performs this data on a block with *writeActive* state. When all pages on the *writeActive* block have been written, this block also moves to the *used* state, and a new *clean* block will be chosen as the current *writeActive* block. Although RBER is consequently higher in *WH*, the number of errors within a code word is not beyond the superior error correction capability of LDPC code. Moreover, the corresponding block is more likely to trigger garbage collection (GC) because of the *write-hot* access characteristic.

Traditional voltage control without the fluctuation of threshold voltages, is applied in *MH* data. These *MH* data will be performed on a block with *mixActive* state. When all pages on the *mixActive* block have been written, it also moves to the *used* state, and VC will chose a *clean* block as the current *mixActive* block. And when a *used* block is chosen by GC, it will be erased and move back to the *clean* state. Similar to hot/cold data separation policy [22,23], separating *readActive, writeActive* and *mixActive* blocks improves the efficiency of garbage collection.

3.3   Overhead Analysis

The implementation of the proposed HIRE approach includes method implemented in the flash buffer manager and information recorded in the flash controller. In the flash buffer manager, we need to maintain the access hotness information. In order to figure out these information, the buffer list adds two attributes, including buffer read and write hit counts. We assume that the most buffer hit read/write counts is N_h, and the buffer size is N_c which specifies the maximum number of pages cached by buffer pool in this work, then the maximal size of storage required by the access hotness information is $\lceil \log_2 N_h \rceil \times 2 \times N_c$

bits. This storage overhead is negligible for a state-of-the-art SSD. In addition, we also extend each mapping entry in the flash translation layer of flash controller with a hotness field, using 2 bits to record three types of access hotness (*RH*, *WH* and *MH*), which is also negligible for a state-of-the-art SSD. Thus, it can be seen that the storage overhead is negligible.

4   Performance Evaluation

In this section, we first present the experimental methodology. Then, the I/O performance and endurance improvement of the proposed voltage optimization are presented. For comparison purpose, we have implemented several works which are closely related to our proposed HIRE approach.

4.1   Methodology

In this paper, we use an event-driven simulator to further demonstrate the effectiveness of the proposed HIRE. We simulate a 128 GB SSD with 8 channels, each of which is connected to 8 flash memory chips. We implement dynamic page mapping scheme between logical and physical locations as the FTL mapping scheme. Greedy garbage collection and dynamic wear-leveling scheme are also implemented in the FTL of the simulator. All these settings are consistent with previous works [3].

Table 1. Parameters in this work

Threshold voltages	Sensing (µs)	Transfer (µs)	Program (µs)
(1.40, 2.85, 3.55, 4.25)	30	40	600
(1.17, 2.37, 2.96, 3.54)	90	80	600
(0.93, 1.90, 2.37, 2.83)	210	100	600

As shown in Table 1, under the traditional voltage control, (1.17, 2.37, 2.96, 3.54) represents the threshold voltage of the four states in the simulated 2 bit/cell MLC NAND flash memory chip, and we use 600 µs as the program latency when ΔV_p is 0.25, 90 µs as memory sensing latency and 80 µs as data transfer latency when using LDPC with seven reference voltages. For the boosted threshold voltages, (1.40, 2.85, 3.55, 4.25) represents the corresponding threshold voltage of the four flash cell states when ΔV_p is 0.3, 30 µs as memory sensing latency and 40 µs as data transfer latency. When the threshold voltages reduce, the threshold voltage of four flash cell states is (0.93, 1.90, 2.37, 2.83) and ΔV_p is 0.2, the sensing latency is 210 µs and the data transfer latency is 100 µs.

For validation, we implement HIRE as well as baseline, HVC and LVC. We treat traditional voltage control strategy without any further targeted optimization as the baseline case in our contrastive experiments. HVC (High Voltage Controller) approach increases threshold voltages of all flash cells to maximize read

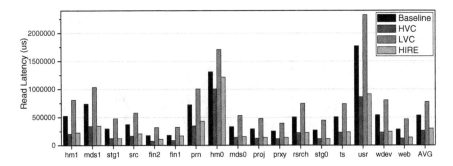

Fig. 3. The read latency under different voltage control approaches.

latency reduction, while LVC (Low Voltage Controller) approach reduces threshold voltages of all the flash cells to maximize wearing reduction. We evaluate our design using real world workloads from the MSR Cambridge traces [18] and two financial workloads [17], which are widely used in previous works to study SSD system performance metrics [19–21].

4.2 Experiment Results

In this section, the experimental results are presented and analyzed. Seventeen datasets were used in the experiments including a variety of application scenarios. To test the performance of our approach, the I/O response time and wearing are presented below.

Figure 3 shows the read latency of the proposed HIRE under different datasets, as compared to baseline, HVC and LVC approaches. It can be seen that HIRE outperforms baseline under all datasets, reducing read latency by 43.49 % on average. From Fig. 3, we can also see that the read performance improvement of HIRE under different datasets is distinctly different. For the *stg1* trace, the percent read latency reduction between baseline and HIRE is 58.59 %. For the *fin1* trace, the percent read latency reduction between baseline and HIRE is 6.89 %. HIRE increases voltages for the *read-hot* data, thus more *read-hot* significantly reduces the read latency. Figure 3 also shows that HVC approach archives the maximize read performance improvement, which is even better than HIRE. This significant improvement achieved for HVC approach is attributed to the fact that persistently increasing voltages leads to the minimize read response time, while HIRE only increases voltages of the *read-hot* data. However, HVC will also get the worst flash wearing at the same time, which can be seen in Fig. 4.

Figure 4 shows the wearing weight for the seventeen traces under four approaches. Wearing weight is invoked as the metric to show the wearing degree of the proposed approach. The lower wearing weight, the longer endurance of storage system. It can be seen that compared with the traditional baseline approach, HIRE achieves significant wearing reduction. HIRE outperforms baseline

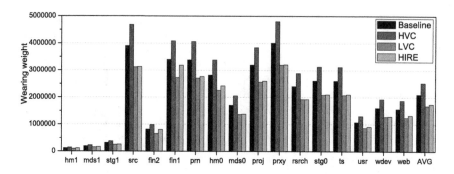

Fig. 4. The wearing weight under four approaches.

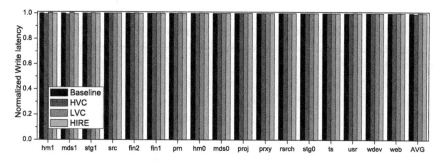

Fig. 5. The normalized write latency under different voltage control strategies.

with wearing reduction by 16.87 % on average. On the other hand, compared to baseline, the greatest wearing reduction observed in *stg1* is 19.99 %, while the smallest reduction observed in *fin2* is only 1.66 %. This is because HIRE drops voltages for the *write-hot* data, thus more *write-hot* data significantly reduces the wearing. Moreover, HVC gets the maximum wearing weight although it realizes the maximum read latency reduction, which has been discussed above.

To further demonstrate that our HIRE approach does not sacrifice the write performance, the normalized write latency in all experiments are measured and presented in Fig. 5. It can be seen that, very intuitively, the write latency of HIRE is comparable to those of the three competitor approaches. We can thus get the conclusion that the voltage control strategy in the proposed HIRE approach does not affect the write latency of the storage system.

5   Conclusion

In this paper, we proposed HIRE, a wearing and read reduction approach, that applies two new management strategies in NAND flash memory storage system: *Hotness Identifier (HI)* captures the hotness characteristics at the flash buffer management level and *Voltage Controller (VC)* manages the appropriate threshold voltages of a flash cell in the flash controller. The key insight behind the design of HIRE is that based on the access hotness characteristics provided by *HI*, *VR* decreases the threshold voltages of a flash cell for the *write-hot* data for wearing reduction and increases these for the *read-hot* data for read latency reduction. Extensive experimental results and detailed comparisons show that the proposed approach is effective in various types of workloads for NAND flash memory storage system. On average, HIRE improves read performance by up to 43.49 % and decreases the wearing of flash memory by up to 16.87 % over previous voltage management approaches. In addition, HIRE does not have a negative write performance effect, and the overhead of the proposed approach is negligible.

Acknowledgment. The authors would like to thank the anonymous reviewers for their detailed and thoughtful feedback which improved the quality of this paper significantly. This work was supported in part by the National Natural Science Foundation of China under grant No. 91330117, the National High-tech R&D Program of China (863 Program) under grant No. 2014AA01A302, the Shaanxi Social Development of Science and Technology Research Project under grant No. 2016SF-428, the Shenzhen Scientific Plan under grant No. JCYJ20130401095947230 and No. JSGG20140519141854753.

References

1. Margaglia, F., Yadgar, G., Yaakobi, E., Li, Y., Schuster, A., Brinkmann, A.: The devil is in the details: implementing flash page reuse with WOM codes. In: Proceedings of Conference on File and Storage Technologies, February 2016
2. Zhang, X., Li, J., Wang, H., Zhao, K., Zhang, T.: Reducing solid-state storage device write stress through opportunistic in-place delta compression. In: Proceedings of Conference on File and Storage Technologies, pp. 111–124, February 2016
3. Cui, J., Wu, W., Zhang, X., Huang, J., Wang, Y.: Exploiting latency variation for access conflict reduction of NAND flash memory. In: 32nd International Conference on Massive Storage Systems and Technology, May 2016
4. Schroeder, B., Lagisetty, R., Merchant, A.: Flash reliability in production: the expected and the unexpected. In: Proceedings of Conference on File and Storage Technologies, pp. 67–80, February 2016
5. Zhao, K., Zhao, W., Sun, H., Zhang, X., Zheng, N., Zhang, T.: LDPC-in-SSD: making advanced error correction codes work effectively in solid state drives. In: Proceedings of Conference on File and Storage Technologies, pp. 243–256 (2013)
6. Dong, G., Xie, N., Zhang, T.: Enabling nand flash memory use soft-decision error correction codes at minimal read latency overhead. IEEE Trans. Circ. Syst. I: Regular Papers **60**(9), 2412–2421 (2013)
7. Wu, G., He, X., Xie, N., Zhang, T.: Exploiting workload dynamics to improve SSD read latency via differentiated error correction codes. ACM Trans. Des. Autom. Electron. Syst. **18**(4), 55 (2013)
8. Jimenez, X., Novo, D., Ienne, P.: Wear unleveling: improving NAND flash lifetime by balancing page endurance. In: Proceedings of Conference on File and Storage Technologies, pp. 47–59 (2014)
9. Pan, Y., Dong, G., Zhang, T.: Error rate-based wear-leveling for NAND flash memory at highly scaled technology nodes. IEEE Trans. Very Large Scale Integration (VLSI) Syst. **21**(7), 1350–1354 (2013)

10. Agrawal, N., Prabhakaran, V., Wobber, T., Davis, J.D., Manasse, M.S., Panigrahy, R.: Design tradeoffs for SSD performance. In: USENIX Annual Technical Conference, pp. 57–70 (2008)

11. Jeong, J., Hahn, S.S., Lee, S., Kim, J.: Lifetime improvement of NAND flash-based storage systems using dynamic program and erase scaling. In: Proceedings of Conference on File and Storage Technologies, pp. 61–74 (2014)

12. Peleato, B., Agarwal, R.: Maximizing MLC NAND lifetime and reliability in the presence of write noise. In: Proceedings of IEEE International Conference on Communications, pp. 3752–3756, June 2012

13. Jeong, J., Hahn, S.S., Lee, S., Kim, J.: Improving NAND endurance by dynamic program and erase scaling. In: USENIX Workshop on Hot Topics in Storage and File Systems, June 2013

14. Pan, Y., Dong, G., Zhang, T.: Exploiting memory device wear-out dynamics to improve NAND flash memory system performance. In: Proceedings of Conference on File and Storage Technologies, p. 18 (2011)

15. Cui, J., Wu, W., Wang, Y., Duan, Z.: PT-LRU: a probabilistic page replacement algorithm for NAND flash-based consumer electronics. IEEE Trans. Consum. Electron. **60**(4), 614–622 (2014)

16. Lin, M., Yao, Z., Xiong, J.: History-aware page replacement algorithm for NAND flash-based consumer electronics. IEEE Trans. Consum. Electron. **62**(1), 23–29 (2016)

17. Storage Performance Council traces. http://traces.cs.umass.edu/storage/

18. Narayanan, D., Thereska, E., Donnelly, A., Elnikety, S., Rowstron, A.: Migrating server storage to SSDs: analysis of tradeoffs. In: Proceedings of the 4th ACM European Conference on Computer Systems, Nuremberg, Germany, pp. 145–158 (2009)

19. Hu, Y., Jiang, H., Feng, D., Tian, L., Luo, H., Zhang, S.: Performance impact and interplay of SSD parallelism through advanced commands, allocation strategy and data granularity. In: Proceedings of the International Conference on Supercomputing, pp. 96–107, May 2011

20. Hu, Y., Jiang, H., Feng, D., Tian, L., Luo, H., Ren, C.: Exploring and exploiting the multilevel parallelism inside SSDS for improved performance and endurance. IEEE Trans. Comput. **62**(6), 1141–1155 (2013)

21. Jung, M., Kandemir, M.: An evaluation of different page allocation strategies on high-speed SSDS. In: Proceedings of USENIX Conference on File and Storage Technologies, p. 9 (2012)

22. Jung, S., Lee, Y., Song, Y.: A process-aware hot/cold identification scheme for flash memory storage systems. IEEE Trans. Consum. Electron. **56**(2), 339–347 (2010)

23. Park, D., Du, D.: Hot data identification for flash memory using multiple bloom filters. In: Proceedings of USENIX Conference on File and Storage Technologies, October 2011

Efficient Management for Hybrid Memory in Managed Language Runtime

Chenxi Wang[1,2], Ting Cao[1(✉)], John Zigman[3], Fang Lv[1,4], Yunquan Zhang[1], and Xiaobing Feng[1]

[1] SKL of Computer Architecture, Institute of Computing Technology, CAS, Beijing, China
{wangchenxi,caoting,flv,zyq,fxb}@ict.ac.cn
[2] University of Chinese Academy of Sciences, Beijing, China
[3] Australia Centre for Field Robotics, AMME, The University of Sydney, Sydney, Australia
john.zigman@sydney.edu.au
[4] State Key Laboratory of Mathematical Engineering and Advanced Computing, Wuxi, China

Abstract. Hybrid memory, which leverages the benefits of traditional DRAM and emerging memory technologies, is a promising alternative for future main memory design. However popular management policies through memory-access recording and page migration may invoke non-trivial overhead in execution time and hardware space. Nowadays, managed language applications are increasingly dominant in every kind of platform. Managed runtimes provide services for automatic memory management. So it is important to adapt them for the underlying hybrid memory.

This paper explores two opportunities, heap partition placement and object promotion, inside managed runtimes for allocating hot data in a fast memory space (fast-space) without any access recording or data migration overhead. For heap partition placement, we quantitatively analyze LLC miss density and performance effect for each partition. Results show that LLC misses especially store misses mostly hit nursery partitions. Placing nursery in fast-space, which is 20 % total memory footprint of tested benchmarks on average, causes only 10 % performance difference from all memory footprint in fast-space. During object promotion, hot objects will be directly allocated to fast-space. We develop a tool to analyze the LLC miss density for each method of workloads, since we have found that the LLC misses are mostly triggered by a small percentage of the total set of methods. The objects visited by the top-ranked methods are recognized as hot. Results show that hot objects do have higher access density, more than 3 times of random distribution for SPECjbb and pmd, and placing them in fast-space further reduces their execution time by 6 % and 13 % respectively.

Keywords: Hybrid memory · Managed runtime · JVM · Memory management

© IFIP International Federation for Information Processing 2016
Published by Springer International Publishing AG 2016. All Rights Reserved
G.R. Gao et al. (Eds.): NPC 2016, LNCS 9966, pp. 29–42, 2016.
DOI: 10.1007/978-3-319-47099-3_3

1   Introduction

As processor cores, concurrent threads and data intensive workloads increase, memory systems must support the growth of simultaneous working sets. However, feature size and power scaling of DRAM is starting to hit a fundamental limit. Different memory technologies with better scaling, such as non-volatile memory (NVM), 3D-stacked and scratchpad memory, are emerging. To leverage the benefits of different technologies, with disparate access-cost modules into an integrated hybrid memory opens up a promising future for memory design. It has the potential to reduce power consumption and improve performance at the same time [1]. However, it exposes the complexity of distributing data to appropriate modules.

Many hybrid memory management policies are implemented in a memory controller with or without OS assistance [2–9]. However, their page migrations can cause time and memory bandwidth overhead. There is also hardware space cost for recording memory access information which limits the size of management granularity too.

For portability, productivity, and simplicity, managed languages such as Java are increasingly dominant in mobiles, desktops, and big servers. For example, popular big data platforms, such as Hadoop and Spark, are all written in managed languages. Managed runtime provides services for performance optimization and automatic memory management. So it is important to adapt managed runtime for hybrid memory system.

This paper explores two opportunities: heap partition placement and object promotion, inside managed runtime for efficient hybrid memory management without additional data migration overhead. Hot objects (objects with high LLC miss density, i.e. LLC misses/object size) identification is conducted offline, thus no online profiling cost. We steal one bit from an object header as a flag to indicate hot object, so no impact on total space usage even at object grain. Our work is orthogonal to the management policies proposed inside an OS or hardware. They can work cooperatively but with reduced cost for managed applications. It can also work alone as a pure software portable hybrid-memory management.

For appropriate heap partition placement, we quantitatively analyze the LLC miss density for each partition of generational GC, including nursery, mature, metadata, and LOS (large object space). We demonstrate that the heap partitions according to object lifetime and characteristics also provide a natural partially classification of hot/cold objects. A 16 MB nursery covers 76 % of total LLC misses, and most of them are store misses. Placing nursery in fast-space use 20 % total memory footprint on average as fast-space, but only 10 % performance difference from all heap in fast-space.

Besides the nursery, for workloads with relatively high LLC misses in mature partition, a small amount of the mature partition is allocated in fast-space to place hot objects during object promotion (which moves long-lived objects from nursery to mature partition). We develop an offline tool using the ASM bytecode manipulation framework [10] to record LLC miss density for each method.

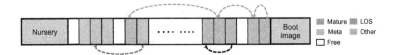

Fig. 1. Virtual memory space partition of Jikes RVM

This information is used to direct JIT-generated machine-code to mark objects dereferenced by top-ranked methods as hot, so that they can later be moved to fast-space during object promotion. Results show that hot objects do have higher LLC miss density, more than 3 times of random distribution for SPECjbb and pmd, and placing them in fast-space further reduces their execution time by 6 % and 13 % respectively, resulting in ultimately 27 % and 31 % faster using our policy compared to the default OS policy of interleaving page allocation.

The structure of the paper is as follows. Sections 2 and 3 are background for managed runtimes and related work. Section 4 is the management scheme we proposed. Section 5 introduces our hybrid memory emulation, and experimental settings. Finally, we discuss and conclude the results.

2   Managed Runtime Background

Managed runtime. Managed-language applications require support services in order to run properly, such as Just-In-Time compilation (JIT) and Garbage collection (GC). Bytecode or only partially optimized code that are frequently executed are translated by the JIT into more optimized code. GC is used to automatically manage memory, including object allocation, and the identification and collection of unreachable objects. Among all types of GC, generational GC is the most popular one as it tends to reduce the overall burden of GC. It does this by partitioning the heap according to object lifetimes.

Generational GC and heap partition. Since most objects have very short lifetimes, generational GC uses a low overhead space (called *nursery* space) for initial allocation and usage, and only moves objects that survive more frequent early collections to a longer lived space (called *mature* space). When a nursery is full, a minor GC is invoked to collect this space. When a minor GC fails due to a lack of space in mature space, a major GC will be performed. Nursery space is normally much smaller than mature space for efficient collection of short-lived objects. Jikes RVM also uses generational GC for its most efficient production configuration. This paper will use this configuration too. Under the production setting for the Jikes RVM, the heap uses a bump-allocation nursery and an Immix [11] mature space.

Other than nursery and mature spaces, Jikes RVM has spaces for large objects (LOS) including stacks, metadata (used by GC), as well as some small spaces for immortal (permanent), non-moving, and code objects, all of which share a discontiguous heap range with the mature space through a memory chunk free list. Figure 1 shows the virtual memory space partition of Jikes RVM. This paper will show how to distribute those partitions to appropriate memory space.

3   Related Work

Different hybrid/heterogeneous main memory structures have been proposed, such as DRAM + NVM [3,4,6,12–15], on-chip memory + off-chip memory [16], and DRAMs with different feature values [8,17]. Though with different technologies, all of them share the common characteristic that different parts of the address space yield different access cost. Many technologies have been proposed to manage this heterogeneity.

Page access monitoring and migration. Most of works use memory controllers to monitor page accesses [3,4,6,16]. The memory controller will then migrate top-ranked pages to fast-space, and OS will update the virtual address mapping table accordingly. However, these research all operate at a fixed grain, mostly on a page level. Besides, page migration invokes time and bandwidth overhead. Bock et al. [12] qualify that page migration can increase execution time by 25 % on average. Our work utilize object promotion for object placement to suitable space, thus does not invoke extra data migration nor time overhead.

Direct data placement. To avoid data migration overhead, there are works that place data in appropriate space directly according to their reference behaviours [8,14,15,17]. Chatterjee et al. [17] organize a single cacheline across multiple memory channels. Critical word (normally the first word) in a cacheline will be placed in a low-latency channel. Wei et al. [15] show that for the groups of objects allocated at the same place in the source code, some of them exhibit similar behaviours, which can be used for static data placement. Li et al. [14] develop a binary instrumentation tool to statistically report memory access patterns in stack, heap, and global data. Liu et al. [18] also implement a tool in OS to collect page access frequency, memory footprint, page re-use time, etc. which can be used to identify hot pages. Phadke and Narayanasamy [8] also profile applications' MLP and LLC misses offline to determine from which memory space each application would benefit the most. There are also works require programmers to help decide data placement [13,19,20]. Our paper uses offline profiling for data placement instead of online monitoring and migration, and does not invoke extra burden to programmers.

Adaption of managed runtime. There are a few works related to the management of hybrid memory particularly for managed applications [21–26]. Shuichi Oikawa's group conduct some preliminary work [21–24]. They state that nursery should be in the fast memory space, but without supporting data, nor for metadata, stacks or other partitions in the heap. They extend write barriers to record the writes to each object online to find hot objects. However that will include write hit to cache which can mislead the data placement. Besides, the process could result in a non-trivial execution overhead. Inoue and Nakatani [25] identify a code pattern in Java applications that can easily causing L1 and L2 cache misses. However, we find the number of memory accesses caused by this pattern is negligible. A series of papers [27–29] describing managed runtime techniques focusing on avoiding page faulting to disk. Those techniques could be applied to vertical hybrid main memory, where fast-space (e.g. DRAM) acts as a cache for slow-space (e.g. NVM). However Dong et al. [16] show that if performance difference between fast-space and slow-space (typically seen in DRAM and NVM) is not obvious, it may not be adequate for vertical hybrid memory to be viable. Hertz et al. [28] keep frequently used partitions such as nursery in memory, preventing them from being swapped, we show that this is still very significant for the nursery even in our context. This paper profiles LLC miss density for each partition and method offline to decide object placement during a GC process.

4   Hybrid Memory Management Scheme

4.1   Overview

The goal of our management system is to enable a machine with a small proportion of fast-space to perform as well as a machine with the same amount of memory where all the memory is fast-space. Specifically, we want hot objects be allocated in fast-space. We exploit two opportunities in managed runtimes: partition placement and object promotion. Analysing the LLC miss density of the various partitions, we determine if all, none or part of a partition is placed in fast-space. Object promotion to the mature partition provides a decision point where an object must be moved, as such, a cheap opportunity for moving to either slow-space or fast-space. Selecting either fast-space or slow-space is driven by offline profiling to determine hot methods (highest LLC miss density) and online marking of objects accessed by those methods. Compared to work before, our scheme does not cause online monitoring or extra data migration, thus no relevant performance overhead.

Heap partition placement. To profile each heap partition, we use numactl library to map virtual memory space to fast-space or slow-space, and use PMU counters to measure LLC load/store misses. As explained in Sect. 2, the nursery is a continuous space, and we map it as a whole. LOS, metadata, and mature partitions share a dis-contiguous memory range divided into chunks. Free chunks are maintained on a list and available for any partition to allocate. To support hybrid memory, we change to two freelists, one for slow-space and one for fast-space. Different partitions will be given the right to access a specific list or both lists. When no free chunks are available in the fast-space list, objects will be allocated from the slow-space list. The overhead of managing the additional list is negligible.

In Sect. 6, we will show that the LLC miss density of the nursery partition is much higher than other partitions, and as such it is mapped to fast-space. A small proportion of the mature partition is mapped to fast-space, and hot objects are moved to that portion when they are promoted.

Object promotion. Minor GC promotes surviving objects from the nursery to the mature partition. During this process, our scheme promotes hot objects to fast-space, and all other surviving objects are promoted to slow-space. Section 3 discusses some related work for finding hot objects. However, our experiments

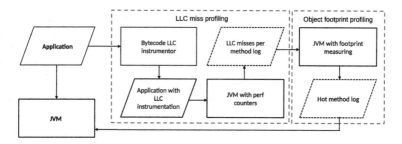

Fig. 2. Offline LLC miss per method profiling feeds into method footprint profiling which is then used to facilitate object promotion during normal execution.

show that they either have a large overhead in time and space, are not effective, or need a programmer to annotate the critical data. Dynamic optimization prevents popular instrumentation tools, such as VTune, from being effective for profiling hardware events.

We develop a tool called HMprof to profile LLC miss density in the mature partition for each method of an application. Since our experiments show that even though each application executes hundreds or thousands of methods, only a dozen of them are responsible for most of the LLC misses, for example 0.4 % and 1 % of the methods in pmd and hsqldb covers 51 % and 54.8 % LLC respectively. This is a result of the particular access patterns and role of those methods. We will describe the implementation details next.

4.2   HMprof Offline Performance Instrumentation

This instrumentation and profiling take place in two phases: first, collecting each method's performance counter statistics of any heap partition by instrumenting the application's java bytecode; and second, collecting the object visitation statistics for the candidate methods by altering the JIT. Figure 2, shows two offline profiling stages, and subsequence execution(s) of the application. These phases are described below.

LLC miss profiling. Performance counter instrumentation is inserted into each method. Since methods may be compiled, and recompiled at runtime it is not possible to use the code location to identify the method, as such each method instrumented is given a unique numeric identifier as part of its instrumentation. The method code is transformed so that it has an additional local variable which is used to record a performance counter entry-value or re-entry value for the method, by invoking perf.readPerf(I)J, see Fig. 3a. Upon exiting the method (either by return from the method, throwing an exception, or invoking a method), the entry-value, performance counter exit-value and the method identifier are logged.

The performance counters read and the values logged are maintained per thread. Logging a measurement is done by invoking perf.updatePerf(IIJ)V, see Fig. 3b, which adds the performance counter delta for that thread to a thread specific array. Each element of the array corresponds to an instrumented thread

```
/** read counter 0, save                /** Update local variable
to local variable e.g. 3 **/            3 for method 576 **/
                                        iconst_0
iconst_0                                sipush   576
invokestatic perf.readPerf(I)J          lload_3
lstore_3                                invokestatic perf.updatePerf(IIJ)V
```

    (a) Execution entry point   (b) Execution exit point

Fig. 3. Example instrumentation in a method.

```
getfield      Result(RefType) = ObjRef, Offset, field
byte_load     t0(B) = ObjRef, HOT_BIT_OFFSET
int_or        t1(B) = t0(B), HOT_BIT_MASK
byte_store    t1(B), ObjRef, HOT_BIT_OFFSET
```

    (a) getfield

```
null_check    Result(GUARD) = Result(RefType)
byte_load     t0(B) = Result(refType), HOT_BIT_OFFSET
int_or        t1(B) = t0(B), HOT_BIT_MASK
byte_store    t1(B), Result(refType), HOT_BIT_OFFSET
```

    (b) null_check

Fig. 4. Example HIR after inserting hot object marking instructions.

identifier. Since there is no interaction between the threads, there is little impact overall, aside from a small perturbation of the cached data.

The statistics accumulated by a particular thread are finally added to the totals when that thread terminates. This imposes some cost on thread termination, but this does not have a significant performance impact. When all threads have terminated the final statistics values are written to a file. We can get a ranked list of methods according to their LLC misses in the mature partition.

Object footprint profiling. Only LLC miss information is not enough to decide the hotness of a method, because the high LLC misses may be because it accesses a large amount of data. So LLC miss density is needed. Object visitation instrumentation is used to track the number of objects visited and their corresponding footprint for the top-ranked methods. An extra word is added to the object header to track which ones of those methods have visited a particular object. When a method visits an object, one corresponding bit will be marked. Because those methods are only a few, one extra word is enough. An extra phase is added to JIT to add marking code, and those methods are forcibly compiled with JIT. Thus, all objects dereferenced by any method that is being tracked are marked.

At the end of execution, the mature partition is scanned for marked objects, this excludes objects that do not survive a nursery collection. The number and footprint of the objects dereferences are accumulated per method. With the LLC miss information from the first step, we can work out the hot method list. Note that all the work above by HMprof is done offline. It will not add overhead to application run.

4.3   Hot Object Marking

After hot methods are found, we will mark the objects they visit as hot and move them to fast-space while an application runs. Similar as Sect. 4.2, we add a new phase in the HIR optimizations of JIT to mark the objects. This one flag bit is stolen from each object header. We target `getfield`, `putfield`, and `call` as three of the most common cases where objects are dereferenced/visited. Importantly a reference that is returned from a call or a getfield has the potential to be dereferenced, if such dereference is to occur then before the return value is dereferenced, the HIR inserts a `null_check`. When a `null_check` of this form is seen then that too is instrumented. In general, these will cover most of the operations that cause object and array dereferencing. Figure 4a shows the additional instructions that are inserted after the `getfield`, note, `ObjRef` reference will already have passed a `null_check` or equivalent to get to this point, so it is safe to use. A similar pattern is used for `putfiled` and `call` (for virtual and interface calls). Similarly, we show in Fig. 4b the additional code added after a `null_check`. In both cases they will set (mark) the hot bit in the object header as `true`, and in later versions will only conditionally set the hot bit.

We used replay compile in our experiment, so the JIT cost will not be counted when the application runs. However, as Cao et al. [30] shows that the JIT can run asynchronously with application threads, the application running time won't be sensitive to the JIT performance.

5   Experimental Methodology

Hybrid memory emulator. Because we do not have hybrid memory products and software simulators are very slow to run complex managed applications, we use a two-socket NUMA server (Intel Xeon X5650) with an interference program to mimic a hybrid memory structure. The interference program only runs on the remote CPUs, which regularly reads data from remote memory to increase the remote access latency and reduce its bandwidth for other applications. Tested benchmarks only run on the local ones.

Running the interference program and also using three channels for the local memory and a single channel for the remote memory, the latency of the mimic slow-space (remote memory) is 3.4 times that of the fast-space (local memory). The fast-space's read and write bandwidth is 5.3 times and 18.2 times those of the slow-space respectively, which is in keeping with current NVM characteristics—the write bandwidth is much worse than read. Those numbers fall within the range of latency and bandwidth characteristics for current NVM technologies [2,9].

LLC size control. The paper is about memory management policy design, and the memory footprint of the benchmarks is not large. To avoid the interference of LLC with the policy evaluation, we need to reduce the LLC size as much as possible. The method we used is mentioned in [31] as cache polluting method to reduce the LLC cache size to 4 MB. Based on the settings above, Fig. 5a shows our emulated experimental platform.

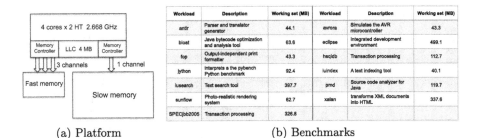

| | (a) Platform | | | | (b) Benchmarks | | |

<table>

Workload	Description	Working set (MB)	Workload	Description	Working set (MB)
antlr	Parser and translator generator	44.1	avrora	Simulates the AVR microcontroller	43.3
bloat	Java bytecode optimization and analysis tool	63.6	eclipse	Integrated development environment	499.1
fop	Output-independent print formatter	43.3	hsqldb	Transaction processing	112.7
jython	Interprets a the pybench Python benchmark	92.4	luindex	A text indexing tool	40.1
lusearch	Text search tool	397.7	pmd	Source code analyzer for Java	119.7
sunflow	Photo-realistic rendering system	62.7	xalan	transforms XML documents into HTML	337.6
SPECjbb2005	Transaction processing	326.8			

</table>

(a) Platform   (b) Benchmarks

Fig. 5. Experimental platform and benchmarks.

Virtual machine configurations. We implemented our approach in the Jikes RVM. The mature space is set so that it is big enough to hold all objects that survive nursery GC eliminating the effects of major GC. We use replay compilation to remove the nondeterminism of the adaptive optimization system. It also means that in our experiments, we will not include any JIT processing time. We use DaCapo and SPECjbb benchmarks [32] for our experiments. Figure 5b describes each benchmark and their working set size.

Default OS memory policy. The default Linux memory policy interleaves allocation across all nodes in a NUMA system [33]. This policy will compare with ours in the performance evaluation. In our experimental platform, we use *mbind()* system call to set a VMA (Virtual Memory Area) policy, and interleave page allocation in a task's virtual address to fast and slow memory modules.

6   Evaluation Results

6.1   Heap Partition Placement

To decide how to place each partition in hybrid memory, we quantitatively evaluate the LLC misses associated with each partition, as well as the performance effect when it is placed in fast-space. Figure 6a shows the LLC miss distribution for each partition. It shows that though nursery is only 16M, it covers the most LLC misses, 76 % on average. This is primarily a result for all objects, except for large objects, being initially allocated in the nursery and causing a significant number of LLC misses during object initialization. We evaluate various nursery sizes from 4M to 128M. Results show that LLC misses due to nursery accesses increase with the nursery size. However, the curve flattens after 16M for most applications, so we pick 16M in the experiments. The mature partition covers 13 % of the LLC misses on average. This percentage is relatively high for SPECjbb, pmd, and hsqldb, 44 %, 27 % and 22 % respectively. The LLC misses hitting other partitions are small. Even though stacks are frequently accessed, they are mostly in cache, so will not cause many LLC misses. With the memory footprint result of total objects allocated in each partition, we compute the LLC miss density of the nursery to be 12.5 times that of the mature partition, 25 times that of LOS, and 33.3 times that of the metadata partition.

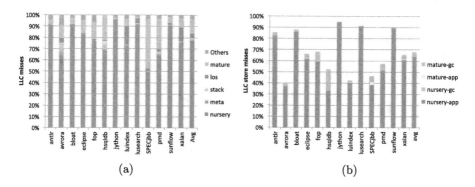

Fig. 6. (a) LLC misses distribution; (b) LLC store misses %.

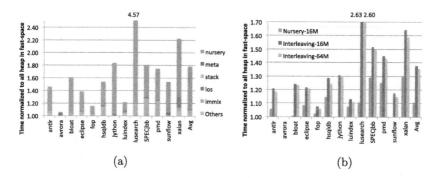

Fig. 7. (a) Time effect of each partition, (b) time comparison between nursery in fast-space and OS interleaving allocation.

Some memory technology like NVM has a large write cost. Our hybrid memory emulator also sets the write bandwidth much smaller than that of the read bandwidth. Figure 6b shows the portion of store misses in total hitting the nursery and the mature partition when an application or GC executes. We can see that: (a) for Java benchmarks, most LLC misses are store misses, 64 % on average; (b) almost all of these store misses hit in the nursery; (c) in the nursery, nearly all store misses happen when application code executes, while in the mature partition, they happen during GC execution. Since the mature partition is set to be large enough that no major GC is triggered, all these store misses are a result of object promotion during minor GCs. So store misses are distributed evenly in the mature partition, which has been confirmed in our experiment results. This is undesirable for hybrid memory management especially for NVM, which expect the existence of write-hot data to put into fast-space.

Figure 7a is a stacked column chart showing the time effect of placing each partition in fast-space. The reference is the time when all heap is placed in fast-space. The total height of a bar shows the relative time when all heap is placed in slow-space. It reflects the LLC miss rate (LLC misses per instruction) of an application. lusearch has the highest LLC miss rate, 7.87 per 1K instructions.

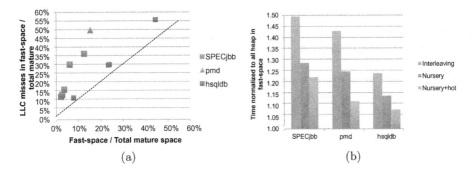

Fig. 8. (a) The correlation of LLC misses hitting in fast-space and the fast-space used, (b) time comparison of interleaving, nursery in fast-space, and nursery plus hot objects of mature partition in fast-space.

The second is xalan, 2.57 per 1K instructions. So when the heap is placed in slow-space, compared to being placed in fast-space, the running time is 4.57 and 2.22 times respectively. avrora has the lowest LLC miss rate, 1.03 per 1K instructions. So the time is basically the same when the heap is either in fast-space or slow-space. The figure also shows that corresponding to Fig. 6a, placing a 16M nursery into fast-space can greatly reduce the time, on average from 1.76 to 1.10, only a 10 % difference from placing all the heap in fast-space. Placing the mature partition in fast-space can further reduce time from 1.08 to almost the same as all in fast-space (1.00) on average. For SPECjbb and pmd, the mature partition in fast-space reduces their normalized running time from 1.29 to 1.01, and 1.23 to 1.00.

We then compare the execution time of the nursery in fast-space with the default page interleaving scheme of OS in Fig. 7b. For the interleaving scheme, we compare both a 16M and larger 64M interleaved fast-space setting with our 16M setting. However, in both instances as interleaving treats every partition evenly, the time is much more than only the 16M nursery in fast-space, 1.38 and 1.35 respectively compared to 1.10 on average.

All the results above suggest that the nursery should be placed directly into fast-space. It will get rid of the online monitoring and page migration costs. For mature space, we will allocate a small amount of fast-space for the hot objects found by our tool HMprof. The results will be analyzed in the next section.

6.2 Hot Object Allocation

Marked hot objects that are promoted to the mature partition are placed in fast-space, if available. In this subsection we show the effectiveness of our scheme, i.e. the objects moved to fast-space have high memory accesses but relatively small space cost. In particular SPECjbb, pmd and hsqldb are examined since they have more LLC misses in the mature partition than other benchmarks.

Figure 8a shows the correlation of fast-space usage and the LLC misses it covers when hot objects in mature partition are allocated in fast-space. pmd benefits most, with the hottest method only using 15 % (12M) of the mature partition objects (by volume) while covering 50 % of the LLC misses. The hottest 12 methods of SPECjbb use 6 % (18M) of the mature partition objects (by volume) and cover 31 % of the LLC misses. After the first 12 methods the thirteenth is proportionally less effective, resulting in a total use of 12 % (36M) of the mature partition objects (by volume) and 37 % of the LLC misses being covered. The remaining methods are not considered hot or account for too few LLC misses. The hot methods for hsqldb are not obvious, and with the 12 hottest methods using 43 % (42M) of the mature partition objects (by volume) while covering 56 % of the LLC misses, only a little better than random promotion. As noted in Sect. 6.1, the distribution of write LLC misses amongst objects in the mature partition is more even than that of read LLC misses, and given the cost difference between read and write, it is adversely affecting our performance improvements.

Figure 8b compares relative execution time of default OS page interleaving policy using 64 MB fast-space, only a 16M nursery in fast-space, and both the 16M nursery and hot objects of mature partition in fast-space. The policy proposed gets the best performance for the three benchmarks. For SPECjbb and pmd only 16 % and 23 % (respectively) of their working sets reside in fast-space (including the nursery partition), while only degrading performance by 23 % and 12 % respectively from that of all the heap in fast-space. Placing 51 % of the working set for hsqldb in fast-space yields a performance degradation of 8 % over than of all the heap in fast-space.

7   Conclusion

Hybrid memory is a promising alternative for future memory systems, however, its complexity challenges effective management. This paper explores unique opportunities inside managed runtimes for efficient and portable hybrid memory management with negligible online overhead. Our policy places the nursery and a small amount of the mature partition in fast-space. Compared to the default OS policy, for SPECjbb and pmd, our scheme is 27 % and 31 % faster. Compared to placing all the heap in fast-space, we place 16 % and 23 % heap in fast-space, but achieve only 23 % and 12 % performance difference respectively for the two benchmarks. In future work, we will target big data applications as test benchmarks.

Acknowledgement. This work is supported by the National High Technology Research and Development Program of China (2015AA011505), the Open Project Program of the State Key Laboratory of Mathematical Engineering and Advanced Computing (2016A03), the China Postdoctoral Science Foundation (2015T80139), the National Natural Science Foundation of China (61202055, 61221062, 61303053, 61432016, 61402445, 61432018, 61133005, 61272136, 61521092, 61502450).

References

1. Xie, Y.: Modeling, architecture, and applications for emerging memory technologies. IEEE Des. Test Comput. **28**(1), 44–51 (2011)

2. Qureshi, M.K., Srinivasan, V., et al.: Scalable high performance main memory system using phase-change memory technology. In: ISCA 2009, pp. 24–33. ACM (2009)
3. Ramos, L.E., Gorbatov, E., et al.: Page placement in hybrid memory systems. In: ICS, pp. 85–95. ACM (2011)
4. Zhang, W., Li, T.: Exploring phase change memory and 3D die-stacking for power/thermal friendly, fast and durable memory architectures. In: PACT 2009 (2009)
5. Li, Y., Choi, J., et al.: Managing hybrid main memories with a page-utility driven performance model. arXiv.org, July 2015
6. Dhiman, G., Ayoub, R., Rosing, T.: PDRAM: a hybrid PRAM and DRAM main memory system. In: DAC 2009, pp. 664–669, July 2009
7. Yoon, H., Meza, J., Ausavarungnirun, R., Harding, R., Mutlu, O.: Row buffer locality aware caching policies for hybrid memories. In: ICCD, pp. 337–344 (2012)
8. Phadke, S., Narayanasamy, S.: MLP aware heterogeneous memory system. In: DATE, pp. 956–961. IEEE (2011)
9. Caulfield, A.M., Coburn, J., et al.: Understanding the impact of emerging nonvolatile memories on high-performance, IO-intensive computing. In: SC (2010)
10. OW2 Consortium: ASM (2015)
11. Blackburn, S.M., McKinley, K.S.: Immix: a mark-region garbage collector with space efficiency, fast collection, and mutator performance. In: PLDI (2008)
12. Bock, S., Childers, B.R., Melhem, R.G., Mossé, D.: Concurrent page migration for mobile systems with OS-managed hybrid memory. In: CF, pp. 31:1–31:10. ACM (2014)
13. Dulloor, S., Roy, A., et al.: Data tiering in heterogeneous memory systems. In: EuroSys, pp. 15:1–15:16. ACM (2016)
14. Li, D., Vetter, J.S., et al.: Identifying opportunities for byte-addressable nonvolatile memory in extreme-scale scientific applications. In: IPDPS, pp. 945–956. IEEE (2012)
15. Wei, W., Jiang, D., McKee, S.A., Xiong, J., Chen, M.: Exploiting program semantics to place data in hybrid memory. In: PACT, pp. 163–173. IEEE (2015)
16. Dong, X., Xie, Y., et al.: Simple but effective heterogeneous main memory with on-chip memory controller support. In: SC, pp. 1–11 (2010)
17. Chatterjee, N., Shevgoor, M., et al.: Leveraging heterogeneity in DRAM main memories to accelerate critical word access. In: MICRO, pp. 13–24. IEEE (2012)
18. Liu, L., Li, Y., Ding, C., Yang, H., Wu, C.: Rethinking memory management in modern operating system: horizontal, vertical or random? IEEE Trans. Comput. **65**(6), 1921–1935 (2016)
19. Hassan, A., Vandierendonck, H., et al.: Software-managed energy-efficient hybrid DRAM/NVM main memory. In: CF, pp. 23:1–23:8. ACM (2015)
20. Malicevic, J., Dulloor, S., et al.: Exploiting NVM in large-scale graph analytics. In: INFLOW, pp. 2:1–2:9. ACM (2015)
21. Nakagawa, G., Oikawa, S.: Preliminary analysis of a write reduction method for non-volatile main memory on Jikes RVM. In: CANDAR, pp. 597–601, December 2013
22. Nakagawa, G., Oikawa, S.: An analysis of the relationship between a write access reduction method for NVM/DRAM hybrid memory with programming language runtime support and execution policies of garbage collection. In: IIAIAAI (2014)
23. Nakagawa, G., Oikawa, S.: Language runtime support for NVM/DRAM hybrid main memory. In: 2014 IEEE COOL Chips XVII, pp. 1–3, April 2014
24. Nakagawa, G., Oikawa, S.: NVM/DRAM hybrid memory management with language runtime support via MRW queue. In: SNPD, pp. 357–362. IEEE (2015)

25. Inoue, H., Nakatani, T.: Identifying the sources of cache misses in Java programs without relying on hardware counters. In: ISMM, pp. 133–142. ACM (2012)
26. Schneider, F.T., Payer, M., Gross, T.R.: Online optimizations driven by hardware performance monitoring. In: PLDI, pp. 373–382. ACM (2007)
27. Yang, T., Hertz, M., Berger, E.D., Kaplan, S.F., Moss, J.E.B.: Automatic heap sizing: taking real memory into account. In: ISMM, pp. 61–72. ACM (2004)
28. Hertz, M., Feng, Y., Berger, E.D.: Garbage collection without paging. In: PLDI, pp. 143–153. ACM (2005)
29. Yang, T., Berger, E.D., Kaplan, S.F., Moss, J.E.B.: CRAMM: virtual memory support for garbage-collected applications. In: OSDI, pp. 103–116. USENIX Association (2006)
30. Cao, T., Blackburn, S.M., et al.: The Yin and Yang of power and performance for asymmetric hardware and managed software. In: ISCA, pp. 225–236. IEEE (2012)
31. Ferdman, M., Adileh, A., et al.: Clearing the clouds: a study of emerging scale-out workloads on modern hardware. In: ASPLOS, pp. 37–48. ACM (2012)
32. Blackburn, S.M., Garner, R., et al.: The DaCapo benchmarks: java benchmarking development and analysis. In: OOPSLA, pp. 169–190. ACM (2006)
33. The Linux Kernel Organization: NUMA memory policy (2015)

Resilience and Reliability

Application-Based Coarse-Grained Incremental Checkpointing Based on Non-volatile Memory

Zhan Shi[✉], Kai Lu, Xiaoping Wang, Wenzhe Zhang, and Yiqi Wang

College of Computer, National University of Defense Technology,
Changsha, People's Republic of China
alec_1994@126.com, lukainudt@163.com,
{xiaopingwang,zhangwenzhe}@nudt.edu.cn, 459046923@qq.com

Abstract. The Mean Time to Failure continues to decrease as the scaling of computing systems. To maintain the reliability of computing systems, checkpoint has to be taken more frequently. Incremental checkpointing is a well-researched technique that makes frequent checkpointing possible. Fine-grained incremental checkpointing minimizes checkpoint size but suffers from significant monitoring overhead. We observe the memory access at page granularity and find that the size of contiguous memory regions visited by applications tends to be proportional to size of corresponding memory allocation. In this paper, we propose the Application-Based Coarse-Grained Incremental Checkpointing (ACCK) that leverages the priori information of the memory allocation to release the memory monitoring granularity in an incremental and appropriate way. This provides better opportunities for balancing the tradeoff between monitoring and copying overhead. ACCK is also assisted by hugepage to alleviate the TLB overhead. Our experiment shows that ACCK presents 2.56x performance improvement over the baseline mechanism.

1 Introduction

As more of high performance computing systems are being deployed in practice, fault-tolerance and self-healing are becoming increasingly important. Large-scale machines are often used by the scientific community to solve computationally intensive applications typically running for days or even months. Fault-tolerance is also a must-have characteristic of large-scale software system used in safety-critical and business-critical domains. However, large systems exponentially increase the total number of failure points and suffer [1, 2]. For instance, if mean-time-to-failure (MTTF) of an individual node is as long as ten years, the MTTF of 64,000 node system is expected to decrease to the order of tens of minutes [5, 12]. Therefore, it is critical to tolerate hardware and software failures with low impact on application performance and avoid re-computation.

Checkpoint-restart is an effective mechanism for preventing applications from restarting from scratch when unexpected system failure or scheduled maintenance occurs [3–5]. A checkpoint is a snapshot of application state in non-volatile devices used for restarting execution after failure. However, the scaling of computing system puts additional pressure on checkpoint mechanism. On the one hand, checkpoint has to be

G.R. Gao et al. (Eds.): NPC 2016, LNCS 9966, pp. 45–57, 2016.
DOI: 10.1007/978-3-319-47099-3_4

taken more frequently [6, 7] relative to the failure rate of the system which, in turn, directly impacts the application execution time and non-volatile storage requirements. On the other hand, the overhead of global checkpoint increases due to the large checkpoint size.

With the emerging non-volatile memory technologies, fast in-memory checkpoint helps alleviate the data transfer bandwidth problem, which is recognized as a major bottleneck of checkpointing. Moreover, in-memory approach allows frequent checkpointing to meet the requirements of large-scale systems. The presence of non-volatile memory provides opportunities for incremental checkpointing technique. Since the in-memory checkpointing makes it possible to take checkpoints every few seconds, it reduces the overhead of incremental checkpointing. As the checkpoint interval decreases, a small number of memory blocks are modified, hence, the average size of an incremental checkpoint decreases. Recent work [3–5] has demonstrated that the incremental checkpointing shows its advantage over full-size checkpointing when the checkpoint interval is within one minute.

To employ an incremental checkpointing technique, dirty page management is required for every page in the DRAM. Page-based incremental checkpointing techniques leverage the hardware page protection to track dirty pages and back up the dirty pages at the end of checkpoint interval [8]. Generally, the overhead of incremental checkpointing is made up of two parts, the monitoring overhead and the copying overhead. These two parts are a pair of trade-off factors and the key to balance the tradeoff is the granularity of the monitor. Finer-grained monitoring identifies the modified data in finer granularity with higher monitoring overhead, but is able to copy less unmodified data. With coarser-grained monitoring, the monitoring overhead is reduced but more unmodified data needs to be copied. Our experiment reveals that page-based incremental checkpointing technique suffers more from significant monitoring overhead. It indicates that a coarser-grained implementation will better balances the tradeoff and boosts the overall performance. However, blindly releasing the granularity does benefit to the monitoring overhead anyway, but results in extremely large checkpoint size which slow both the checkpoint and restart processes.

We observe the memory access characteristics at page granularity and find that the size of contiguous memory regions visited by applications tends to be proportional to the size of corresponding memory allocation. It indicates that the memory allocation information can be leveraged to appropriately release the monitoring granularity. Based on this observation, we propose Application-Based Coarse-Grained Incremental Checkpointing (ACCK) mechanism that strikes the balance between the monitoring overhead and copying overhead in incremental checkpointing. Based on the relationship between contiguous memory regions visited by applications and the corresponding memory allocation, ACCK mechanism releases the monitoring granularity by not monitoring the memory regions that the applications tend to visit. Since page-based incremental checkpointing works with normal-size pages to enable fine-grained monitoring, it inevitably increases the TLB overhead. We implement merge and split operation in Linux kernel which merges normal-size pages (4 Kbyte) to huge-size page (2 Mbyte) and splits huge-size page back to normal-size pages. ACCK merges normal-size pages when it decides to keep them unmonitored and splits huge-size page at checkpoint time to maintain fine-grained monitoring. This effectively alleviates the TLB overhead during the runtime.

Compared to traditional page-grained incremental checkpointing, ACCK mechanism largely reduces the monitoring overhead with bearable increase in copying overhead. The experimental results show that the performance of memory access monitoring, which accounts for around 70 % of the checkpointing time, improves 9x on average. As a result, ACCK presents a 2.5x performance improvement over the baseline page-grained based incremental checkpointing mechanism with the copying overhead increases by 7 % and the TLB overhead alleviated.

The remainder of this paper is organized as follows: Sect. 2 introduces the background and our motivation. We describe the design and implementation of ACCK in detail in Sect. 3. Section 4 gives the experiments results. Related work is discussed in Sect. 5 and we conclude in Sect. 6.

2   Background and Motivation

2.1   Non-volatile Memory

Non-volatile memory (NVM) is maturing fast in recent years. NVM features fast access, non-volatile, large capacity, and byte-addressable. Currently, phase change memory (PCM) is the most developed non-volatile memory technology [8–10]. The read speed of PCM is comparable with DRAM, while the write speed is much slower (typically 10x slower). There are many studies at architecture level focusing on mitigating the write latency [11, 12]. In this paper, we emulate the slow write by adding latency to test its performance on supporting checkpoint.

HDD data transfer bandwidth has long been a main concern for checkpointing technologies [11]. NVM allows in-memory copy to accelerate checkpointing. With the NVM support, the age-old checkpoint/restart mechanism seems more attractive due to its simplicity and low cost. Recent work [11] has shown that PCM-supported in-memory checkpointing is 50 times faster than the conventional in-HDD checkpointing. We assume the non-volatile memory can be directly accessed by CPUs via load and store instructions. It shares the same physical address with DRAM.

2.2   Incremental Checkpointing with Non-volatile Memory

As the scaling of computing systems, MTTF continues to decrease from days to hours, and to several minutes [11, 12]. The checkpoint interval decreases with MTTF since if the checkpoint time surpass the failure period, it means the possibility of ending up with infinite execution time. As noticed by previous work [11], frequent checkpointing is only possible by using PCRAM and is critical to benefit from incremental checkpointing schemes. As the checkpoint interval decreases, the probability of polluting a clean page becomes smaller, hence, the incremental checkpointing shows advantages over full-size checkpointing in terms of average checkpoint size.

Incremental checkpointing features user-transparency, decent portability and flexibility [3, 5, 11]. It requires a memory access monitor to track the dirty data and periodically backs them up to non-volatile memory or hard-disk. Existing researches leverage the hardware page protection mechanism to monitor write operations and back up the data in the granularity of pages. At the beginning of each checkpoint interval, all the writable pages are marked as read-only using mprotect system call. When an mprotected page is written, a page fault exception occurs and sends the SIGSEGV signal. The memory access monitor receives the signal and call the page fault exception handler to save the address of the dirty page in an external data structure. The page fault signal handler also marks the written page as writable by calling unprotect system call. At the end of the checkpoint interval, the monitor scans the data structure that tracks the dirty pages and backs up all the dirty pages. In this paper, we implement this page-protection based memory access monitor in runtime level and trigger checkpoint operation with the time interval of 5 s.

2.3 The Problem with Current Checkpoint

Generally, the overhead of incremental checkpointing is decided by the granularity of memory access monitoring [13]. The finer the granularity, the more page faults will be triggered but less data will be copied. The coarser the granularity, the less page fault occurs but more unmodified data has to be moved. The ideal case falls somewhere between which involves the least overhead to the total system performance.

The widely supported page sizes in operating system are 4K and 2M. Page-based incremental checkpointing works with 4K memory pages. 2M page is too coarse for monitoring which largely increases the checkpoint size. This will make incremental checkpoint fall back to full-size checkpoint with useless monitoring. However, current incremental checkpointing suffers from significant monitoring overhead (as well as TLB overhead) with 4K pages. Once a page is visited, a page fault occurs to handle the fault and the page will be copied at the checkpoint time. We quantify the monitoring overhead and copying overhead to clear our motivation. The rdtsc instruction is used to reckon the page-fault handler by time. We estimate the data movement from DRAM to PCRAM to simulate the copying overhead where each 8 byte atomic writes costs 600 ns. Note that both monitoring and copying overhead are generic and application-independent. Table 1 shows the average monitoring overhead and copying overhead at 4K and 2M granularity. Monitoring overhead is around 2.5x the time of copying at 4K level while copying data accounts for the most of overhead (~200x) with 2M huge page.

Table 1. Comparison of monitoring and copying overhead at 4K and 2M granularity

Granularity	Monitoring overhead	Copying overhead
4K	~100 us per 4 KByte	< 40 us per 4 KByte
2M	~0.2 us per 4 KByte	< 40 us per 4 KByte

Our experiments in Sect. 4 shows that monitoring overhead accounts for around 70 % of total checkpointing time. Therefore, a key to optimize the incremental checkpointing performance is finding a way to minimize the monitoring overhead. Specifically, a coarser-grained monitor that adapts well to the memory access pattern of applications will yield much better results. Previous work [13] has tried some intuitive methods to reduce the number of page faults during checkpoint interval, such as leaving the pages around the written pages unmonitored. However, these methods without priori information shows marginal improvement.

3   Design and Implementation

3.1   Contiguous Memory Regions to be Visited

Since no priori information is used to predict the memory regions to be visited, previous page-based incremental checkpointing has to track every write operation that trigger the page fault. We observe the memory access pattern of PARSEC and SPLASH benchmark suites at 4 K granularity and find that the size of contiguous memory regions visited by applications tends to be proportional to the size of the corresponding memory allocation. For example, if an application malloc a chunk of memory space sizing 100 pages, usually a 30 % or 50 % of pages will be contiguously visited, which are 30 and 50 pages. Given the same ratio (30 % or 50 %), for applications typically allocate thousands of pages, these numbers (30 and 50 pages in last example) will be proportionally increased. In this experiment, the total size of applications' memory allocation is divided into 2n pieces where n can be a reasonably large integer, such as 6 or 7. Each piece is regarded as "hot" piece if more than 80 % of pages inside the piece has been visited. In this definition of "hot" piece, we do not put strict limitation that all pages have to be visited in order to cover some more flexible memory access patterns.

Figure 1 shows the cumulative distribution function (CDF) and histogram of the priori information we are interested, which is the proportion between contiguous memory space visited by applications and the size of memory allocation, and their corresponding frequency. We run and statistic all applications in PARSEC and SPALSH2 to make this observation more reliable and generic. The parameter n is set to 6 so each memory allocation is divided into 64 pieces. In the histogram and CDF figures, the x-axis shows the ratio between the contiguous pieces visited by applications and the total pieces of memory allocation and y-axis shows the frequency or the proportion of corresponding ratio for memory allocations in all applications. It is noticeable that nearly 30 % has no "hot" pieces at all. Around 18 % (from 27 % to 45 %) of allocation has "hot" pieces between 30 % and 40 % of total pieces allocated while around 17 % of allocation has "hot" pieces between 60–70 % of total pieces allocated. This observation sheds new light on memory access pattern which can be utilized to appropriately loose the monitoring granularity to achieve better performance of incremental checkpointing for applications with large memory footprint.

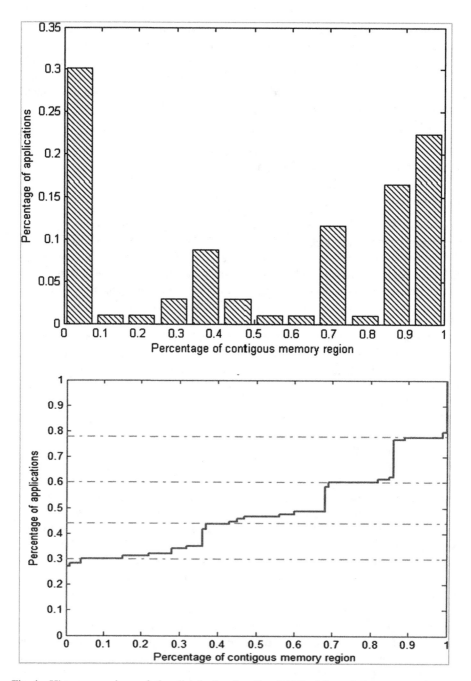

Fig. 1. Histogram and cumulative distribution function (CDF) of the ratio between contiguous memory pieces visited by applications and total allocated pieces

3.2 Application-Based Coarse-Grained Checkpoint: Loose Monitoring Granularity for "Hot" Applications

Our observation shows that applications tend to visit contiguous memory regions with its length often proportional to the size of the corresponding memory allocation. Based on this observation, we propose Application-Based Coarse-Grained Incremental Checkpointing (ACCK) that looses monitoring granularity for "hot" applications. ACCK first records of the start address and size of memory regions applied by applications. ACCK keeps track of the memory access pattern at 4K page granularity and divides the memory allocation into 2n pieces (at least one page for each piece). Here, we adopt a new definition of "hot" piece that for each piece of memory, if more than 80 % pages out of first 10 % of pages are visited, it is marked as a potential "hot" piece.

ACCK releases the monitoring granularity incrementally and gradually. Given that there are 2n pieces for each memory allocation, ACCK leaves the pieces unmonitored based on the memory access pattern at the pace of (20, 21, …, 2n − 3), (20, 21 …, 2n − 3), …, (20, 21, …, 2n − 3) pieces. Specifically, at the beginning of checkpoint, every piece is monitored. If a monitored piece becomes a potential "hot" piece, it will be left unmonitored by unprotecting all the pages inside the piece. If the following piece become a potential "hot" piece again, this piece and the following piece (a total of 21 = 2 pieces) will left unmonitored. Similarly, if following piece becomes potential "hot", ACCK leaves the following pieces unmonitored at the pace of 22, 23…until 2n − 3 pieces, then it repeat this process from the pace 20 to prevent over coarse granularity. For example, if an application visits all pieces in order, ACCK mechanism (with n = 6) releases the monitor at the pace of (1, 2, 4, 8) pieces and repeat until the end of memory regions. Figure 2 (a) shows the ACCK example for an in-order memory access pattern and Fig. 2(b) shows an ACCK example for an any-order memory access pattern. The dotted areas in Fig. 2 denote the recognized potential "hot" pieces, which trigger the following arrows. Note that the arrows in Fig. 2 does not have to occur in order.

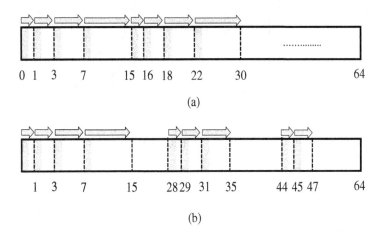

(a)

(b)

Fig. 2. Example of ACCK mechanism for in-order and any-order memory access pattern

3.3 Huge Page Support

2M huge page has a theoretical 512x performance improvement in terms of TLB performance over 4K page. However, previous researches are cautious about the use of huge pages. If huge pages are not used appropriately, a large amount of unmodified data has to be copied at the end of checkpoint interval.

In this work, we implement a kernel patch to Linux kernel 3.18 to provide merge and split operations between 4K pages and 2M huge pages. A merge operation merges 512 contiguous, 2M-alined 4K pages into a huge page (Fig. 3 top). A split operation splits a 2M huge page into 512 4K pages (Fig. 3 bottom). These functions are exposed to runtime library via system calls.

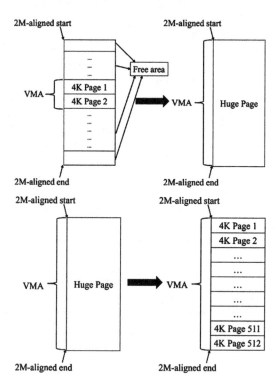

Fig. 3. An example of the merge (top) and split (bottom) operation done by modification on Linux.

In ACCK mechanism, if a large number of pieces with more than 512 4K pages in total will be unmonitored, these pages will be merged into huge pages if possible (note that huge pages to be merged into must be 2M-aligned). If the merge succeeds, ACCK turns off the page protection of the huge pages to leave it unmonitored. If the merge fails, ACCK remains to work in the traditional 4K granularity. In order to monitor in fine granularity at the beginning of checkpoint interval, the merged huge pages will be split into 4K pages at the end of checkpoint interval. The benefits of huge page comes from low TLB miss rate and penalty during runtime.

4 Experiments

This paper introduces Application-Based Coarse-Grained Incremental Checkpointing (ACCK). This section mainly evaluates and compares the performance of ACCK mechanism with the page-grained incremental checkpointing techniques.

4.1 Experimental Setup and Benchmarks

Our experiment platform is an AMD sever equipped with 2.2 GHz 12-core CPU and 16 GB of physical memory. The operating system is Linux 4.2. Our benchmarks come from PARSEC and SPLASH benchmark suite [14]. It focuses on programs from all domains, including HPC applications and server applications. The largest "native" input set is used.

4.2 Performance Metrics and Corresponding Results

Monitoring Overhead. ACCK mechanism mainly focuses on reducing the significant monitoring overhead of incremental checkpoint. Given the fact that the unit monitoring overhead is around 2.5x of unit copying overhead (application-independent), ACCK mechanism appropriately release the monitoring granularity with useful priori information. Figure 4 shows the significant performance improvement in terms of monitoring overhead in incremental checkpointing. As can be seen, ACCK mechanism lowers the monitoring overhead for all applications. The improvement can be as significant as 10x for most applications. The application freqmine is an exception with its reduction not

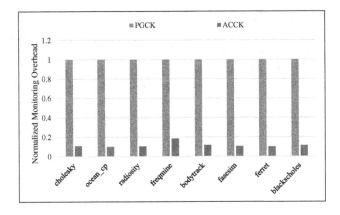

Fig. 4. Monitoring overhead

as significant as other applications. The reason behind is that there is not enough potential "hot" pieces in its memory allocation, which does not satisfy the requirements to trigger ACCK mechanism. In this case, the discrete memory access pattern will cause ACCK to fall back to the baseline incremental checkpointing. However, due to negligible management overhead of ACCK, the monitoring overhead of ACCK is always much better than traditional page-grained incremental checkpointing.

Copying Overhead. As mentioned in the previous section, the copying overhead is not as significant as monitoring overhead per memory page. ACCK mechanism releases monitoring granularity and increases copying overhead during checkpoint. However, our experimental results proves that the additional copying overhead is minimal compared to the improved monitoring performance. Figure 5 shows the total copying overhead of ACCK and the baseline incremental checkpoint. Only an average of 7.4 % more data has to be copied. Moreover, we argue that the preCopy mechanism [12] to pre-move data before checkpoint time reduces the memory pressure at checkpoint time. Therefore, the additional copying overhead can be effectively amortized.

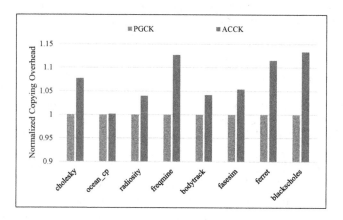

Fig. 5. Copying overhead

TLB Overhead. We also evaluate the performance of the page size adjustment. ACCK mechanism merge 4K pages into huge pages if a large number of pieces with more than 512 4K pages in total will be unmonitored. The use of huge page helps improve the TLB performance since each TLB entry maps much larger memory region with huge page. We use oprofile profiling tool to evaluate the data TLB miss using DTLB_MISS counter where the sampling count is set to 500. Figure 6 shows the normalized data TLB miss of ACCK mechanism with and without huge page support. Note that the merged pages will fall back to 4K pages at checkpoint time to maintain fine-grained monitoring at start.

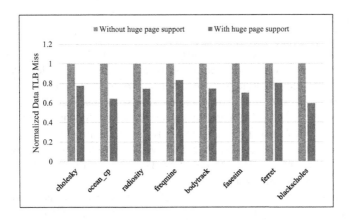

Fig. 6. Normalized data TLB miss with and without huge page support

Overall Checkpointing Performance. Generally, the overhead of incremental checkpoint consists of the monitoring overhead and the copying overhead. ACCK mechanism sacrifices the copying overhead for significant reduction in monitoring overhead and our experimental results prove it to be very effective in terms of overall checkpointing performance. Figure 6 gives the overall checkpointing performance of ACCK mechanism and the baseline incremental checkpoint. The overall checkpointing performance is defined as the reciprocal of the summation of the monitoring overhead and copying overhead. ACCK mechanism achieves 2.56x performance improvement over the baseline incremental checkpointing. It is noticeable that the performance improvement of each benchmark is pretty average, with the highest improvement 2.79x (ocean_cp) and lowest improvement 2.2x (freqmine) (Fig. 7).

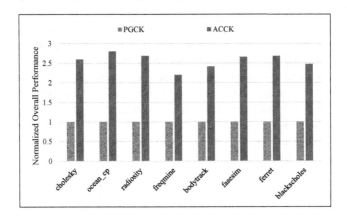

Fig. 7. Overall performance

5   Related Work

As checkpoint-restart is the commonly-used technique for fault-tolerance, the related research is abundant. Non-volatile memory sheds new light on fault tolerance. Previous work [11, 12] leverages the byte persistency of non-volatile memory to do in-memory copy to accelerate checkpointing. To address the slow write speed and limited bandwidth during checkpoint, [11] proposes a preCopy mechanism to move checkpoint data to non-volatile memory before checkpoint time to amortize the memory bandwidth pressure at checkpoint time. [12] proposes a 3D PCMDRAM design at architectural level to facilitate data movement between DRAM and PCM. These two studies both focus on hiding the long write latency of non-volatile memory.

Most of related work of reducing the checkpoint size uses the incremental checkpointing technique [15] that only saves the dirty data between two consecutive checkpoints. Since then, the hardware memory management mechanism has been leveraged to monitor the dirty data. However, incremental checkpoint technique still suffers from significant monitoring overhead and struggle with the granularity of memory access monitor. This paper propose a novel monitoring mechanism which can reduce the monitoring overhead with bearable increase in checkpoint size. Our work is orthogonal to previous studies (e.g. pre-copy mechanism [12]) and can be combined to achieve better performance.

6   Conclusion

Checkpoint-restart has been an effective mechanism to guarantee the reliability and consistency of computing systems. Our work mainly addresses the significant monitoring overhead of current incremental checkpointing technique. This paper proposes Application-Based Coarse-Grained Incremental Checkpointing (ACCK) mechanism based on non-volatile memory. We observe the memory access characteristics and find that the size of contiguous memory regions heavily visited by applications tends to be proportional to the size of allocated memory space. ACCK leverages the priori information of the memory allocation to release the memory monitoring granularity in an incremental and appropriate way. The experimental results shows that ACCK largely reduces the monitoring time and presents 2.56x overall checkpointing performance improvement. This work can be applied to frequent checkpoint of a wide range of applications and databases and can be combined with other work (e.g. pre-copy mechanism) to achieve better checkpoint performance.

Acknowledgments. This work is partially supported by National High-tech R&D Program of China (863 Program) under Grants 2012AA01A301 and 2012AA010901, by program for New Century Excellent Talents in University, by National Science Foundation (NSF) China 61272142, 61402492, 61402486, 61379146, 61272483, and by the State Key Laboratory of High-end Server and Storage Technology (2014HSSA01). The authors will gratefully acknowledge the helpful suggestions of the reviewers, which have improved the presentation.

References

1. Reed, D.: High-End Computing: The Challenge of Scale. Director's Colloquium, May 2004
2. Schroeder, B., Gibson, G.A.: Understanding failures in petascale computers. J. Phys.: Conf. Ser. **78**(1), 012022 (2007). IOP Publishing
3. Plank, J.S., Xu, J., Netzer, R.H.: Compressed differences: an algorithm for fast incremental checkpointing. Technical report, CS-95-302, University of Tennessee at Knoxville, August 1995
4. Princeton University Scalable I/O Research. A checkpointing library for Intel Paragon. http://www.cs.princeton.edu/sio/CLIP/
5. Plank, J.S., Beck, M., Kingsley, G., Li, K.: Libckpt: transparent checkpointing under unix. In: Usenix Winter Technical Conference, pp. 213–223, January 1995
6. Vaidya, N.H.: Impact of checkpoint latency on overhead ratio of a checkpointing scheme. IEEE Trans. Comput. **46**, 942–947 (1997)
7. Plank, J.S., Elwasif, W.R.: Experimental assessment of workstation failures and their impact on checkpointing systems. In: 28th International Symposium on Fault-Tolerant Computing, June 1998
8. Koltsidas, I., Pletka, R., Mueller, P., Weigold, T., Eleftheriou, E., Varsamou, M., Ntalla, A., Bougioukou, E., Palli, A., Antanokopoulos, T.: PSS: a prototype storage subsystem based on PCM. In: Proceedings of the 5th Annual Non-volatile Memories Workshop (2014)
9. Coburn, J., Caulfield, A.M., Akel, A., Grupp, L.M., Gupta, R.K., Jhala, R., Swanson, S.: NV-heaps: making persistent objects fast and safe with next-generation, non-volatile memories. ACM SIGARCH Comput. Archit. News **39**(1), 105–118 (2011). ACM
10. Bautista-Gomez, L., Tsuboi, S., Komatitsch, D., Cappello, F., Maruyama, N., Matsuoka, S.: FTI: high performance fault tolerance interface for hybrid systems. In: Proceedings of 2011 International Conference for High Performance Computing, Networking, Storage and Analysis. ACM (2011)
11. Dong, X., Muralimanohar, N., Jouppi, N., Kaufmann, R., Xie, Y.: Leveraging 3D PCRAM technologies to reduce checkpoint overhead for future exascale systems. In: Proceedings of the Conference on High Performance Computing Networking, Storage and Analysis. ACM (2009)
12. Kannan, S., Gavrilovska, A., Schwan, K., Milojicic, D.: Optimizing checkpoints using NVM as virtual memory. In: 2013 IEEE 27th International Symposium on Parallel and Distributed Processing (IPDPS). IEEE (2013)
13. Zhang, W.Z., et.al.: Fine-grained checkpoint based on non-volatile memory, unpublished
14. Bienia, C., Kumar, S., Singh, J.P., Li, K.: The PARSEC benchmark suite: characterization and architectural implications. In: Proceedings of the 17th International Conference on Parallel Architectures and Compilation Techniques. ACM (2008)
15. Sancho, J.C., Petrini, F., Johnson, G., Frachtenberg, E.: On the feasibility of incremental checkpointing for scientific computing. In: Proceedings of the 18th International Parallel and Distributed Processing Symposium. IEEE (2004)
16. Nam, H., Kim, J., Hong, S.J., Lee, S.: Probabilistic checkpointing. In: IEICE Transactions, Information and Systems, vol. E85-D, July 2002
17. Agbaria, A., Plank, J.S.: Design, implementation, and performance of checkpointing in NetSolve. In: Proceedings of the International Conference on Dependable Systems and Networks, June 2000

DASM: A Dynamic Adaptive Forward Assembly Area Method to Accelerate Restore Speed for Deduplication-Based Backup Systems

Chao Tan[1], Luyu Li[1], Chentao Wu[1(✉)], and Jie Li[1,2]

[1] Shanghai Key Laboratory of Scalable Computing and Systems,
Department of Computer Science and Engineering,
Shanghai Jiao Tong University, Shanghai 200240, China
wuct@cs.sjtu.edu.cn
[2] Department of Computer Science,
University of Tsukuba, Tsukuba, Ibaraki 305-8577, Japan

Abstract. Data deduplication yields an important role in modern backup systems for its demonstrated ability to improve storage efficiency. However, in deduplication-based backup systems, the consequent exhausting fragmentation problem has drawn ever-increasing attention over in terms of backup frequencies, which leads to the degradation of restoration speed. Various Methods are proposed to address this problem. However, most of them purchase restore speed at the expense of deduplication ratio reduction, which is not efficient.

In this paper, we present a Dynamic Adaptive Forward Assembly Area Method, called DASM, to accelerate restore speed for deduplication-based backup systems. DASM exploits the fragmentation information within the restored backup streams and dynamically trades off between chunk-level cache and container-level cache. DASM is a pure data restoration module which pursues optimal read performance without sacrificing deduplication ratio. Meanwhile, DASM is a resource independent and cache efficient scheme, which works well under different memory footprint restrictions. To demonstrate the effectiveness of DASM, we conduct several experiments under various backup workloads. The results show that, DASM is sensitive to fragmentation granularity and can accurately adapt to the changes of fragmentation size. Besides, experiments also show that DASM improves the restore speed of traditional LRU and ASM methods by up to 58.9 % and 57.1 %, respectively.

Keywords: Data deduplication · Restore speed · Reliability · Cache policy · Performance evaluation

1 Introduction

Data deduplication is an effective technique used to improve storage efficiency in modern backup systems [2,13]. A typical deduplication-based backup system partitions backup streams into variable-size or fixed-size chunks. Each data

G.R. Gao et al. (Eds.): NPC 2016, LNCS 9966, pp. 58–70, 2016.
DOI: 10.1007/978-3-319-47099-3_5

chunk is identified by fingerprints calculated using cryptographic methods, such as SHA-1 [11]. Two chunks are considered to be duplicates if they have identical fingerprints. For each chunk, deduplication system employs Key-Value Store, also referred to fingerprint index, to identify possible duplicates. Only new fresh chunks are physically stored in containers while duplicates are eliminated.

However, in backup systems, the deviation between physical locality and logical locality increases when backup frequencies are improved, which leads to the physical dispersion of subsequent backup streams. The consequent exhausting fragmentation problem has drawn ever-increasing attention, which results in the degradation of restoration speed and expensive garbage collection operations [8,10].

In the past decade, various methods are proposed to address this problem [7,9]. Most of them purchase restore speed by sacrificing the deduplication ratio, which is costly [6,12]. Traditional restoration method employs LRU algorithm to cache chunk containers. In many scenarios, LRU buffers a large amount of unuseful chunks within containers. Besides, unlike some other applications, we have perfect pre-knowledge of future access informations during restoration, which cannot be well utilized by LRU. A few advanced approaches like ASM [6] employs a forward assembly area to prefetch data chunks within a same container. Nevertheless, ASM is a chunk-level restoration method which limits its read performance due to the one-container cache regulation.

In this paper, we present a Dynamic Adaptive Forward Assembly Area Method, called DASM, to accelerate restore speed for deduplication-based backup systems. DASM exploits the fragmentation information within the restored backup streams and dynamically trades off between chunk-level cache and container-level cache. DASM is a pure data restoration module which pursues optimal read performance without sacrificing deduplication ratio. Meanwhile, DASM works well under different memory footprint restrictions.

The main contributions of this paper are summarized as follows,

- We propose a novel Dynamic Adaptive Forward Assembly Area method (DASM) for deduplication-based backup systems, which outperforms prior approaches in terms of restoration speed. DASM performs well in different scenarios, such as various memory restrictions and backup workloads.
- We conduct several experiments to demonstrate the effectiveness of DASM. The results show that DASM sharply improves the restore speed in various workloads.

The remainder of the paper is organized as follows. Section 2 reviews the background and the motivation of DASM. Section 3 illustrates the details of our DASM. Section 4 evaluates the performance of our scheme compared with other popular restoration cache algorithms. Finally we conclude our work in Sect. 5.

2   Background and Motivation

In this section, firstly, we introduce data deduplication briefly. Then we explore the fragmentation problem and how it impacts restoration speed. After that, an elaborate investigation of existing solutions and the motivation of our approach are exhibited.

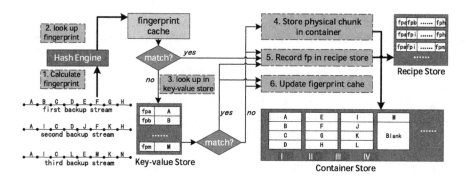

Fig. 1. Data deduplication system architecture.

2.1 Data Deduplication

In backup systems, data deduplication can significantly improve storage efficiency [2,13]. Figure 1 illustrates a typical data deduplication system architecture [4].

Two chunks are considered to be duplicates if they have identical fingerprints. A typical deduplication system employs Key-Value Store, referred to fingerprint index as well, to identify possible duplicates. The key-value store maps each fingerprint to the corresponding physical location of data chunks. The recipe store is used to record logical fingerprint sequences according to the order of the original data stream, in case of future data restoration. And container store is a log-structured storage warehouse. After deduplication, data chunks are aggregated into fixed-sized containers (usually 4 MB) and stored in a container store.

As shown in Fig. 1, original backup streams are partitioned into several variable or fixed-size chunks. The hash engine calculates a fingerprint for each data chunk using cryptographic methods, such as SHA-1 [11].

Once a fingerprint is produced, the system takes following steps to eliminate duplicates: (1) Look up in the fingerprint cache. (2) If it is a cache hit, it means that a duplicate data chunk has already existed. In this situation, we can only record the fingerprint into recipe store and terminate the deduplication process. (3) If cache misses, it looks up in the key-value store for further identification. (4) If there is a match, jump to step 5. Otherwise, the data chunk is considered to be a new fresh and stored into containers in the container store. (5) Record the fingerprint in the recipe store. (6) Update fingerprint cache to explore data localities.

2.2 Fragmentation Problem and Restoration Speed

Fragmentation is one of the exhausting problems caused by typical deduplication scheme. As we can see in Fig. 1, physical chunks are stored sequentially in order of their appearance. In the essence, the physical locality is similar to the logical locality for the first backup stream. However, this deviation increases as time goes because duplicate chunks are eliminated, which leads to the physical dispersion of subsequent backup streams.

Fragmentation problems is troublesome in many aspects. First, it degrades the restoration speed [8]. In deduplication systems, read and write operations are executes with basic granularity of container. Thus data restoration should be faster with consecutive physical distribution. Besides, chunks could become invalid because of data deletion operations. Physical dispersion results in holes within the containers, which leads to the emergence of inefficient garbage collection [10].

Various methods are proposed to address these problems. On one hand, several methods accelerate the restore speed via decreasing deduplication ratio [3]. iDedup [6] selectively deduplicates only sequences of disk blocks and replaces the expensive, on-disk, deduplication metadata with a smaller, in-memory cache. These techniques enable it to tradeoff deduplication ratio for performance. The context-based rewriting (CBR) minimizes drop in restore performance for latest backups by shifting fragmentation to older backups, which are rarely used for restore [5].

Traditional restoration method employs LRU algorithm to cache chunk containers. However, LRU is a container-level cache policy which buffers a large amount of unused chunks within containers. Besides, unlike other data access pattern, we have perfect pre-knowledge of future access information during restoration, which is not utilized by LRU. ASM [6] employs a forward assembly area to prefetch data chunks within a same container. Nevertheless, ASM is a chunk-level restoration method which limits its read performance since the one-container cache regulation.

2.3 Forward Assembly Area

Forward Assembly Area (ASM) is a chunk-level restoration method which caches chunks rather than containers for better cache performance. Figure 2 depicts the basic functions of ASM.

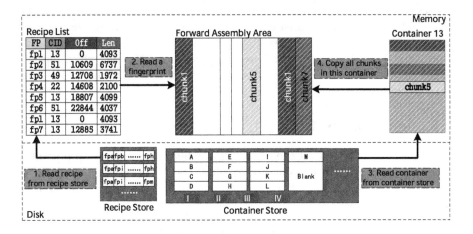

Fig. 2. Forward Assembly Area (ASM) Method.

ASM employs a large forward assembly area to assemble M bytes of the restored backup. Meanwhile, it utilizes two dedicated buffers, a recipe buffer to cache recipe streams and a chunk-container-sized buffer to cache proper containers that is being used.

In a simple case shown in Fig. 2, firstly, ASM reads the recipes from their related recipe store preserved in disk into the recipe buffer. Then, ASM obtains the top n recipes which hold at most M bytes of the restored data. After that, ASM finds the earliest unrestored chunk and loads the corresponding container into its I/O buffer. For $chunk1$ with fingerprint $fp1$, the corresponding container $container13$ is loaded into the container buffer. Then, all the chunks belongs to $container13$ in the top n recipe items will be restored, which are $chunk1$, $chunk5$, $chunk7$ in this case. ASM repeats this procedure until the M bytes are completely filled. Finally, ASM flushes these M bytes of restored data into disk.

ASM restores M bytes every time and only one container is loaded into memory during each recovery, which improves the cache performance. However, the one-container regulation may degrade the read performance since each container have to wait until the last one finishes restoration of all chunks.

2.4 Our Motivation

Many previous literatures attempt to figure out the fragmentation problem through deduplication procedures, such as rewriting. These methods purchase restore speed at the expense of deduplication ratio reduction, which is unworthy. From the restoration's perspective purely, traditional LRU cache policy ignores the perfect pre-knowledge of future access information during restoration and holds plenty of useless chunks in memory, which is a big resource waste. ASM is a chunk-level restoration method which limits its read performance since the one-container cache regulation.

To address this problem, we propose a novel Dynamic Adaptive Forward Assembly Area method (DASM) for deduplication-based backup systems, which arms ASM with a multiple-container-sized cache. DASM adaptively adjusts the size of the forward assembly area and the container cache according to the fragmentation level of the restored backup streams to pursue optimal restoration performance. DASM is resource independent and cache efficient, which outperforms prior approaches under different memory footprint restrictions and various backup workloads.

3   Design of DASM

To overcome the shortages of the forward assembly area method, we present a Dynamic Adaptive Forward Assembly Area method (DASM) which arms ASM with a multiple-container-sized cache. Figure 3 exhibits the overall architecture of DASM.

Different from ASM, DASM carries a multiple-container-sized cache called Container Cache, which buffers multiple containers. To reduce the resource dependencies and increase cache efficiencies, we impose restrictions on memory footprint by bounding the overall size of the ASM area and the container cache.

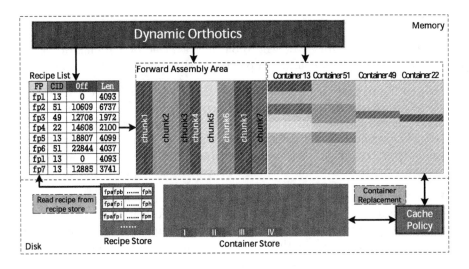

Fig. 3. Overview of Dynamic Adaptive Forward Assembly Area Method (DASM).

Besides the original ASM area and the new joint container cache, DASM involves other two main components as below,

- **Dynamic Orthotics**

  Dynamic Orthotics is a calculation model which exploits future access information to pursue optimal restoration performance within the restriction of finite memory footprint. It regards the fragmentation rate as a major criterion and dynamically adjusts the proportion of the ASM area to the container cache. Details are discussed in Sect. 3.1.

- **Cache Policy**

  Cache Policy module depicts the cache replacement policies carried out in the container cache. It works as a centralized scheduler which dispatches containers legitimately to reduce cache miss and minimize the bandwidth requirement.

DASM abides by the following steps,

(1) Tradeoff the ASM area and the container cache according to the fragmentation rate, which are typically done by Dynamic Orthotics module. After Dynamic Orthotics completes the tradeoff, the top n chunks within C containers are restored at this time.

(2) Load the required C containers into the container cache. If there is a cache miss, DASM selects appropriate cache policies for container replacement.

(3) Execute the ASM restoration schemes policies repeatedly: find the earliest unrestored chunk and copy all the chunks pertains to its corresponding container to the forward assembly area.

(4) Flush all the restored data to disks and restart from step 1.

3.1 Dynamic Orthotics

Restoration speed is strongly depended on the fragmentation granularity of the restored data stream. We consider two extreme situations,

(1) Lowest fragmentation granularity for the first backup: as for the first backup. In this scenario, we can shrink container caches to a single container size since almost all consecutive chunks belong to a same container.
(2) Highest fragmentation granularity that almost all unique chunks are placed in different containers with each other: Under this circumstance, we have to shrink ASM area to acquire as large container cache area as possible.

Based on these observations, we propose a mathematical model called Dynamic Orthotics, which exploits future access information to pursue optimal restoration performance within the restriction of finite memory footprint. It regards fragmentation rate as the major criterion and dynamically adjusts the proportion of the ASM area to container cache.

For clarity, we define a few symbols as shown in Table 1.

Table 1. NOTATIONS OF DASM

Notation	Description
ASM	Forward assembly area whose size is donated by $|ASM|$
CC	Container cache whose size is donated by $|CC|$
CS	Container Size
MFP	Overall memory footprint whose size is donated by $|MFP|$
$chunksize_i$	Chunk size of the ith chunk in the recipe stream
C_i	The overall number of containers required by the top i chunks
n	The number of chunks waiting to be restored at a time
$rate$	Fragmentation Rate

Suppose there are n chunks waiting to be restored in the forward assembly area and they belong to C_n containers. To obtain optimal restoration performance, ASM area should hold exactly $\sum_{i=1}^{n} chunksize_i$ bytes while container cache has the ability to load accurately C_n containers. The relationships between these notations can be formulated by the following equations:

$$|ASM| = \sum_{i=1}^{n} chunksize_i \tag{1}$$

$$|CC| = C_n * CS \tag{2}$$

$$|ASM| + |CC| \leq |MFP| \tag{3}$$

We define fragmentation rate by the following equation,

$$fragmentation\ rate = \frac{|CC|}{|MFP|} \tag{4}$$

As shown in Algorithm 1, Dynamic Orthotics reads chunk information sequentially from the recipe buffer. For each chunk, dynamic orthotics calculates whether it can be pushed into ASM. If Eqs. 1, 2 and 3 still holds, then add the chunk into ASM. Otherwise, terminate and adjust $|ASM|$ and $|CC|$ according to the returned value.

Algorithm 1. Dynamic Orthotics

Aim: Dynamically adjust the proportion of the ASM area to container cache according to the fragmentation rate.

while *(chunk ← RecipeBuffer.head)≠ null* **do**
    C'_n = chunk.CID in CC? $C_n : C_n + 1$
    if *(ASM.size+chunk.size)+C'_n *CS ≤ MFP.size* **then**
        ASM.size+=chunk.sie
        $C_n=C'_n$
    else
        return $ASM.size, C_n$

3.2 Near-Optimal Cache Policy

To reduce container cache miss penalty as much as possible, we implement a variant of Belady's optimal replacement cache policy [1].

Belady's policy evicts the cached container that will be accessed in the farthest future. With foreseeable container access information, it is oversimplified to achieve optimality. However, with fragmentation rate high enough, we may have to traverse along the recipe list for a long time to find a victim, which is expensive. Therefore we establish several cache policies which could achieve near-optimal performance under framework of DASM.

- If a container has already existed in the container cache and it will be reused during the next round, keep it in the cache.
- If there exists no such containers, evict all containers in the container cache.

DASM dynamically adapts the size of container cache and reserve exactly C_n containers' size for the containers required. Since containers which are not reused during the next round will be evicted no matter how, we just evict them without considering replacement order.

4 Performance Evaluation

To demonstrate the effectiveness of DASM, we conduct several experiments using various backup datasets to evaluate the performance of DASM and compare it with traditional restore methods such as LRU and ASM.

4.1 Evaluation Methodology

(1) Evaluation Platform. We utilize an open-source deduplication platform called Deduplication Framework (DeFrame) [4], for comprehensive data deduplication evaluation. DeFrame implements the entire parameter space discussed in a modular and extensible fashion; this enables apple-to-apple comparisons among both existing and potential solutions [4].

We implement and evaluate a DASM prototype on DeFrame under the Ubuntu 14.10 operating system, with linux kernel version 3.13.0, running on a quad-core Intel i5-4430 processor at 3.00 GHz, with a 12 GB RAM, a 1 TB 7200RPM hard disk drive.

(2) Traditional Restoration Methods for Comparison. This evaluation employs LRU, ASM as the contrasts. As illustrates in Sect. 2, traditional restoration method employs LRU algorithm to cache chunk containers. ASM employs a forward assembly area to prefetch data chunks within a same container.

(3) Evaluation Metrics. In this paper, we exploit restoration speed as our major evaluation metric. Restore speeds are measured in term of encoding time in seconds. Besides, we explores fragmentation rate to show that DASM is sensitive to fragmentation degree and can adapt to fragmentation change accurately. The fragmentation rate is defined in Sect. 3.1 as:

$$fragmentation\ rate = \frac{|CC|}{|MFP|} \tag{5}$$

(4) Evaluation Datasets. We choose three real-world files as our datasets: ubuntu-14.04.3, ubuntu-14.10 and ubuntu-15.04. These datasets are firstly stored as the 1st, 2nd and 3rd backup streams in the deduplication systems, respectively. After that, we evaluates performance of LRU, ASM and our DASM methods by restoring each original backup streams. Table 2 lists some detailed information about these datasets.

Table 2. DETAILED INFORMATION ABOUT DATASETS

Backup data	Bytes	Chunks	Average chunk size	Containers
ubuntu-14.04.3	1054867456	228791	4610	255
ubuntu-14.10	1186529280	257945	4599	378
ubuntu-15.04	1150844928	250609	4592	480

4.2 Experimental Results

In this section, we give the experimental results of DASM and compare it with LRU and ASM under three backup streams to illustrate its benefits.

Table 3. Comparison among LRU, ASM and DASM under different cache size in terms of restore speed.

	128M			256M			1G		
	1st	2nd	3rd	1st	2nd	3rd	1st	2nd	3rd
DASM	4.733	6.047	5.982	4.552	5.689	5.329	4.34	5.937	4.947
LRU	11.507	12.233	12.311	8.173	8.245	7.874	9.081	9.461	10.114
Improvement	58.9 %	50.6 %	51.4 %	44.3 %	31.0 %	32.3 %	52.2 %	57.2 %	51.1 %
ASM	8.341	9.491	9.623	8.453	8.127	6.693	9.572	10.692	11.544
Improvement	43.3 %	36.3 %	37.8 %	46.1 %	30.0 %	20.3 %	54.7 %	44.5 %	57.1 %

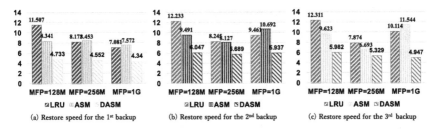

Fig. 4. Comparison among LRU, ASM and DASM under different cache size in terms of restore speed.

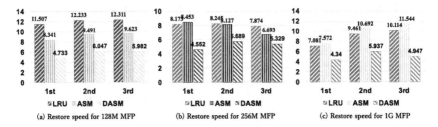

Fig. 5. Comparison among LRU, ASM and DASM under different backup streams in terms of restore speed.

(1) Restore Speed Under Different Cache Size. Table 3 and Fig. 4 describe the comparison between restore speed among LRU, ASM and DASM under different cache size. Experiments show that DASM improves the restore speed of traditional LRU and ASM methods by up to 58.9 % and 57.1 %, respectively.

(2) Restore Speed Under Different Backup Streams. Figure 5 illustrates the comparison between restore speed among LRU, ASM and DASM under different backup streams. Since the first backup is stored sequentially among the containers, which means that it carries the lowest fragmentation problem, it is restored fastest under arbitrary circumstances. As shown in the Figure, DASM outperforms LRU and ASM under any backup streams.

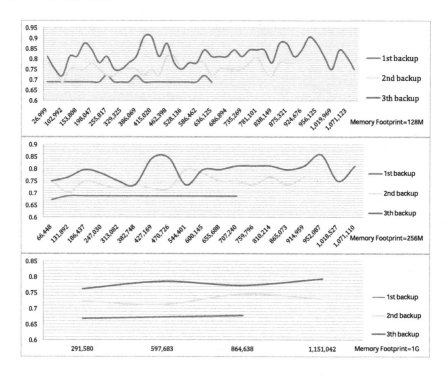

Fig. 6. Fragmentation rate curves under different backup streams

(3) Fragmentation Rate. Figure 6 depicts the fragmentation rate changing curves under different backup streams. As we can see in the figure, regardless of the size of memory footprint, as backup time increases, the average fragmentation rate rises with amplitude aggrandizament (3rd > 2nd > 1st). This phenomenon implies that our DASM can effectively and accurately detect fragmentation changes and adjust accordingly.

4.3   Analysis

Traditional LRU cache policy ignores the perfect pre-knowledge of future access information during restoration and holds plenty of useless chunks in memory, which is a big resource waste. ASM is a chunk-level restoration method which limits its read performance since the one-container cache regulation.

From the results in the previous subsections, it is clear that DASM approach has many advantages on restore speed in backup systems compared to the previous restore methods: LRU and ASM. There are several reasons to achieve these gains. First, DASM integrates container cache which can effectively enhance the hit ratio of chunks and reduce read latency. Second, DASM can accurately capture current fragmentation granularity and dynamically adjust ASM area size and container cache size to achieve the best performance. Therefore, DASM outperforms LRU and ASM enormously.

5   Conclusions

In this paper, we present a Dynamic Adaptive Forward Assembly Area Method, called DASM, to accelerate restore speed for deduplication-based backup systems. Different from previous approaches, DASM is a pure data restoration module which pursue optimal read performance without sacrificing deduplication ratio. DASM exploits the fragmentation information within the restored backup streams and dynamically trades off between chunk-level cache and container-level cache which leverages both advantages of LRU and ASM. Experiments results show that DASM is sensitive to fragmentation degree and can adapt to fragmentation change accurately. Besides, experiments also show that DASM improves the restore speed of traditional LRU and ASM methods by up to 58.9 % and 57.1 %, respectively.

Acknowledgement. We thank anonymous reviewers for their insightful comments. This work is partially sponsored by the National 863 Program of China (No. 2015AA015302), the National 973 Program of China (No. 2015CB352403), the National Natural Science Foundation of China (NSFC) (No. 61332001, No. 61303012, and No. 61572323), the Scientific Research Foundation for the Returned Overseas Chinese Scholars, and the CCF-Tencent Open Fund.

References

1. Belady, L.A.: A study of replacement algorithms for a virtual-storage computer. IBM Syst. J. **5**, 78–101 (1966)
2. Asaroand, T., Biggar, H.: Data de-duplication, disk-to-disk backup systems: technical and business considerations. The Enterprise Strategy Group
3. Fu, M., Feng, D., et al.: Accelerating restore and garbage collection in deduplication-based backup systems via exploiting historical information. In: USENIX Annual Technical Conference 2014
4. Fu, M., Feng, D., et al.: Design tradeoffs for data deduplication performance in backup workloads. In: Proceedings of the USENIX FAST 2015
5. Kaczmarczyk, M., Barczynski, M., et al.: Reducing impact of data fragmentation caused by in-line deduplication. In: Proceedings of the 5th Annual International Systems and Storage Conference
6. Lillibridge, M., Eshghi, K., Bhagwat, D.: Improving restore speed for backup systems that use inline chunk-based deduplication. In: Proceedings of the USENIX FAST 2013
7. Mandagere, N., Zhou, P., et al.: Demystifying data deduplication. In: Proceedings of the ACM/IFIP/USENIX Middleware 2008 Conference Companion
8. Nam, Y.J., Lu, G.L., et al.: Chunk fragmentation level: an effective indicator for read performance degradation in deduplication storage. In: High Performance Computing and Communications (HPCC) 2011
9. Paulo, J., Pereira, J.: A survey and classification of storage deduplication systems. ACM Comput. Surv. (CSUR) **47**(1), 11 (2014)
10. Preston, W.C.: Restoring deduped data in deduplication systems. SearchDataBackup.com (2010)

11. Quinlan, S., Dorward, S.: Venti: a new approach to archival storage. In: Proceedings of the USENIX FAST 2002
12. Srinivasan, K., Bisson, T., et al.: iDedup: latency-aware, inline data deduplication for primary storage. In: Proceedings of the USENIX FAST 2012
13. Wallace, G., Douglis, F., et al.: Characteristics of backup workloads in production systems. In: Proceedings of the USENIX FAST 2012

Scheduling and Load-Balancing

A Statistics Based Prediction Method for Rendering Application

Qian Li$^{(\boxtimes)}$, Weiguo Wu, Long Xu, Jianhang Huang, and Mingxia Feng

Department of Computer Science and Technology,
Xi'an Jiaotong University, Xi'an 710049, China
qian.l@stu.xjtu.edu.cn, wgwu@mail.xjtu.edu.cn, longxu20145@gmail.com,
huangjhsx@gmail.com, b833167720163.com

Abstract. As an interesting commercial application, rendering plays an important role in the field of animation and movie production. Generally, render farm is used to rendering mass images concurrently according to the independence among frames. How to scheduling and manage various rendering jobs efficiently is a significant issue for render farm. Therefore, the prediction of rendering time for frames is relevant for scheduling, which offers the reference and basis for scheduling method. In this paper a statistics based prediction method is addressed. Initially, appropriate parameters which affect the rendering time are extracted and analyzed according to parsing blend formatted files which offers a general description for synthetic scene. Then, the sample data are gathered by open source software Blender and J48 classification algorithm is used for predicting rendering time. The experimental results show that the proposed method improve the prediction accuracy about 60 % and 75.74 % for training set and test set, which provides reasonable basis for scheduling jobs efficiently and saving rendering cost.

Keywords: Rendering · Prediction · Statistics · Classification · Render farm

1 Introduction

High performance computing (HPC) provides a chance for scientists to use large scale computing resources to settle problems in intensive computation application [15]. Gradually, researchers concentrate on how to manage what application could be applied on HPC platforms to maximize the performance. As an intensive computation and massive data access application, rendering with the feature of independence among frames is suitable for parallel processing in HPC environment. Rendering is the process of creating an image from a model by means of computer programs [2,16], which is used widely on many field, for example, animation design, development of games, simulation [3], etc.

With the rapid development of animation industry, rendering is widely used in movie production and directly determines the visual effect of animation works.

© IFIP International Federation for Information Processing 2016
Published by Springer International Publishing AG 2016. All Rights Reserved
G.R. Gao et al. (Eds.): NPC 2016, LNCS 9966, pp. 73–84, 2016.
DOI: 10.1007/978-3-319-47099-3_6

For an animation production, rendering a photo-realistic image with high resolution of 4K to 6K can be exceptionally costly, often taking days, or even weeks. Generally, render farm, which is a cluster of interconnected computers used for rendering images in parallel [4], is used by companies to rendering mass images concurrently, which has been proven to be quite effective way to cutting down hours of render time into minutes.

When using the render farm, users just submit their rendering jobs which includes the requirement of number of rendering resources, types of rendering software, budget and deadline etc. through web portal or client. The render farm with a pool of finite rendering resources receives the rendering jobs, chooses appropriate resources according to the demands of rendering users and scheduling rendering jobs according to some policies. Generally speaking, the research spot is focus on optimizing and design of scheduling policy [9,19,26]. But many issues are based the on the premise of obtaining the application running time in advance or have not a-priori knowledge on execution time prediction [17], which will negatively impacts the efficiency of scheduling policy, especially for the static policy from the view of system. And from the view of users, without prediction, users have no idea how long they will be waiting for finish rendering jobs, users cannot obtain better experience on rendering service and choose an economical way to employ rendering resources. Therefore, how to predict running time of applications and improve prediction accuracy is significant topic for render farm.

In this paper, we propose a statistics based prediction method to provide a guidance for scheduling policy in render farm. The proposed method extracts and analyzes firstly the appropriate parameters which affect the rendering time by the way of parsing blend formatted files. Then, the sample data are gathered by open source software Blender and we use J48 classification algorithm to train and predict rendering time. And the test result indicate that our method improves the prediction accuracy about 60 % and 75.74 % for training set and test set respectively.

The rest of this paper is organized as follows: related works are introduced in Sect. 2. In Sect. 3, we describe the system design and proposed method. Section 4 presents the experimental results. And conclusion and future works are provided in Sect. 5.

2   Related Works

Rendering is one of the most important research topics in computer graphics, and it is closely related to the other technologies. Rendering plays an important role in the field of animation and movie production. The execution time prediction for rendering is necessary for scheduling and user's Qos. Obviously for this schedule to be effective and experience to be better, a good prediction of the execution time for rendering is required.

Many researchers have explored the use of various time models to predict execution time. According to auto-regressive model a time series based prediction method [21] is also proposed. For physically-based medical simulation, a multirate output-estimation method using the ARMAX model [11] is presented to improve the computational speed and accuracy. By rigid model, Liu et al. [14] proposes a proxy position prediction method using the geometric patch. The patch is calculated from the real-time contact region prediction method. Hou and Sourina [8] present a new prediction method based on auto-regressive model for smooth haptic rendering [22] to overcome the low update rate of the physical simulation with complex or deformable models. Schnitzer et al. [17] predict the individual execution time of graphics commands using models for the main three commands relevant for rendering, namely, FLUSH, CLEAR, and DRAW.

And then, prediction ideology is also be used for various types of render. For remote image-based rendering (IBR) [12] in mobile virtual environments, Lazeml et al. [10] propose a prefetching scheme that predicts the client potential path based on the movement history using a linear prediction model. The server then sends one predicted image with every position update for the client, which reduces the server load and improves the system scalability. In Depth image-based rendering (DIBR), a combined hole-filling approach [25] with spatial and temporal prediction is presented.

Considering the workload in the process of rendering, Wimmer and Wonka [20] present an estimation approach based on sampling rendering times, and an improved mathematical heuristics based on a cost function. They propose two hardware extensions, i.e. a time-stamping function and a conditional branch mechanism, which make rendering time estimations more robust. Meantime, the proposed estimation method for rendering time can also be used to calculate efficient placement of impostors in complex scenes. Doulamis et al. [7] address the method of 3D rendering workload prediction based on a combined fuzzy classification and neural network model. Litke et al. [13] predict computational workload of jobs assigned for execution 3D image rendering on commercially exploited Grid. And Doulamis et al. [6] propose an efficient non-linear task workload prediction mechanism with a non-linear model incorporated with a fair scheduling algorithm for task allocation and resource management in Grid computing. The history-based motion prediction method [23] aims at high file hits and predicts the future motion according to the historical ones, which produces better results when interpolation is added. Son et al. [18] propose a new approach for predicting and identifying the load condition of agents to solve load balancing problem. However, these methods only works for static model but ignore the influence of the parameters used in render files.

3 Proposed Strategy

3.1 System Design

A workflow of prediction a rendering process is depicted in Fig. 1. The input scene files are encoded on BLEND format which is standard format support by Blender. Blender is the free and open source 3D creation suite. It supports

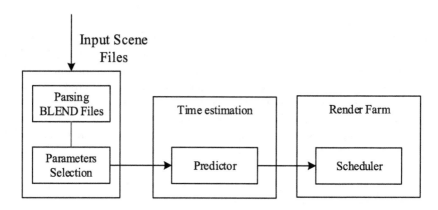

Fig. 1. Workflow of prediction

the entirety of the 3D pipeline-model, rigging, animation, simulation, rendering, compositing and motion tracking, even video editing and game creation [1]. And the scene file offers a general framework for describing the structure of a synthetic world and uses the minimum information required of interacting the rendering environment. Also it describes the rendering algorithm as well as respective parameters used for performing the rendering. To identify the parameters that impact the rendering process and the algorithm used, the scene files are parsed. In this way, a set of candidate parameters is constructed, which is responsible for selecting the most significant parameters among all candidates, i.e., a feature vector of appropriate attributes is constructed to predict the rendering time.

The predictor predicts the time of a rendering process by taking into consideration the feature vector. The J48 classification algorithm is used for training and predicting rendering time. And then, scheduler will scheduling rendering jobs according to exploiting information provided by the previous prediction result. In the paper, we mainly focus the process of prediction.

3.2   Parsing of Parameters

A BLEND file usually contains many parameters which describe the rendering attributes, and some parameters may have less impact on rendering time. We use Blender's API for Python scripting to parse parameters and the scene image is shown in Fig. 2. And Table 1 shows the initial parsing result.

We use the method of control variable to select the parameters and change the corresponding value of parameter to get rid of the parameters with less impact on the rendering time. The rendering time is an average value obtained by 20 times rendering. As shown in Table 1, the change of parameters value has less impact on the rendering time. Except that, the vertex, edge and face of object is fixed in a scene and the impact of these factors is included in that of no. of Mesh. And then three parameters are also rejected. Therefore, at the processing of prediction we don't consider these parameters. Then, we will introduce the parameters which mainly impact on the rendering time.

Fig. 2. The scene image for prediction

Table 1. The parameters with less impact on rendering time

Parameter	Variation range	Rendering time
Intensity of illuminant	[1.01–11]	[55.0401–59.9534]
No. of camera	[1–10]	[55.0572–55.6572]
Absorption types of ambient light	[MULTIPLY, ADD]	[50.3848–55.6572]
Absorption intensity of ambient light	[1–10]	[50.3848–55.6572]
Types of diffuse reflection	5 types	[50.1567–55.6572]
Types of highlight	5 types	[50.1688–55.6572]
Types of anti-aliasing filter	7 types	[55.6572–58.8323]

– Shadow [5], Blender provides two types of shadow, Ray-Tracing Shadow and Buffer Shadow. Table 2 shows the relationship between rendering time and types of Buffer Shadow. When an image is rendered, the rendering time with different types of Buffer Shadow is different.

– Light type, there are five types of light, point light, sun light, spot, hemi light and area light. Hemi light has no sampling value so it is rejected. We use formula (1) to indicate the influence of light types on rendering time. And the coefficient is empirical value.

$$Light\_s = \tfrac{1}{7} * Point\_s + \tfrac{1}{7} * Sun\_s \\ + \tfrac{1}{7} * Spot\_s + Aera\_s \tag{1}$$

Table 2. The rendering time with different types of shadows

Types	Rendering time
Regular	49.7928
Irregular	50.6198
Halfway	52.3219
Deep	50.3958

– Number of light, which is an important factor on rendering time. In a scene, there includes various types of light corresponding to different number of light. We use formula (2) to indicate the influence on rendering time. And the coefficient is empirical value.

$$
\begin{aligned}
NLight\_s = &\tfrac{1}{5} * NPoint\_s + \tfrac{1}{5} * NSun\_s \\
&+ \tfrac{1}{10} * NSpot\_s + \tfrac{1}{10} * NHemi\_s \\
&+ Aera\_s
\end{aligned}
\tag{2}
$$

– Ambient light, there are two types, raytrace and approximate. The approximate is rarely used and we use raytrace as the main factor. The raytrace usually includes three types, CONSTANT_QMC, ADAPTIVE_QMC, CONSTANT_JITTERED. We use formula (3) to indicate the influence on rendering time. And the coefficient is empirical value.

$$
\begin{aligned}
Ambientlight = &5 * CONSTANT\_QMC \\
&+ 3.5 * ADAPTIVE\_QMC \\
&+ 1.4 * CONSTANT\_JITTERED
\end{aligned}
\tag{3}
$$

– Pixel value, which is the product of resolution ratio, the more pixels the more elaborate image, and the rendering time is longer. In the paper, we use 17 types of resolution ratio.

– Tile size, the more tile size, the longer rendering time. Usually, the tile size is approximate number of resolution ratio.

– Number of object, the object has many attributes and in the paper we just consider the influence of number of object. The more objects the longer rendering time.

– Anti-aliasing, there are 4 types of Anti-aliasing sample values, 5, 8, 11, 16. And the value 0 means that the anti-aliasing is not used. The impact is shown in Table 3.

– Raytrace method, there include 6 types, AUTO, OCTREE, BLIBVH, VBVH, SIMD_SVBVH and SIMD_QBVH. The impact with different types is shown in Table 4.

Table 3. The rendering time with different types of Anti-aliasing sample values

Value	Rendering time
0	14.5008
5	55.6572
8	85.4189
11	116.9777
16	171.1598

Table 4. The rendering time with different types of Anti-aliasing sample values

Type	Rendering time
AUTO	55.6572
OCTREE	162.5122
BLIBVH	138.0688
VBVH	78.2354
SIMD_SVBVH	56.6742
SIMD_QBVH	59.0663

3.3 Strategy Description

In this section, we will introduce the prediction strategy according to the parameters parsed in above section. We use Weka as tool and J48 classification algorithm [24]. The J48 has the following advantages.

- Easy understand for rules. Each branch of the decision tree in J48 corresponds to a classification rule, and the total rules set is easy to understand.
- The fast running. The time complexity of J48 algorithm is $O(n^3)$, n is sample size.
- The higher accuracy.

4 Experimental Results

At the beginning, we need dispose the original data. The inactive data is to be rejected. And then, the rendering time set need to be discretized, which is helpful to classification and prediction. We sort the rendering time set with descending order, and each 5 second as a subsection.

The disposed data is input into Weka and Fig. 3 shows the visualization result. The rendering time is automatically discretized into 20 classes.

We use the J48 algorithm provided by Weka and the accuracy rate of training set is 49.14 % after 10 times of cross validation. And the accuracy rate of test set is 66.67 %. The classification matrix is shown in Figs. 4 and 5.

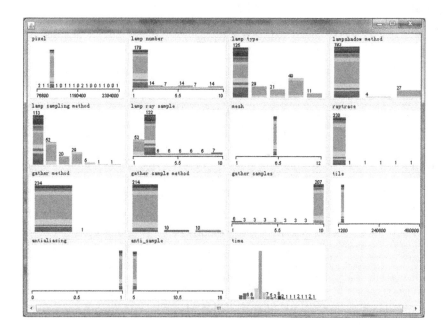

Fig. 3. The visualization result of discretized data

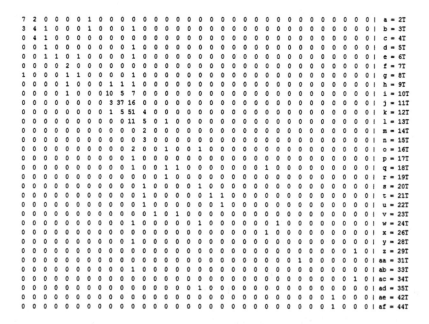

Fig. 4. The classification matrix of training set

```
 10  0  0  0  0  0  0  0  0  0  0  0  0  0  0  0  0  0  0  0  0  0  0  0  0  0  0  0  0  0  0 |  a = 2T
  3  6  0  0  0  0  0  0  0  0  1  0  0  0  0  0  0  0  0  0  0  0  0  0  0  0  0  0  0  0  0 |  b = 3T
  0  0  4  0  1  0  0  0  0  0  0  0  0  0  0  0  0  0  0  0  0  0  0  0  0  0  0  0  0  0  0 |  c = 4T
  0  0  0  0  1  0  0  0  0  0  1  0  0  0  0  0  0  0  0  0  0  0  0  0  0  0  0  0  0  0  0 |  d = 5T
  1  0  0  0  2  0  0  0  0  0  1  0  0  0  0  0  0  0  0  0  0  0  0  0  0  0  0  0  0  0  0 |  e = 6T
  0  0  0  0  0  2  0  0  0  0  0  0  0  0  0  0  0  0  0  0  0  0  0  0  0  0  0  0  0  0  0 |  f = 7T
  1  0  0  0  1  1  0  0  0  0  1  0  0  0  0  0  0  0  0  0  0  0  0  0  0  0  0  0  0  0  0 |  g = 8T
  0  0  0  0  0  2  0  0  2  0  0  0  0  0  0  0  0  0  0  0  0  0  0  0  0  0  0  0  0  0  0 |  h = 9T
  0  0  0  0  1  0  0 17  2  3  0  0  0  0  0  0  0  0  0  0  0  0  0  0  0  0  0  0  0  0  0 |  i = 10T
  0  0  0  0  0  0  0  3 41 12  0  0  0  0  0  0  0  0  0  0  0  0  0  0  0  0  0  0  0  0  0 |  j = 11T
  0  0  0  0  0  0  0  1  4 53  3  0  0  0  0  0  0  0  0  0  0  0  0  0  0  0  0  0  0  0  0 |  k = 12T
  0  0  0  0  0  0  0  0  4 13  0  0  0  0  0  0  0  0  0  0  0  0  0  0  0  0  0  0  0  0  0 |  l = 13T
  0  0  0  0  0  0  0  0  1  1  0  0  0  0  0  0  0  0  0  0  0  0  0  0  0  0  0  0  0  0  0 |  m = 14T
  0  0  0  0  0  0  0  0  2  1  0  0  0  0  0  0  0  0  0  0  0  0  0  0  0  0  0  0  0  0  0 |  n = 15T
  0  0  0  0  0  0  0  2  1  0  0  1  0  0  0  0  0  0  0  0  0  0  0  0  0  0  0  0  0  0  0 |  o = 16T
  0  0  0  0  0  0  0  1  0  0  0  0  0  0  0  0  0  0  0  0  0  0  0  0  0  0  0  0  0  0  0 |  p = 17T
  0  0  0  0  0  0  0  1  1  0  0  1  0  1  0  0  0  0  0  0  0  0  0  0  0  0  0  0  0  0  0 |  q = 18T
  0  0  0  0  0  0  0  0  0  0  0  1  0  0  0  0  0  0  0  0  0  0  0  0  0  0  0  0  0  0  0 |  r = 19T
  0  0  0  0  0  0  0  0  1  0  0  0  1  0  0  0  0  0  0  0  0  0  0  0  0  0  0  0  0  0  0 |  s = 20T
  0  0  0  0  0  0  0  0  1  0  0  0  1  1  0  0  0  0  0  0  0  0  0  0  0  0  0  0  0  0  0 |  t = 21T
  0  0  0  0  0  0  0  0  0  1  0  0  0  0  1  0  0  0  0  0  0  0  0  0  0  0  0  0  0  0  0 |  u = 22T
  0  0  0  0  0  0  0  0  0  1  0  0  0  0  1  0  0  0  0  0  0  0  0  0  0  0  0  0  0  0  0 |  v = 23T
  0  0  0  0  0  0  0  0  0  1  0  0  0  0  1  0  0  0  0  0  0  0  0  0  0  0  0  0  0  0  0 |  w = 24T
  0  0  0  0  0  0  0  0  0  0  0  0  0  0  0  1  0  0  0  0  0  0  0  0  0  0  0  0  0  0  0 |  x = 26T
  0  0  0  0  0  0  0  0  1  0  0  0  0  0  0  0  0  0  0  0  0  0  0  0  0  0  0  0  0  0  0 |  y = 28T
  0  0  0  0  0  0  0  0  0  0  0  0  0  0  0  0  0  0  0  0  1  0  0  0  0  0  0  0  0  0  0 |  z = 29T
  0  0  0  0  0  0  0  0  0  0  0  0  0  0  0  0  0  0  0  0  1  0  0  0  0  0  0  0  0  0  0 | aa = 31T
  0  0  0  0  0  0  0  0  1  0  0  0  0  0  0  0  0  0  0  0  0  0  0  0  0  0  0  0  0  0  0 | ab = 33T
  0  0  0  0  0  0  0  0  0  0  0  0  0  0  0  0  0  0  0  0  0  0  0  0  0  1  0  0  0  0  0 | ac = 34T
  0  0  0  0  0  0  0  0  0  0  0  0  0  0  1  0  0  0  0  0  0  0  0  0  0  0  0  0  0  0  0 | ad = 35T
  0  0  0  0  0  0  0  0  0  0  0  0  0  0  0  0  0  0  0  0  0  0  0  0  0  1  0  0  0  0  0 | ae = 42T
  0  0  0  0  0  0  0  0  0  0  0  0  0  0  0  0  0  0  0  0  0  0  0  0  0  1  0  0  0  0  0 | af = 44T
```

Fig. 5. The classification matrix of test set

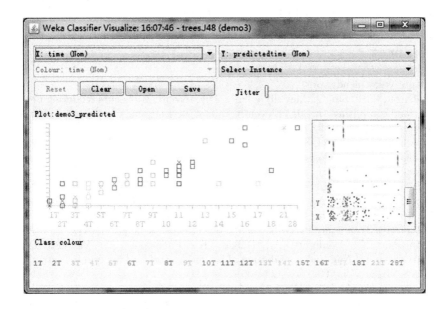

Fig. 6. The comparison of rendering time and prediction result.

The low accuracy rate is due to the less change range for each parameter. The useful data in each classification is less and unrepresentative. Therefore, we can suitably reduce the accuracy of the classification for rendering time and use 10 second as a subsection and discretize rendering time set again. And the accuracy rate of training set and test set is 60 % and 75.74 % respectively. The prediction result is shown in Fig. 6. The comparison result shows that the J48 classification algorithm can obtain the accurate prediction result for rendering time according to the main parameters parsed from scene files.

5   Conclusion and Future Work

In this paper, we present a statistics based prediction method for rendering application. The scene files with BLEND format are parsed to extract and analyze the parameters which affect the rendering time. And we use Blender to gather the sample data and J48 classification algorithm to predict rendering time. The experimental results show that the proposed method improve the prediction accuracy about 60 % and 75.74 % for training set and test set respectively, which provides reasonable guide for scheduling jobs efficiently and saving rendering cost.

Acknowledgments. This work is supported by Natural Science Foundation of China (61202041, 91330117), National High-Tech R&D (863) Program of China (2012AA01A306, 2014AA01A302) and the Key Technologies Program for Social Development of Shaanxi Province (2016SF-428). Computational resources have been made available on Xi'an High Performance Computing Center.

References

1. http://www.blender.org/
2. Baharon, M.R., Shi, Q., Llewellyn-Jones, D., Merabti, M.: Secure rendering process in cloud computing. In: 2013 Eleventh Annual International Conference on Privacy, Security and Trust (PST), pp. 82–87. IEEE (2013)
3. Chapman, W., Ranka, S., Sahni, S., Schmalz, M., Moore, L., Elton, B.: A framework for rendering high resolution synthetic aperture radar images on heterogeneous architectures. In: 2014 IEEE Symposium on Computers and Communication (ISCC), pp. 1–6. IEEE (2014)
4. Chong, A., Sourin, A., Levinski, K.: Grid-based computer animation rendering. In: Proceedings of the 4th International Conference on Computer Graphics and Interactive Techniques in Australasia and Southeast Asia, pp. 39–47. ACM (2006)
5. Doulamis, N., Doulamis, A., Dolkas, K., Panagakis, A., Varvarigou, T., Varvarigos, E.: Non-linear prediction of rendering workload for grid infrastructure. Mach. Graph. Vis. **13**(1/2), 123–136 (2004)
6. Doulamis, N., Doulamis, A., Litke, A., Panagakis, A., Varvarigou, T., Varvarigos, E.: Adjusted fair scheduling and non-linear workload prediction for QoS guarantees in grid computing. Comput. Commun. **30**(3), 499–515 (2007)

7. Doulamis, N.D., Doulamis, A.D., Panagakis, A., Dolkas, K., Varvarigou, T., Varvarigos, E., et al.: A combined fuzzy-neural network model for non-linear prediction of 3-D rendering workload in grid computing. IEEE Trans. Syst., Man, Cybern., Part B: Cybern. **34**(2), 1235–1247 (2004)
8. Hou, X., Sourina, O.: A prediction method using interpolation for smooth six-DOF haptic rendering in multirate simulation. In: 2013 International Conference on Cyberworlds (CW), pp. 294–301. IEEE (2013)
9. Khan, A.R., Saleem, M., Banday, S.A.: Improving the performance of hierarchical scheduling for rendering. In: 2014 Innovative Applications of Computational Intelligence on Power, Energy and Controls with Their Impact on Humanity (CIPECH), pp. 457–460. IEEE (2014)
10. Lazem, S., Elteir, M., Abdel-Hamid, A., Gracanin, D.: Prediction-based prefetching for remote rendering streaming in mobile virtual environments. In: 2007 IEEE International Symposium on Signal Processing and Information Technology, pp. 760–765. IEEE (2007)
11. Lee, K., Lee, D.Y.: Real-time haptic rendering using multi-rate output-estimation with armax model. In: International Conference on Control, Automation and Systems, ICCAS 2007, pp. 1821–1826. IEEE (2007)
12. Leung, W.H., Chen, T.: Compression with mosaic prediction for image-based rendering applications. In: 2000 IEEE International Conference on Multimedia and Expo, ICME 2000, vol. 3, pp. 1649–1652. IEEE (2000)
13. Litke, A., Tserpes, K., Varvarigou, T.: Computational workload prediction for grid oriented industrial applications: the case of 3D-image rendering. In: IEEE International Symposium on Cluster Computing and the Grid, CCGrid 2005, vol. 2, pp. 962–969. IEEE (2005)
14. Liu, Y., Chou, W., Yan, S.: Proxy position prediction based continuous local patch for smooth haptic rendering. J. Comput. Inf. Sci. Eng. **12**(3), 031004-1–031004-9 (2012)
15. Mochocki, B.C., Lahiri, K., Cadambi, S., Hu, X.S.: Signature-based workload estimation for mobile 3D graphics. In: Proceedings of the 43rd Annual Design Automation Conference, pp. 592–597. ACM (2006)
16. Monte, C.F.P., Piccoli, F., Luciano, C., Rizzi, S., Bianchini, G., Scutari, P.C.: Estimation of volume rendering efficiency with gpu in a parallel distributed environment. Procedia Comput. Sci. **18**, 1402–1411 (2013)
17. Schnitzer, S., Gansel, S., Durr, F., Rothermel, K.: Concepts for execution time prediction of 3D GPU rendering. In: 2014 9th IEEE International Symposium on Industrial Embedded Systems (SIES), pp. 160–169. IEEE (2014)
18. Son, B.H., Lee, S.W., Youn, H.Y.: Prediction-based dynamic load balancing using agent migration for multi-agent system. In: 2010 12th IEEE International Conference on High Performance Computing and Communications (HPCC), pp. 485–490. IEEE (2010)
19. Tamm, G., Kruger, J.: Hybrid rendering with scheduling under uncertainty. IEEE Trans. Vis. Comput. Graph. **20**(5), 767–780 (2014)
20. Wimmer, M., Wonka, P.: Rendering time estimation for real-time rendering. In: Rendering Techniques, pp. 118–129 (2003)
21. Wu, J., Song, A., Li, J.: A time series based solution for the difference rate sampling between haptic rendering and visual display. In: IEEE International Conference on Robotics and Biomimetics, ROBIO 2006, pp. 595–600. IEEE (2006)
22. Xiao-peng, H., Cheng-jun, C., Yi-qi, Z.: Contact elements prediction based haptic rendering method for collaborative virtual assembly system. In: WRI Global Congress on Intelligent Systems, GCIS 2009, vol. 4, pp. 259–263. IEEE (2009)

23. Xiaohong, Z., Shengzhong, F., Jianping, F.: A history-based motion prediction method for mouse-based navigation in 3D digital city. In: Seventh International Conference on Grid and Cooperative Computing, GCC 2008, pp. 686–690. IEEE (2008)
24. Yadav, A.K., Chandel, S.: Solar energy potential assessment of western Himalayan Indian state of Himachal Pradesh using J48 algorithm of WEKA in ANN based prediction model. Renew. Energy **75**, 675–693 (2015)
25. Yu, W., Wang, W., He, G., Goto, S.: Combined hole-filling with spatial and temporal prediction. In: 2013 20th IEEE International Conference on Image Processing (ICIP), pp. 3196–3200. IEEE (2013)
26. Yu, X., Zhang, X., Liu, L., Hwang, J.N., Wan, W.: Dynamic scheduling and real-time rendering for large-scale 3D scenes. J. Sig. Process. Syst. **75**(1), 15–21 (2014)

IBB: Improved K-Resource Aware Backfill Balanced Scheduling for HTCondor

Lan Liu[✉], Zhongzhi Luan, Haozhan Wang, and Depei Qian

Sino-German Joint Software Institute, Beihang University, Beijing 100191, China
{liulan,07680,wanghaozhan,depeiq}@buaa.edu.cn

Abstract. HTCondor, a batch system characterized by its matchmaking mechanism, schedules job in FCFS way, so its performance is not ideal as expected. Backfilling is a technique to address the above problem. Most backfilling algorithms are based on CPU information and have large room for improvements with considering other resource information. The K-resource aware scheduling algorithm Backfill Balanced (BB) selects backfill job which can best balance the usage of all resources and achieve better performance compared with the classical backfilling algorithm. However, BB does not realize that small jobs' impacts on resource utilization are negligible and they mainly contribute to reduce the average response time. Here we propose the IBB algorithm, which utilizes the characteristics of small jobs to guide a better job selection. We implemented IBB on HTCondor to improve its performance. Experiments results show that IBB can provide up to 60 % performance gains in most performance metrics compared with BB.

1 Introduction

HTCondor, a high-throughput distributed system, can produce high job throughput and reliable system performance by using a flexible mechanism ClassAd [1]. However, its dedicated scheduler performs in FCFS which may result in lots of resource fragmentations when the current job is too large. It provides another way called "Best-fit" to skip the current blocked job. However, the blocked job may suffer from starvation when the subsequent jobs are quite small.

An effective way to handle the above problem is backfilling which schedules low-priority small jobs after the current blocked one into execution to utilize the resource fragmentations. There are two typical backfilling methods: Conservative backfilling and EASY backfilling [2]. William Leinberger et al. proposed the K-resource aware scheduling algorithm Backfill Balanced (BB) which can use the additional resource information to select backfill jobs more intelligently than typical backfilling methods [3]. However, BB does not realize that the influence differences on system resource utilization and global system resource status diagram exerted by large jobs and small ones. What's more, it can only select one job to backfill in one traversal.

Our contribution is to provide a variant of backfilling algorithm termed Improved Backfill Balanced (IBB) based on BB. IBB can make use of the additional resource information and the characteristic of small jobs to make more intelligent decisions on

G.R. Gao et al. (Eds.): NPC 2016, LNCS 9966, pp. 85–92, 2016.
DOI: 10.1007/978-3-319-47099-3_7

the selection of backfilling jobs. And we implemented IBB on HTCondor which can further improve its job throughput.

This paper is organized as follows: Sect. 2 describes the related work of past research in parallel job scheduling. Section 3 presents the core thought and application of IBB. Experiments and evaluations are given in Sect. 4. The conclusion and future work are provided in Sect. 5.

2   Related Work

As mentioned in Sect. 1, the system resource utilization and job throughput of HTCondor are not ideal enough. How to utilize the resource fragmentations effectively in parallel job scheduling is one of its most difficult problems.

Backfilling is well known in parallel job scheduling to increase system resource utilization and job throughput. Conservative backfilling can select a small job to backfill from the back of the queue as long as it does not delay the start time of all the jobs in front of it. EASY takes a more aggressive way and selects a job to backfill if it will not delay the start time of the first job in the queue [2]. It is obvious that Conservative backfilling is not as flexible as EASY since it is under the limitation that all front queued jobs cannot be delayed for execution.

Aside from methods mentioned above, a number of variants based on backfilling have been put forward recent years, including Slack-Based backfilling, Relaxed back-filling, etc. [4–7]. Those variants were shown to have lower average slowdown than EASY. However, they may result in worse wait time and higher time complexity. Most important of all, none of them takes any additional job resource requirements and system resource information into consideration, which can easily lead to unbalanced resource utilization and finally harm system performance.

William Leinberger et al. put forward Backfill Balanced (BB) which provides K-resource aware job selection heuristics. BB uses the additional job resource requirements and current system resource status information to guide job selection for backfilling. It can make efficient use of all the available system resource information and experiments show that its performance gains in average response time can up to 50 % over classical backfilling scheduling methods.

3   Improved Backfill Balance Scheduling

3.1   Thought of IBB

The classical backfilling algorithms can improve system resource utilization and job throughput by selecting small jobs to execute on resource fragmentations. However, none of them takes any other available resource information into consideration except CPU. The performance degrades since there may be lots of other resource being wasted. BB can achieve better system performance than classical backfilling methods by providing K-resource aware job selection heuristics. BB selects job based on the overall ability to balance the system resource utilization, its general notion is that if all the resource usages are kept balanced, then more jobs will likely fit into the system, creating a larger backfill candidate pool. BB's evaluation mechanism showed in (1) includes two parts: a balance measure and a fullness modifier. The balance measure showed on the left part of (1) is used to score each backfill job candidate which aims at achieving the best resource utilization balance. The fullness modifier showed on the right is applied to relax the balance criteria as the system gets full by allowing a larger job which achieves a worse balance to be selected over a smaller one which achieves a better balance when the larger one can nearly full the machine. The job with the lowest score indicates a best balance it can up to by the time. The goal of BB is to improve the average response time of the system by improving the response time of small jobs which can best balance the usage of all system resource [3].

$$
\frac{\max_i(S_i + R_i^j)}{\sum_{i=1}^{K}\left(S_i + R_i^j\right)/K} * \left\{ 1.0 - \frac{\sum_{i=1}^{K}\left(S_i + R_i^j\right)}{K} \right\} \tag{1}
$$

The notations are explained in Table 1:

Table 1. Notation explanation

Notation	Explanation
K	The number of resource types
S_i	The current utilization of resource i in the system S
R_i^j	The requirement for resource i by job j

The BB algorithm can significantly improve system performance compared with the classical backfilling algorithms. However, transient imbalance of resource utilization can be neglected, since it is often caused by the execution of a small number of large jobs and will come out of the circumstance once the large jobs terminate. Long-duration imbalance of resource utilization is often caused by successive execution of many large jobs, and it can only be relieved by the execution of large jobs which are complementary in resource requirements as small jobs characterized by short execution time and tiny resource needs can usually do little improvement for the ease of imbalanced resource utilization situation.

As described above, we found that BB doesn't realize the fact that the small jobs' influence on system resource utilization is negligible for their resource requirement is tiny and the execution time is very short relative to large jobs. Another flaw in BB is that in one traversal of the job queue, it can only select one job to backfill, which lowers the efficiency of backfilling and thus affects the average job response time and job throughput.

Here we put forward the Improved Backfill Balanced (IBB) algorithm based on BB. The same with BB, it is K-resource aware as it takes all available resource infor-mation into consideration for backfill job selection. Our standpoint is trying to back-fill more small jobs as far as possible by taking all available resource information and the characteristics of small jobs into consideration, which, in return, can achieve considerable performance gains over BB. The difference of IBB from BB mainly lies in the points listed below:

- If the job meets the basic backfilling requirements and will not worsen the resource imbalance in the system, it can be selected.
- In one traversal of the job queue, backfill all the jobs meet the above requirement.

The evaluation mechanism in IBB is shown in (2), if the evaluation result is true, then we select the job for backfilling, skip it if not:

$$\frac{\max_i \left(S_i + R_i^j \right)}{\sum_{i=1}^{K} \left(S_i + R_i^j \right)/K} \leq \frac{\max_i \left(S_i \right)}{\sum_{i=1}^{K} S_i/K} \tag{2}$$

The reason for performance improvement which IBB gains over BB lies in the fact that we realized the influence difference on system resource utilization and global system resource status diagram exerted by large jobs and small ones, and try to backfill more small jobs as far as possible to reduce the average response time and improve job throughput more significantly. The algorithm is given in Algorithm 1.

Algorithm 1. Improved Backfill Balanced Algorithm

```
procedure schedule_jobs()
  schedule_head_of_list()
  backfill_jobs()
procedure schedule_head_of_list()
  for all jobs in queue do
    pivot <- first job in the queue
    if   pivot requires <= current idle resource   then
      start job immediately
    else
      break
    end if
  end for
procedure backfill_jobs()
  pivot <- first job in the queue
  t <- time when sufficient resource will be available for pivot
  extra <- extra resource at t not required by pivot job
  cur_avg_util <- currently average resource utilization
  for each job in queue except the first do
    idle_res <- currently idle resource
    if job requires <= idle_res and will finish by t, or job_requires <=
         min(idle_res, extra) then
      avg_util <- average resource utilization with job being backfilled
      if avg_util <= cur_avg_util then
        start job immediately
      end if
    end if
  end for
```

3.2 Apply Backfilling to HTCondor

HTCondor's simple and novel matchmaking algorithm which can produce high system reliability and high job throughput makes it become more and more attractive. However, to ensure simplicity and reliability, its scheduling strategy for parallel jobs just basically follows the FCFS principle and limits the improvement of system performance. Actually backfilling has little impact on system reliability and simplicity since it only needs to traverse the job queue to select jobs for backfilling when the first job in the queue got blocked, with no other complex algorithm and communications needed.

To further improve HTCondor's system performance, we implement IBB on it, the performance gains over the original FCFS and Best-fit scheduling methods are substantial as expected.

4   Experiments and Evaluations

This subsection describes the experiments conducted to evaluate the IBB. As the scale of real environment is limited, we first make performance comparison by simulating to prove the feasibility and effectiveness of IBB on large scale computing systems. As there is little information about jobs' requirements for disk, network, etc., we only consider CPU and memory here. Then we implemented IBB on HTCondor to improve its job throughput, job response time and system resource utilization, which also proves the effectiveness of IBB in modern RJMS.

4.1   Simulation Experiments

We make performance comparison by simulating to prove the feasibility and effectiveness of IBB on large scale computing systems. As the simulator [10] does not provide job throughput and system resource utilization information, we list them as future work and here just provide results for average wait time, average response time and average slowdown. We simulated on the following two kinds of workloads.

- Workload composed of the same job type which we call as Pure Workload.
- Workload composed of mixed type of jobs. We refer it as Mixed Workload.

By simulating on the above two kinds of workloads, we can prove that our algorithm works well in both scenarios, which, to some extent, can generalize all kinds of workloads in real environments.

Pure Workload. This workload is provided by the Los Alamos National Lab (LANL) called LANL-CM5. It contains detailed information about job's actual CPU and memory usage, as well as the arrival time and execution time. We simulated the experiments in a 1024-node cluster with 1 GB memory per node.

Figure 1 depicts the performance results for pure workload. The relative load means the experimental system load relative to the workload's original experiment load. The results indicate that IBB is far better than BB. For the average wait time and average response time, the performance gains can up to 65 %. The average slowdown has relative lower gains since it mainly depends on the execution of large jobs. The results show that IBB can work well in environment with a single workload type.

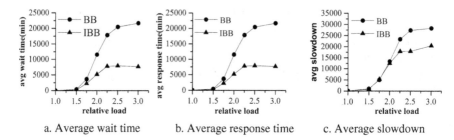

a. Average wait time   b. Average response time   c. Average slowdown

Fig. 1. Average wait time, response time, slowdown under different load with pure workload

Mixed Workload. To verify that IBB can also work well with mixed types of jobs, we selected two traces to synthetic a mixed workload. The first trace is LANL-CM5 introduced above. The second one called MetaCentrum is memory-intensive and contains several months' worth of accounting records. We processed the synthetic workload in the same way as LANL-CM5.

Figure 2 depicts the average wait time, average response time and average slowdown for Mixed Workload. The system load changes in the same way as experiment conducted on Pure Workload. The performance gains for the three metrics can up to 60 %. Experiment results show that IBB can be applied to mixed job types well and even produces better performance gains than it does on Pure Workload.

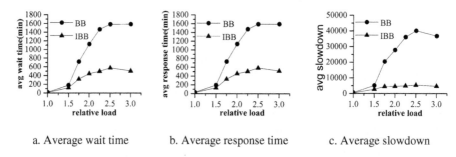

a. Average wait time   b. Average response time   c. Average slowdown

Fig. 2. Average wait time, response time, slowdown under different load with mixed workload

4.2 Experiments Conducted on HTCondor

Experiment was also conducted on HTCondor to evaluate the performance gains of IBB over its default FCFS and Best-fit scheduling algorithm in real environment. Experiment results prove that IBB can significantly improve HTCondor's performance. The experiment was conducted on a four-node cluster. The job queue was composed of 54 MPI jobs from the NAS Parallel Benchmark and the time interval between each job is one second. Figure 3 depicts each job's wait time, response time and slowdown. From Fig. 3(a) and (b) we can see that the job parallelism degree scheduled by IBB is much higher than FCFS with quite a number of small jobs being packed to execute on the resource fragmentations while almost no large jobs suffering from starvation. Although the Best-fit scheduling method can get almost the same performance as IBB in job parallelism degree, it can easily make large jobs suffer from starvation, which means it cannot guarantee fairness well. Figure 3(c) shows that each job's slowdown is almost the same for IBB, which means the wait time of each job endured is negligible compared with its execution time. However, the slowdown is uneven distributed with FCFS scheduling algorithm which indicates worse average job response time.

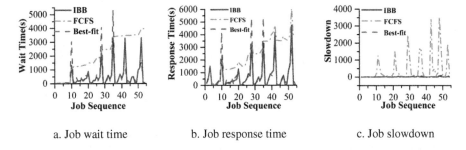

a. Job wait time   b. Job response time   c. Job slowdown

Fig. 3. Job wait time, response time, slowdown on HTCondor

4.3 Discussion

To summarize, the experiment conducted on HTCondor are somewhat inconclusive and depend on the job queue. As the scale of our HTCondor pool is limited and the job queue we designed may not strictly conform to the real scenario, the performance gains of IBB in real environment is much better than it got by simulation. To some extent, the experiments conducted on simulator can reflect the true performance of IBB. The success of IBB indicates that taking the characteristic of small jobs and overall system resource information into consideration is reasonable and can select small jobs to backfill in a more efficient way.

5   Conclusion and Future Work

In this paper, we improved the K-resource aware backfilling algorithm by utilizing the characteristics of small jobs and all available resource information, and proposed a new model to select jobs for backfilling more effectively. Meanwhile, we implement backfilling algorithm on HTCondor, which can significantly improve its performance.

The success of IBB shows that small jobs' influence on system resource status diagram is negligible and its contribution to reduce average response time is attractive. IBB can perform a better job packing of the small jobs while maintaining sufficient progress of the large jobs.

While our algorithm performs better than almost all existing backfilling algorithms, it still has some drawbacks. For example, it has to do scheduling based on the job resource requirements information and estimated execution time given by users which may be inaccurate and affect system performance. Future work will focus on putting forward a way to provide appropriate estimation of job resource requirements and execution time to further improve system resource utilization and job throughput.

Acknowledgments. This research is supported by the National Key R&D Program (Grant No. 2016YFB0201403) and the National Natural Science Foundation of China (Grant Nos. 61361126011, 61133004, 61502019). And here we would like to thank the HTCondor team and the father of HTCondor Miron Livny for providing us help in understanding and using HTCondor.

References

1. Wright, D.: Cheap cycles from the desktop to the dedicated cluster: combining opportunistic and dedicated scheduling with Condor. In: Conference on Linux Clusters: The HPC Revolution, Champaign - Urbana, IL, June 2001
2. Mu'Alem, A.W., Feitelson, D.G.: Utilization, predictability, workloads, and user runtime estimates in scheduling the IBM SP2 with backfilling. IEEE Trans. Parallel Distrib. Syst. **12**(6), 529–543 (2001)
3. Leinberger, W., Karypis, G., Kumar, V.: Job scheduling in the presence of multiple resource requirements. In: SC Conference IEEE Computer Society, pp. 47–47 (1999)
4. Talby, D., Feitelson, D.G.: Supporting priorities and improving utilization of the IBM SP scheduler using slack-based backfilling. In: 13th International and 10th Symposium on Parallel and Distributed Processing (1999)
5. Ward, W.A., Mahood, C.L., West, J.E.: Scheduling jobs on parallel systems using a relaxed backfill strategy. In: Feitelson, D.G., Rudolph, L., Schwiegelshohn, U. (eds.) JSSPP 2002. LNCS, vol. 2537, pp. 88–102. Springer, Heidelberg (2002). doi:10.1007/3-540-36180-4_6
6. Nissimov, A., Feitelson, D.G.: Probabilistic Backfilling: Job Scheduling Strategies for Parallel Processing, pp. 102–115. Springer, Heidelberg (2007)
7. Jackson, D., Snell, Q., Clement, M.: Core algorithms of the Maui scheduler. In: Feitelson, D.G., Rudolph, L. (eds.) JSSPP 2001. LNCS, vol. 2221, pp. 87–102. Springer, Heidelberg (2001). doi:10.1007/3-540-45540-X_6
8. Lawson, B.G., Smirni, E., Puiu, D.: Self-adapting backfilling scheduling for parallel systems. In: International Conference on Parallel Processing, pp. 583–592 (2002)
9. Litzkow, M.: Remote unix – turning idle workstations into cycle servers. In: Proceedings of Usenix Summer Conference, pp. 381–384 (1987)
10. Cappello, F., Kramer, W., Jette, M.: Contributions for resource and job management in high performance computing. Thesis (2010)
11. Yi, S., et al.: Combinational backfilling for parallel job scheduling. In: International Conference on Education Technology and Computer, pp. V2-112–V2-116 (2010)
12. Siyambalapitiya, R., Sandirigama, M.: New backfilling algorithm for multiprocessor scheduling with gang scheduling. IUP J. Comput. Sci. (2011)
13. Thain, D., Tannenbaum, T., Livny, M.: Distributed computing in practice: the condor experience. Concurr. Comput. Pract. Exp. **17**(2–4), 323–356 (2005)

Multipath Load Balancing in SDN/OSPF Hybrid Network

Xiangshan Sun, Zhiping Jia[✉], Mengying Zhao, and Zhiyong Zhang

School of Computer Science and Technology,
Shandong University, Jinan, China
jzp@sdu.edu.cn

Abstract. Software defined network (SDN) is an emerging network architecture that has drawn the attention of academics and industry in recent years. Affected by investment protection, risk control and other factors, the full deployment of SDN will not be finished in the short term, thus it results into a coexistence state of traditional IP network and SDN which is named hybrid SDN. In this paper, we formulate the SDN controller's optimization problem for load balancing as a mathematical model. Then we propose a routing algorithm Dijkstra-Repeat in SDN nodes which can offer disjoint multipath routing. To make it computationally feasible for large scale networks, we develop a new Fast Fully Polynomial Time Approximation Schemes (FPTAS) based Lazy Routing Update (LRU).

1 Introduction

Load balancing is a key technique for improving the performance and scalability of the Internet. It aims to distribute traffic so as to optimize some performance criteria. Load balancing using OSPF may cause network congestion as they are non-traffic-aware. The chief problem is that very often many comparable traffic flows are misled to converge on bottleneck links since these algorithms are oblivious to traffic characteristics and link loading.

SDN is an emerging innovator to the traditional networking paradigm, which unleashes a powerful new paradigm offering flow-level traffic control and programmable interfaces to network operators. However, fully deploying the SDN in the network is by no means an easy job. We may encounter economical, organizational and technical challenges [1]. As a result, a full deployment of SDN, i.e., all the router nodes support SDN and can be centrally controlled by the controllers, in the network will not work out in the short term. Thus a hybrid SDN deployment, i.e., SDN/OSPF hybrid network is a better choice. We adopt the hybrid architecture as the research background in this work. In a hybrid SDN, only the SDN nodes can be controlled by the centralized controller, while the legacy nodes still use the traditional shortest path routing protocol OSPF to forward packets.

[2] is the first paper to address network performance issues in an incrementally deployed SDN network. It formulates the load balancing as a linear programming problem and refines a FPTAS algorithm to solve it. But [2] only uses a single shortest path to optimize the traffic passing through SDN nodes and the SDN controller must

G.R. Gao et al. (Eds.): NPC 2016, LNCS 9966, pp. 93–100, 2016.
DOI: 10.1007/978-3-319-47099-3_8

recompute the routing after forwarding one flow. The network performance is thus limited. We propose disjoint multipath calculation in SDN nodes. For the flows directed to the same destination, the SDN controller can map them to disjoint paths which could ensure that the flows do not aggregate until they reach the destination node. We also formulate the SDN controller's optimization problem for load balancing and develop a Lazy Routing Update (LRU) scheme for solving these problems, which belongs to Fast Fully Polynomial Time Approximation Schemes (FPTAS). LRU can decrease the routing calculation in the SDN controller. It does this by spreading traffic load across all feasible links in the network. In simpler terms it means placing traffic where the capacity exists.

2   Problem Formulation

2.1   Hybrid Network Scenario

In the SDN/OSPF hybrid network, a centralized SDN controller computes the forwarding table for a set of SDN nodes. The first packet of every flow passing through SDN nodes is sent to the SDN controller, and the following operations are done by the SDN controller. The rest of the nodes in the network run traditional network protocol OSPF and forward packets along the shortest paths. In addition to forwarding packets, the SDN nodes forward some traffic measurement information to the SDN controller. The controller uses these information along with information disseminated in the network by OSPF-TE to dynamically map the routing tables to the SDN nodes in order to change traffic conditions. Note that in OSPF-TE, the nodes also exchange available bandwidth information on the links in the network. Therefore the controller knows the current OSPF costs as well as the amount of traffic flow on each link (averaged over some time period).

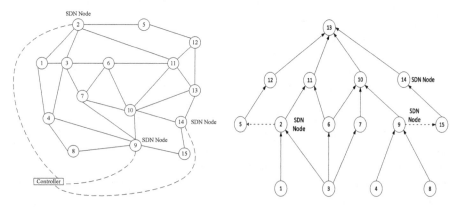

Fig. 1. A hybrid network scenario   **Fig. 2.** Shortest path tree to node 13

Figure 1 shows an example of hybrid network topology from [2]. Nodes 2, 9, 14 are SDN nodes and the rest nodes are legacy nodes. SDN nodes 2, 9, 14 are controlled externally. We will use this network to illustrate some of the concepts that we outline in the rest of the paper. We assume that all the links in the network are bidirectional and all links have the same OSPF cost. Each flow enters the network at its ingress node and has to visit a set of nodes before egressing the network at its egress node. The traffic that goes from source to destination without transiting through a SDN node will be referred to as uncontrollable traffic. If the source of a packet is a SDN node, or if it passes through at least one SDN node before it reaches its destination then the traffic will be called controllable traffic. In other words, controllable traffic comprises of packets that pass through at least one SDN node if the packets are routed using standard OSPF. There is at least an opportunity at the SDN nodes to manipulate the path of controllable traffic (Fig. 2).

2.2 Optimization Problem Definition

Given a directed graph $G = (N, E)$, where the N and E are set of n nodes and set of m edges, respectively, with each edge capacity retrievable from a function $c(e)$. The background traffic $b(e)$ on each link e is readily retrieved or estimated by the controller through the dynamic information disseminated by OSPF-TE [6]. $g(e)$ is the edge residual capacity and $g(e) = c(e) - b(e)$. There are h flows defined as a set of ingress-egress pairs, $K = \{(s_i, t_i) : s_i, t_i \in N, i = 1, ..., h\}$ and associated to them are demands, $D = \{d(k) : k \in K\}$. Note that we use edge to represent network link. Let P_k be the set of paths between s_k to t_k in G, and let $P = \cup P_k$. Let $f(p)$ denotes the amount of flow along path p.

The primal linear program (LP) formulation is

max φ

$$\sum_{p \in P_k} f(p) \geq \varphi d(k), \forall k \in K \tag{1}$$

$$\sum_{p \in P_k} f(p) \leq g(e), \forall e \in E \tag{2}$$

$$f(p) \geq 0, \forall p \in P \tag{3}$$

(1) denotes that the sum of flows on all paths in P_k is greater than the demand of ingress-egress pairs. (2) enforces the edge capacity constraints which ensure that the total flow on the edge is less than the difference between the edge capacity $c(e)$ and the background traffic $b(e)$. (3) ensures non-negative flow on each candidate path. The goal is to maximize the throughput φ while not violating capacity constraints. If the optimal $\varphi > 1$ then the current flow can be routed at the SDN nodes while ensuring that all edge utilizations are less than one.

We now associate dual variables $l(e)$ with each edge capacity constraint (5) and $z(k)$ for the demand constraint (4). It is interesting to note that its dual LP problem of the above can be shown to be

$$\min \sum_{e \in E} l(e)g(e)$$

$$\sum_{e \in P} l(e) \geq z(k), \forall k \in K, \forall p \in P \qquad (4)$$

$$\sum_{k} z(k)d(k) \geq 1 \qquad (5)$$

$$l(e) \geq 0, \forall e \in E \qquad (6)$$

$$z(k) \geq 0, \forall k \in K \qquad (7)$$

Note that this problem is a constrained version of the maximum concurrent flow problem, we can adapt the Fully Polynomial Time Approximation Scheme (FPTAS) developed for a generic maximum concurrent flow problem [3] to this case at SDN controller.

3   Load Balancing in Hybrid SDN Network

3.1   Disjoint Multipath Calculation

The proposed disjoint multipath scheme determines paths as follows. First, a path between nodes i and j is found as the shortest path by Dijkstra algorithm. The Dijkstra algorithm is then repeated after excluding network links used in the first shortest path to calculate the second shortest path. After that, Dijkstra algorithm is further repeated after excluding those network links used in the first or second shortest path. This process is repeated until no more paths are obtained. The algorithm of disjoint multipath calculation is named Dijkstra-Repeat in the following of this paper. Obviously, the Dijkstra-Repeat algorithm for computing the routing table for the SDN nodes could ensure that routing will be along loop-free shortest paths while minimizing the congestion in the network.

Forwarding is a method which maps incoming packets to outgoing links. The SDN nodes act basically as forwarding elements. If there are multiple next hops for a given destination, then the SDN nodes can split traffic to the destination in a pre-specified manner across the multiple next hops, subject to load balancing.

3.2   LRU: A New FPTAS Algorithm

We assume that the traffic matrix and the topology of the network are steady for a short period. The locations and number of the SDN nodes can be fixed and determined based on greedy algorithms [2]. The δ is defined as the same value in [2], which is a function of the desired accuracy level ω, the number of nodes n and the number of edges m. The algorithm then operates iteratively. At the beginning of each cycle, the controller schedules controllable traffic with awareness of background traffic $b(e)$ on each link by OSPF-TE, so as to optimize the overall load balancing. The dual weight of each edge $e \in E$ is initialized to $l(e) = \delta/g(e)$, where $g(e)$ is the remaining capacity of each edge.

In each iteration, it first computes the multiple admissible paths P_{ut} between SDN nodes u and other nodes t with Dijkstra-Repeat. For the primal problem, the algorithm forwards flow along the path p, while p is selected from P_{ut} with hashing. The amount of flow $f(u)$ sent along the path p is determined by the minimum remaining link capacity $g(e)$ on p and the controllable traffic demand $d(u)$ between the two terminals of the path. As a result, the primal variable R_{ut} and the primal flow demand $d(u)$ is updated by $f(u)$, respectively. After updating the primal variables, the algorithm continues to update the dual variables $l(e)$ related to path p. The algorithm stops when $D_L \geq 1$.

```
Algorithm for Load Balancing
   D_L←0
   l(e)←δ/g(e),e∈E   R_ut←0,u∈SN,t∈N
   while D_L<1 do
      for each demand d(u) having the same destination t∈N
         P_ut: admissible paths set with Dijkstra-Repeat
         while D_L<1 and d(u)>0 do
            select path p from P_ut with hashing
            c=min_e∈p g(e)
            f(u)=min{d(u),c},∀u
            Route f(u) flow from each u to t
            R_ut=R_ut+f(u)
            d(u)=d(u)-f(u)
            l(e)=l(e)(1+ωf(u)/c(e))
            Recompute D_L=Σ_e∈E g(e)/l(e)
         end while
      end for
   end while
   φ=min R_ut/D
Output: φ
```

The algorithm follows in the similar vein as [3]. The correctness of the algorithm as well as the running time analysis is identical to the results in the paper and is therefore omitted. Actually, the computational complexity of the FPTAS algorithm is at most a polynomial function of the network size and $1/\omega$ [3]. Thus, the computational complexity of our approximation algorithm is also polynomial. There are however some key differences in the implementation of the algorithm. One key difference is that we use disjoint multipath while [3] uses a single shortest path. In fact, multipath routing can significantly reduce congestion in hot spots by distributing traffic to unused network resources instead of routing all the traffic on a single path. That is, multipath routing offers better load balancing and makes full utilization of network resources [4].

The other key difference is that our FPTAS algorithm is based on Lazy Routing Update. In each iteration, [3] has to compute the lightest admissible path from all SDN nodes to a given destination using path finding algorithm with the dual weights $l(e)$ (not OSPF costs). The most time consuming step in practical cases is the shortest path computation. In [3], the SDN controller recomputes the shortest path after routing one flow, resulting in frequent updates on routers, which is a so time consuming process in each iteration of FPTAS algorithm that it doesn't fit in such an online routing algorithm. So in our scenario, at the beginning of each cycle, the controller calculates admissible paths set using Dijkstra-Repeat algorithm with the traffic information from OSPF-TE. And in a short period, the SDN controller maps the flows aggregated at SDN nodes to multiple admissible paths with hashing. This process of augmenting flow is repeated until the problem is dual feasible. We call that Lazy Routing Update (LRU), as shown in Algorithm for Load Balancing.

4   Experiments and Evaluation

In this section, we conduct the simulation experiments. We ran two groups of experiments to check the effectiveness of the algorithm using the following two topologies: (i) The Geant (Europe) topology from [5]. This topology has 22 nodes and 36 links; (ii) The Abilene topology from [5]. This topology has 12 nodes and 30 links. For Geant and Abilene topology, the link weights and the link capacities are given, and we can also get the traffic matrices of the two topologies from [5]. The number of SDN nodes for the two topologies are determined as 6 and 3, respectively. The location of the SDN nodes are decided by the incremental greedy approach stated in [2].

For Geant and Abilene topology, we carry out twenty experiments with twenty traffic matrices from [5] on each topology to compare with the maximum link utilization in OSPF, HSTE [2] and our LRU. We carry out the two groups of experiments to illustrate the practicality of our algorithm, as the two topologies used in the experiments are real and the traffic is actually measured. The results are shown in Figs. 3 and 4. As the figures illustrate, our algorithm LRU in the figures obtains a lower

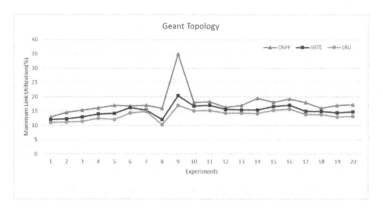

Fig. 3. Comparison of maximum link utilization of geant

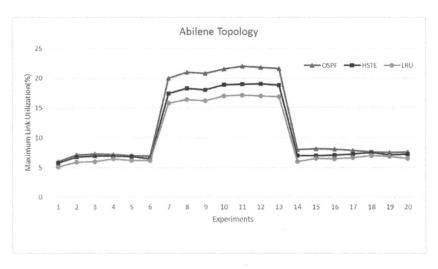

Fig. 4. Comparison of maximum link utilization of abilene

maximum link utilization compared with the other two algorithms. Compared with HSTE, LRU can reduce the overall maximum link utilization by 10 % and 9 % for Geant and Abilene topologies, respectively. Compared with OSPF, the reductions are 20 % and 17 %.

5 Conclusion

The SDN/OSPF hybrid network load balancing is a popular problem that raises people's attention worldwide. It deviates from the traditional load balancing scenario, where the flows are always routed along the shortest paths. The emerging of SDN provides a new method to solve the load balancing problem. It can centrally control the flows that directed to the outgoing links of the SDN nodes, which is similar with the model of multi-commodity. In this paper, we propose a new FPTAS algorithm LRU to solve the load balancing problems in SDN/OSPF hybrid network. Compared with other load balancing algorithms, the proposed algorithm reduces the SDN calculation and obtains a lower maximum link utilization. In the future work, we will carry out the experiments on the testbed and consider more hybrid SDN network types.

Acknowledgments. This research is sponsored by the State Key Program of National Natural Science Foundation of China No. 61533011, Shandong Provincial Natural Science Foundation under Grant No. ZR2015FM001, the Fundamental Research Funds of Shandong University No. 2015JC030.

References

1. Vissicchio, S., Vanbever, L., Bonaventure, O.: Opportunities and research challenges of hybrid software defined networks. ACM SIGCOMM Comput. Commun. Rev. **44**(2), 70–75 (2014)
2. Agarwal, S., Kodialam, M., Lakshman, T.: Traffic engineering in software defined networks. In: Proceedings of the IEEE INFOCOM, pp. 2211–2219 (2013)
3. Garg, N., Konemann, J.: Faster and simpler algorithms for multicommodity flow and other fractional packing problems. SIAM J. Comput. **37**(2), 630–652 (2007)
4. Dasgupta, M., Biswas, G.: Design of multi-path data routing algorithm based on network reliability. Comput. Electr. Eng. **38**(6), 1433–1443 (2012)
5. SDNlib. http://sndlib.zib.de/home.action
6. Nascimento, M.R., Rothenberg, C.E., Salvador, M.R., Corrêa, C.N., de Lucena, S.C., Magalhaes, M.F.: Virtual routers as a service: the routeflow approach leveraging software-defined networks. In: Proceedings of the 6th International Conference on Future Internet Technologies, pp. 34–37. ACM (2011)

Heterogeneous Systems

A Study of Overflow Vulnerabilities on GPUs

Bang Di, Jianhua Sun$^{(\boxtimes)}$, and Hao Chen

College of Computer Science and Electronic Engineering,
Hunan University, Changsha 410082, China
{dibang,jhsun,haochen}@hnu.edu.cn

Abstract. GPU-accelerated computing gains rapidly-growing popularity in many areas such as scientific computing, database systems, and
cloud environments. However, there are less investigations on the security
implications of concurrently running GPU applications. In this paper, we
explore security vulnerabilities of CUDA from multiple dimensions. In
particular, we first present a study on GPU stack, and reveal that stack
overflow of CUDA can affect the execution of other threads by manipu-
lating different memory spaces. Then, we show that the heap of CUDA
is organized in a way that allows threads from the same warp or different
blocks or even kernels to overwrite each other's content, which indicates
a high risk of corrupting data or steering the execution flow by overwriting function pointers. Furthermore, we verify that integer overflow
and function pointer overflow in *struct* also can be exploited on GPUs.
But other attacks against format string and exception handler seems not
feasible due to the design choices of CUDA runtime and programming
language features. Finally, we propose potential solutions of preventing
the presented vulnerabilities for CUDA.

Keywords: GPGPU · CUDA · Security · Buffer overflow

1 Introduction

Graphics processing units (GPUs) were originally developed to perform complex mathematical and geometric calculations that are indispensable parts of
graphics rendering. Nowadays, due to the high performance and data parallelism, GPUs have been increasingly adopted to perform generic computational
tasks. For example, GPUs can provide a significant speed-up for financial and
scientific computations. GPUs also have been used to accelerate network traffic processing in software routers by offloading specific computations to GPUs.
Computation-intensive encryption algorithms like AES have also been ported to
GPU platforms to exploit the data parallelism, and significant improvement in
throughput was reported. In addition, using GPUs for co-processing in database
systems, such as offloading query processing to GPUs, has also been shown to
be beneficial.

  With the remarkable success of adopting GPUs in a diverse range of real-
world applications, especially the flourish of cloud computing and advancement

© IFIP International Federation for Information Processing 2016
Published by Springer International Publishing AG 2016. All Rights Reserved
G.R. Gao et al. (Eds.): NPC 2016, LNCS 9966, pp. 103–115, 2016.
DOI: 10.1007/978-3-319-47099-3_9

in GPU virtualization [1], sharing GPUs among cloud tenants is increasingly becoming norm. For example, major cloud vendors such as Amazon and Alibaba both offer GPU support for customers. However, this poses great challenges in guaranteeing strong isolation between different tenants sharing GPU devices.

As will be discussed in this paper, common well-studied security vulnerabilities on CPUs, such as the stack and heap overflow and integer overflow, exist on GPUs too. Unfortunately, with high concurrency and lacking effective protection, GPUs are subject to greater threat. In fact, the execution model of GPU programs consisting of CPU code and GPU code, is different from traditional programs that only contains host-side code. After launching a GPU *kernel* (defined in the following section), the execution of the GPU code is delegated to the device and its driver. Therefore, we can know that the GPU is isolated from the CPU from the perspective of code execution, which means that the CPU can not supervise its execution. Thus, existing protection techniques implemented on CPUs are invalid for GPUs. On the other hand, the massively parallel execution model of GPUs makes it difficult to implement efficient solutions tackling security issues. Unfortunately, despite GPU's pervasiveness in many fields, a thorough awareness of GPU security is lacking, and the security of GPUs are subject to threat especially in scenarios where GPUs are shared, such as GPU clusters and cloud.

From the above discussion, we know that GPUs may become a weakness that can be exploited by adversaries to execute malicious code to circumvent detection or steal sensitive information. For example, although GPU-assisted encryption algorithms achieve high performance, information leakage such as private secrete key has been proven to be feasible [2]. In particular, in order to fully exert the computing power of GPUs, effective approaches to providing shared access to GPUs has been proposed in the literature [3,4]. However, without proper mediation mechanisms, shared access may cause information leakage as demonstrated in [2]. Furthermore, we expect that other traditional software vulnerabilities on CPU platforms would have important implications for GPUs, because of similar language features (CUDA programming language inherits C/C++). Although preliminary experiments has been conducted to show the impact of overflow issues on GPU security [5], much remains unclear considering the wide spectrum of security issues. In this paper, we explore the potential overflow vulnerabilities on GPUs. To the best of our knowledge, it is the most extensive study on overflow issues for GPU architectures. Our evaluation was conducted from multiple aspects, which not only includes different types of attacks but also considers specific GPU architectural features like distinct memory spaces and concurrent kernel execution. Although we focus on the CUDA platform, we believe the results are also applicable to other GPU programming frameworks.

The rest of this paper is organized as follows. Section 2 provides necessary background about the CUDA architecture. In Sect. 3, we perform an extensive evaluation on how traditional overflow vulnerabilities can be implemented on GPUs to affect the execution flow. Possible countermeasures are discussed in Sect. 4. Section 5 presents related work, and Sect. 6 concludes this paper.

2   Background on CUDA Architecture

CUDA is a popular general purpose computing platform for NVIDIA GPUs. CUDA is composed of device driver (handles the low-level interactions with the GPU), the runtime, and the compilation tool-chain. An application written for CUDA consists of host code running on the CPU, and device code typically called *kernels* that runs on the GPU. A running kernel consists of a vast amount of GPU *threads*. Threads are grouped into *blocks*, and blocks are grouped into *grids*. The basic execution unit is *warp* that typically contains 32 threads. Each thread has its own program counters, registers, and local memory. A block is an independent unit of parallelism, and can execute independently of other thread blocks. Each thread block has a private per-block shared memory space used for inter-thread communication and data sharing when implementing parallel algorithms. A grid is an array of blocks that can execute the same kernel concurrently. An entire grid is handled by a single GPU.

The GPU kernel execution consists of the following four steps: (i) input data is transferred from the host memory to GPU memory through the DMA; (ii) a host program instructs the GPU to launch a kernel; (iii) the output is transferred from the device memory back to the host memory through the DMA.

CUDA provides different memory spaces. During execution, CUDA threads may access data from multiple memory spaces. Each thread maintains its own private local memory that actually resides in global memory. Automatic variables declared inside a kernel are mapped to local memory. The on-chip shared memory is accessible to all the threads that are in the same block. The shared memory features low-latency access (similar to L1 cache), and is mainly used for sharing data among threads belonging to the same block. The global memory (also called device memory) is accessible to all threads, and can be accessed by both GPU and CPU. There are two read-only memory spaces accessible by all threads, i.e. constant and texture memory. Texture memory also offers different addressing models, as well as data filtering, for some specific data formats. The global, constant, and texture memory spaces are optimized for different memory usages, and they are persistent across kernel launches by the same application.

3   Empirical Evaluation of GPU Vulnerabilities

In this section, we first introduce the testing environment. Then, we discuss specific vulnerabilities for stack overflow, heap overflow, and others respectively, with a focus on the heap overflow because of its potential negative impact and significance in scenarios where multiple users share GPU devices. Due to the proprietary nature of the CUDA platform, we can only experimentally confirm the existence of certain vulnerabilities. And further exploration about inherent reasons and such issues is beyond the scope of this paper, which may require a deeper understanding of the underlying implementation of CUDA framework and hardware device intricacy.

```
1    typedef unsigned long(*pFdummy)(void);
2    __device__ __noinline__ unsigned long normal1() {
3      printf("Normal\n");
4      return 0;
5    }
6    __device__ __noinline__ unsigned long malicious() {
7      printf("Attack!\n");
8      return 0;
9    }
10   __device__ int overf[100];
11   //================================================================
12     for(int i = 0; i < length; i++) {overf[i] = input[i];}
13     unsigned int buf[16];
14     pFdummy fp[8];
15     fp[0]=normal1; fp[1]=normal2; fp[2]=normal3; fp[3]=normal4;
16     fp[4]=normal5; fp[5]=normal6; fp[6]=normal7; fp[7]=normal8;
17     for(int i = 0; i < length; i++) {buf[i] = overf[i];}
18     fp[5];
```

Fig. 1. A code snippet of stack overflow in device.

3.1 Experiment Setup

The machine conducting the experiment has a Intel Core i5-4590 CPU clocked at
3.30 GHz, and the GPU is NVIDIA GeForce GTX 750Ti (Maxwell architecture)
that has compute capability 5.0. The operating system is Ubuntu 14.04.4 LTS
(64 bit) with CUDA 7.5 installed. *nvcc* is used to compile CUDA code, and
NVIDIA visual profiler is adopted as a performance profiling tool. CUDA-GDB
allows us to debug both the CPU and GPU portions of the application simultaneously. The source code of all implemented benchmarks is publicly available at
https://github.com/aimlab/cuda-overflow.

3.2 Stack Overflow

In this section, we investigate the stack overflow on GPUs by considering different
memory spaces that store adversary-controlled data, and exploring all possible
interactions among threads that are located in the same block, or in different
blocks of the same kernel, or in distinct kernels.

The main idea is as follows. The adversary formulates malicious input data
that contains the address of a malicious function, and assign it to variable a that
is defined in global scope. Two stack variables b and c are declared in a way to
make their addresses adjacent. If we use a to assign values to b to intentionally
overflow b and consequently corrupt the stack variable c that stores function
pointers. Then, when one of the function pointers of c is invoked, the execution
flow would be diverted to the adversary-controlled function. Note that there
is a difference of the stack between the GPU and CPU. In fact, the storage
allocation of GPU stack is similar to the heap, so the direction of overflow is
from low address to high address.

We explain how a malicious kernel can manipulate a benign kernel's stack with an illustrating example that is shown in Fig. 1. In the GPU code, we define 9 functions containing 1 malicious function (used to simulate malicious behavior) and 8 normal functions (only one is shown in Fig. 1, and the other 7 functions are the same as the function *normal1* except the naming). The *__device__* qualifier declares a function that is executed on the device and callable from the device only. The *__noinline__* function qualifier can be used as a hint for the compiler not to inline the function if possible. The array *overf[100]* is declared globally to store data from another array *input[100]* that is controlled by the malicious kernel. Given the global scope, the storage of *overf[100]* is allocated in the global memory space, indicating both the malicious kernel and benign kernel can access. In addition, two arrays named *buf* and *fp* are declared one after another on the stack to ensure that their addresses are consecutively assigned. The *fp* stores function pointers that point to the normal functions declared before, and the data in *overf[100]* is copied to *buf* (shown at line 17) to trigger the overflow. The *length* variable is used to control how many words should be copied from *overf* to *buf* (shown at line 17). It is worth noting that the line 12 is only executed in the malicious kernel to initialize the *overf* buffer. If we set *length* to 26 and initialize *overf* with the value1 **0x590** (address of the *malicious* function that can be obtained using *printf("%p",malicious)* or CUDA-GDB [5]), the output at line 18 would be string "**Normal**". This is because with value 26, we can only overwrite the first 5 pointers in *fp* ($sizeof(buf) + sizeof(pFdummy) * 5 == 26$). However, setting *length* to 27 would cause the output at line 18 to be "**Attack!**", indicating that *fp[5]* is successfully overwritten by the address of the *malicious* function. This example demonstrates that current GPUs have no mechanisms to prevent stack overflow like stack canaries on the CPU counterpart (Fig. 2).

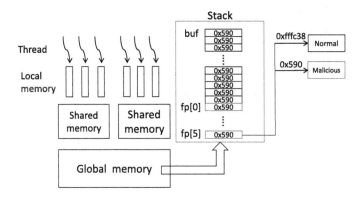

Fig. 2. Illustration of stack overflow.

It is straightforward to extend our experiments to other scenarios. For example, by locating the array *overf* in the shared memory, we can observe that the attack is feasible only if the malicious thread and benign thread both reside in the same block. While if *overf* is in the local memory, other threads has no way to conduct malicious activities. In summary, our evaluation shows that attacking a GPU kernel based on stack overflow is possible, but the risk level of such vulnerability depends on specific conditions like explicit communication between kernels.

3.3   Heap Overflow

In this section, we study a set of heap vulnerabilities in CUDA. We first investigate the heap isolation on CUDA GPUs. Then, we discuss how to corrupt locally-allocated heap data when the malicious and benign threads co-locate in the same block. Finally, we generalize the heap overflow to cases where two kernels are run sequentially or concurrently.

```
1   // ============== a virtual table of the device code ================
2   class Vtable {
3   public:
4     __device__ virtual unsigned long v1() {printf("Normal\n");return 0;}
5     __device__ virtual unsigned long v2() {printf("Normal\n");return 0;}
6     __device__ virtual unsigned long v3() {printf("Normal\n");return 0;}
7     __device__ virtual unsigned long v4() {printf("Normal\n");return 0;}
8   };
9   //====================== malicious function =====================
10  __device__ __noinline__ unsigned long malicious() {
11    printf("Attack!\n");
12    return 0;
13  }
14  //============== a snippet code of memory isolation of heap ==========
15    __shared__ unsigned long *buf;
16    if(threadIdx.x == 0)
17    buf = (unsigned long *) malloc(sizeof(unsigned long) * 8);
18    Vtable *fp = new Vtable;
19    if(threadIdx.x == 0)
20      for(int i = 0; i < length; i++) {buf[i] = input[i];}
21    if(threadIdx.x == 1)
22      printf("%lx", buf[0]);
23  //============= a snippet code of exploiting of 'global' heap =========
24    unsigned long *buf;
25    buf = (unsigned long *) malloc(sizeof(unsigned long) * 8);
26    Vtable *fp = new Vtable;
27    printf("malicious %p\n", malicious);
28    for(int i = 0; i < length; i++) {buf[i] = input[i];}
29    res=fp->v1(); res=fp->v2(); res=fp->v3(); res=fp->v4();
```

Fig. 3. A code snippet of heap overflow

Heap Isolation. Similar to the description of stack overflow, we also use a running example to illustrate heap isolation from two aspects. First, we consider the case of a single kernel. As shown in Fig. 3 (from line 15 to 22), suppose we have two independent threads t_1 and t_2 in the same block, and a pointer variable *buf* is defined in the shared memory. We can obtain similar results when *buf* is defined in the global memory. For clarity, we use buf_1 and buf_2 to represent the

buf in t_1 and t_2. buf_1 is allocated by calling *malloc* as shown at lines 16 and 17. Our experiments show that t_2 can always access buf_1 (line 21 to 22) unless buf is defined in the local scope. Second, we consider the case of two kernels (not shown in the figure). Kernel a allocates memory space for *buf*, and assigns the input value to it. If a returns without freeing the memory of *buf*, another kernel b can always read the content in *buf* if b also has a variable *buf* defined in either shared memory or global memory (no memory allocation for *buf* in b). This is because the GPU assigns the same address to *buf* for b, which makes it possible to access the not freed content of *buf* in b. In summary, for globally-defined heap pointer, the memory it points to can be freely accessed by threads that are not the original allocator. It is not the case for locally-defined heap pointers, but it may still be possible if we can successfully guest the addresses of local heap pointers (we leave this to future work). Most importantly, when a heap pointer is globally visible and the corresponding memory is not properly managed (freed), arbitrary memory accesses across kernels would be possible.

Heap Exploitation. In this experiment, we present that because the heap memory for different threads or kernels is allocated contiguously, overflowing one thread's local buffer may lead to the corruption of another thread's heap data.

We first consider heap memory allocated in local scope. As shown in Fig. 3 (from line 24 to 29), like before, suppose we have two threads t_1 and t_2 in the same block. For t_1, we use *malloc* and *new* to allocate memory for buf_1 and fp_1 respectively (we use these notations to clarify our discussion). fp_1 just stores the **start address** of the four virtual functions (the addresses is contained in the VTABLE). buf_1 and fp_1 are declared locally. t_2 is the same as t_1. After initializing t_1 and t_2, the memory layout of buf_1, fp_1, buf_2, and fp_2 looks like that shown in Fig. 4. Assume t_2 has malicious intention. The *input* in t_1 consists of normal data, and the *input* in t_2 consists of four addresses of the *malicious* function (**0x138**), and the remaining contents of *input* are the address of buf_2 (**0x50263f920**). When *length* is less than 11 (not 9 due to alignment), both t_1 and t_2 will print the string "**Normal**". However, when *length* is set to 11, the virtual table address in fp_1 would be modified to the start address of buf_2 where the four addresses of the *malicious* function are stored. So the output of t_1 will be the string "**Attack!**". When *length* is set to 21 (this value is relative to fp_1), both t_1 and t_2 will invoke the *malicious* function. Similarly, assuming t_1 is the malicious thread, both t_1 and t_2 will output "**Normal**" when *length* is less than 21. By assigning 21 to *length*, only t_1 will print "**Attack!**". And when the value of *length* is 31, both t_1 and t_2 will invoke the *malicious* function.

Based on the analysis above, we can conclude that the memory allocated from the heap in CUDA is globally accessible from different GPU threads without proper access control, and no protection is provided by the runtime system to prevent buffer overflow of heap-allocated memory. The addresses of heap pointers are often guessable, which makes it easy for a adversary to conduct attacks. Because of the closed-source nature of CUDA, further investigation about the implementation-level details is left as future work. In the following, we extend our analysis to the scenario where two kernels are considered when experimenting buffer overflow.

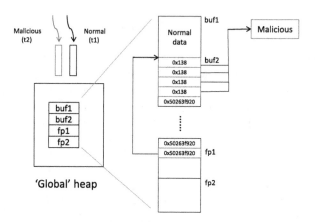

Fig. 4. A heap overflow: t_1 and t_2 represent the benign and malicious thread respectively.

Heap Exploitation Between Kernels. First, we consider the overflow between sequentially launched kernels. The experiment setup is similar to the previous section except that the host launches serially two kernels, $kernel_1$ (launched first) and $kernel_2$. $kernel_1$ simulates behaviors of an adversary and initializes the thread t_1. $kernel_2$ represents a benign user. t_1's input data consist of four addresses of malicious function, and its remaining contents are the address of buf_1. $kernel_1$ intentionally overflows buf_1 by using a large value of $length_1$, and then terminates. $kernel_2$ allocates memory for buf_2 and fp_2, but does not assign any value to them. When accessing one element in fp_2 as a function call, we will observe the output of string "**Attack!**". This is because the GPU assigns the same addresses of pointer variables to the second kernel, and the contents used in the first kernel are remained in GPU memory unchanged.

Second, we analyze the situation of two concurrently running kernels as shown in Fig. 5. This is the typical case of sharing GPUs in cloud or cluster environment, where different users may access the GPU at the same time. $kernel_1$ and $kernel_2$ must be in different streams. $cudaMemcpyAsync$ is called to receive data from the host that allocates *page-locked* memory. The *sleep()* function is used to perform a simple synchronization between kernels to make our experiments more deterministic. t_1 in $kernel_1$ mimics a malicious user's behavior. When buf_2 and fp_2 are initialized (from line 9 to 12) and at the same time t_1 has finished the execution of the *for* loop (at line 20), we will observe the output of string "**Attack!**" from t_2 if it continues to run after the pause at line 13. Based on these observations, we can conclude that multiple kernels, regardless of serially or concurrently running, have the opportunity to intentionally manipulate the heap memory of each other.

```
1    //==================== sleep function ====================
2    __device__ void sleep(int64_t num_cycles) {
3        int64_t cycles = 0;
4        int64_t start = clock64();
5        while (cycles < num_cycles)
6                cycles = clock64() - start;
7    }
8    //==================== normal kernel ====================
9        unsigned long *buf;
10       buf = (unsigned long *) malloc(sizeof(unsigned long) * 8);
11       Vtable *fp = new Vtable;
12       for(int i = 0; i < length; i++) {buf[i] = input[i];}
13       sleep(10000000);
14       res=fp->v1(); res=fp->v2(); res=fp->v3(); res=fp->v4();
15    //==================== malicious kernel ====================
16       unsigned long *buf;
17       buf = (unsigned long *) malloc(sizeof(unsigned long) * 8);
18       Vtable *fp = new Vtable;
19       sleep(1000000);
20       for(int i = 0; i < length; i++) {buf[i] = input[i];}
21       res=fp->v1(); res=fp->v2(); res=fp->v3(); res=fp->v4();
```

Fig. 5. A code snippet of concurrent kernel execution.

3.4   Other Vulnerabilities

In this section, we discuss the issues of *struct* and integer overflow that are demonstrated in one example. In this case, the attacker can exploit the characteristics of integer operations. Because of the two's complementary representation of integers, integer operations may produce undesirable results when an arithmetic operation attempts to produce a numeric value that is too large to be representable with a certain type.

In this experiment (Fig. 6), we define two variables *input[10]* and *length*, which stores user data and data size respectively. The device code for functions *normal* and *malicious* are the same as defined in Fig. 5. In addition, we define a *struct unsafe*, which contains an array *buf[6]* and a function pointer of type *normal*. The *init()* (line 6) function is used to initialize the structure defined above. The *if* statement (line 12) performs array-bounds check to prevent out-of-bound access. Suppose that the address of the *malicious* function is **0x43800000438** that is assigned to *input[10]* as input data by a malicious user. The variable *length* whose type is **unsigned char** is set to 0 by the attacker. The *if* branch would be executed because the value of *length* (0) is smaller than 6. But, the value of *length* will be 255 after it is decremented by one, which causes that the assignment at line 15 overflows the array *buf* and corrupt the function pointer in *struct unsafe*. This experiment shows that *struct* and integers can both be exploited in CUDA. In particular, both overflow and underflow of integer arithmetic operation are possible, which exposes more opportunities for the adversaries.

Format string and exception handling vulnerabilities have been studied on CPUs. However, our experiments show that they currently are not exploitable

```
1   // =================== a snippet of the device code ===================
2   struct unsafe {
3     unsigned long buf[6];
4     void (*normal)();
5   };
6   __device__ __noinline__ void init(struct unsafe *data) {
7     data->normal = normal;
8   }
9   __global__ void test_kernel(unsigned long *input, unsigned char length) {
10    struct unsafe cu;
11    init(&cu);
12    if (length < 6) {
13      length = length - 1;
14      for (int i = 0; i < length; i++)
15        cu.buf[i] = input[i];
16    }
17    cu.normal();
    }
```

Fig. 6. A snippet code of *struct* and integer vulnerabilities

on the GPU due to the limited support in CUDA. For format string, the format-ted output is only supported by devices with compute capability 2.x and higher. The in-kernel *printf* function behaves in a similar way to the counterpart in the standard C-library. In essence, the string passed in as format is output to a stream on the host, which makes it impossible to conduct malicious behavior through *printf* to expose memory errors on the GPU. For the exception han-dling in C++, it is only supported for the host code, but not the device code. Therefore, we can not exploit the security issues of exception handling on CUDA GPUs currently.

4   Discussions and Countermeasures

This section discusses potential countermeasures that can prevent or restrict the impact of the described vulnerabilities. Basically, most discussed weaknesses have limited impact on current GPUs if considered from the security point of view. For example, stack overflow and in-kernel heap overflow can only corrupt the memory data from within the same kernel. It is difficult to inject executable code into a running kernel to change its control flow under the GPU program-ming model. Of course, it may not be the case when more functionalities are integrated to make developing GPU applications more like the CPU counter-parts [6]. However, exploitable vulnerabilities for concurrent kernels pose real and practical risks on GPUs, and effective defenses are required for a secure GPU computing environment.

For security issues of the heap, calling the *free()* function, to a certain extent, can offer necessary protection for heap overflows. When an attacker wants to exploit vulnerabilities to corrupt the heap memory that belongs to other threads and has been freed, error message is reported and the application is terminated.

But this is hard to guarantee in environments where multiple kernels are running concurrently. The bounds check can be used to prevent overflow for both the stack and heap, but the performance overhead is non-trivial if frequently invoked at runtime. In addition, integer overflow may be leveraged to bypass the bounds check. Therefore, a multifaceted solution is desired to provide full protection against these potential attacks. For example, standalone or hybrid dynamic and static analysis approaches can be designed to detect memory and integer overflows. Ideally, such protections should be implemented by the underlying system such as the runtime system, compiler, or hardware of GPU platforms, as many countermeasures against memory errors on CPUs, such as stack canaries, address sanitizers, and address randomization, have been shown to be effective and practical. Unfortunately, similar countermeasures are still missing on GPUs.

CUDA-MEMCHECK [7] can identify the source and cause of memory access errors in GPU code, so it can detect all the heap related overflows in our experiments. But it fails to identify the stack overflows. CUDA-MEMCHECK is effective as a testing tool, but the runtime overhead makes it impractical to be deployed in production environments. Most importantly, when multiple mutually untrusted users share a GPU device, dynamic protection mechanisms are indispensable. Thus, we argue that research endeavors should be devoted to the design of efficient approaches to preventing security issues for GPUs.

A wide range of defensive techniques has been proposed to prevent or detect buffer overflows on CPUs. Compiler-oriented techniques including canaries, bounds checking, and tagging are especially useful in our context. Given that CUDA's backend is based on the LLVM framework and Clang already supports buffer overflow detection (AddressSanitizer) through compiler options, we believe these existing tools can be leveraged to implement efficient defenses against GPU-based overflow vulnerabilities.

5   Related Work

Recently, using GPUs in cloud environment has been shown to be beneficial. The authors of [4] present a framework to enable applications executing within virtual machines to transparently share one or more GPUs. Their approach aims at energy efficiency and do not consider the security issues as discussed in this work. For GPU-assisted database systems, the study in [8] shows that data in GPU memory is retrievable by other processes by creating a memory dump of the device memory. In [9], it is demonstrated feasible to recover user-visited web pages in widely-used browsers such as Chromium and Firefox, because these web browsers rely on GPUs to render web pages but do not scrub the content remained on GPU memory, leading to information leakage. The paper [10] highlights possible information leakage of GPUs in virtualized and cloud environments. They find that GPU's global memory is zeroed only when ECC (Error Correction Codes) is enabled, which poses high risk of private information exposure when ECC is disabled or not available on GPUs. In [2], the authors present a detailed analysis of information leakage in CUDA for multiple memory spaces including the global memory, shared memory, and register. A real case study is performed on a GPU-based AES encryption implementation to reveal the vulnerability of leaking private keys.

However, all existing studies on GPU security have less considered vulnerabilities that are more extensively studied on CPUs. The paper [5] presents a preliminary study of buffer overflow vulnerabilities in CUDA, but the breadth and depth are limited as compared to our work. For example, we put more emphasis on heap overflows between concurrently running kernels, which we believe deserves special attentions in future research of securing shared GPU access.

6 Conclusion

In this paper, we have investigated the weakness of GPUs under malicious intentions with a focus on the CUDA platform. We believe the experiments conducted in this work are also applicable to other GPU frameworks such as OpenCL to reveal the potential security vulnerabilities. Particularly, we have confirmed the existence of stack and heap overflows through a diversified set of experiments, and also uncovered how integer overflow can be used in overwriting a function pointer in a *struct*. Other security issues such as format string and exception handling are also investigated. Although direct exploitation of these potential vulnerabilities is not feasible on current CUDA platform, care must be taken when developing applications for future GPU platforms, because GPU programming platforms are evolving with a fast pace. We hope this study can not only disclose real security issues for GPUs but stimulate future research on this topic especially for scenarios where GPU devices are shared among untrusted users.

Acknowledgment. This research was supported in part by the National Science Foundation of China under grants 61272190, 61572179 and 61173166.

References

1. Shi, L., Chen, H., Sun, J., Li, K.: vCUDA: GPU-accelerated high-performance computing in virtual machines. IEEE Trans. Comput. **61**(6), 804–816 (2012)
2. Pietro, R.D., Lombardi, F., Villani, A.: CUDA leaks: a detailed hack for CUDA and a (partial) fix. ACM Trans. Embedded Comput. Syst. **15**(1), 15 (2016)
3. Pai, S., Thazhuthaveetil, M.J., Govindarajan, R.: Improving GPGPU concurrency with elastic kernels. In: Architectural Support for Programming Languages and Operating Systems, ASPLOS 2013, Houston, TX, USA, 16–20 March 2013, pp. 407–418 (2013)
4. Ravi, V.T., Becchi, M., Agrawal, G., Chakradhar, S.T.: Supporting GPU sharing in cloud environments with a transparent runtime consolidation framework. In: Proceedings of the 20th ACM International Symposium on High Performance Distributed Computing, HPDC 2011, San Jose, CA, USA, 8–11 June 2011, pp. 217–228 (2011)

5. Miele, A.: Buffer overflow vulnerabilities in CUDA: a preliminary analysis. J. Comput. Virol. Hacking Techn. **12**(2), 113–120 (2016)
6. Silberstein, M., Ford, B., Keidar, I., Witchel, E.: GPUfs: integrating a file system with GPUs. In: Proceedings of the Eighteenth International Conference on Architectural Support for Programming Languages and Operating Systems. ASPLOS 2013, pp. 485–498. ACM (2013)
7. NVIDIA: CUDA-MEMCHECK. https://developer.nvidia.com/cuda-memcheck
8. Breß, S., Kiltz, S., Schäler, M.: Forensics on GPU coprocessing in databases - research challenges, first experiments, and countermeasures. In: Datenbanksysteme für Business, Technologie und Web (BTW), - Workshopband, 15. Fachtagung des GI-Fachbereichs "Datenbanken und Informationssysteme" (DBIS), 11–15 March 2013, Magdeburg, Germany. Proceedings, pp. 115–129 (2013)
9. Lee, S., Kim, Y., Kim, J., Kim, J.: Stealing webpages rendered on your browser by exploiting GPU vulnerabilities. In: 2014 IEEE Symposium on Security and Privacy, SP 2014, Berkeley, CA, USA, 18–21 May 2014, pp. 19–33 (2014)
10. Maurice, C., Neumann, C., Heen, O., Francillon, A.: Confidentiality issues on a GPU in a virtualized environment. In: Christin, N., Safavi-Naini, R. (eds.) FC 2014. LNCS, vol. 8437, pp. 119–135. Springer, Heidelberg (2014). doi:10.1007/978-3-662-45472-5_9

Streaming Applications on Heterogeneous Platforms

Zhaokui Li$^{(\boxtimes)}$, Jianbin Fang, Tao Tang, Xuhao Chen, and Canqun Yang

Software Institute, College of Computer,
National University of Defense Technology, Changsha, China
zhaokuili@yeah.net, {j.fang,tangtao84,chenxuhao,canqun}@nudt.edu.cn

Abstract. Using multiple streams can improve the overall system performance by mitigating the data transfer overhead on heterogeneous systems. Currently, very few cases have been streamed to demonstrate the streaming performance impact and a systematic investigation of *streaming necessity* and *how-to* over a large number of test cases remains a gap. In this paper, we use a total of 56 benchmarks to build a statistical view of the data transfer overhead, and give an in-depth analysis of the impacting factors. Among the heterogeneous codes, we identify two types of *non-streamable* codes and three types of *streamable* codes, for which a streaming approach has been proposed. Our experimental results on the CPU-MIC platform show that, with multiple streams, we can improve the application performance by up 90 %. Our work can serve as a generic flow of using multiple streams on heterogeneous platforms.

Keywords: Multiple streams · Heterogeneous platforms · Performance

1 Introduction

Heterogeneous platforms are increasingly popular in many application domains [13]. The combination of using a host CPU combined with a specialized processing unit (e.g., GPGPUs or Intel Xeon Phi) has been shown in many cases to improve the performance of an application by significant amounts. Typically, the host part of a heterogeneous platform manages the execution context while the time-consuming code piece is offloaded to the coprocessor. Leveraging such platforms can not only enable the achievement of high peak performance, but increase the *performance per Watt ratio*.

Given a heterogeneous platform, how to realize its performance potentials remains a challenging issue. In particular, programmers need to explicitly move data between host and device over PCIe before and/or after running kernels. The overhead counts when data transferring takes a decent amount of time, and determines whether to perform offloading is worthwhile [2,3,5]. To hide this overhead, overlapping kernel executions with data movements is required. To this end, *multiple streams* (or *streaming mechanism*) has been introduced, e.g., CUDA Streams [12], OpenCL Command Queues [16], and Intel's

© IFIP International Federation for Information Processing 2016
Published by Springer International Publishing AG 2016. All Rights Reserved
G.R. Gao et al. (Eds.): NPC 2016, LNCS 9966, pp. 116–129, 2016.
DOI: 10.1007/978-3-319-47099-3_10

hStreams [8]. These implementations of *multiple streams* spawn more than one streams/pipelines so that the data movement stage of one pipeline overlaps the kernel execution stage of another[1].

Prior works on multiple streams mainly focus on GPUs and the potential of using multiple streams on GPUs is shown to be significant [4,7,9,17]. Liu et al. give a detailed study into how to achieve optimal task partition within an analytical framework for AMD GPUs and NVIDIA GPUs [9]. In [4], the authors model the performance of asynchronous data transfers of CUDA streams to determine the optimal number of streams. However, these studies have shown very limited number of cases, which leaves two questions unanswered: (1) whether each application is required and worthwhile to use multiple streams on a given heterogeneous platform?, (2) whether each potential application is *streamable* or *overlappable*? If so, how can we stream the code?

To systematically answer these questions, we (1) build a statistical view of the data transfer (H2D and D2H) fraction for a large number of test cases, and (2) present our approach to stream different applications. Specifically, we statistically show that more than 50 % test cases (among 223) are not worthwhile to use multiple streams. The fraction of H2D varies over platforms, applications, code variants, and input configurations. Further, we identify two types of *non-streamable* codes (Iterative and SYNC) and three categories of *streamable* code based on task dependency (embarrassingly independent, false dependent, and true dependent). Different approaches are proposed to either eliminate or respect the data dependency. As case studies, we stream 13 benchmarks of different categories and show their streaming performance impact. Our experimental results show that using multiple streams gives a performance improvement ranging from 8 % to 90 %. To the best of our knowledge, this is the first comprehensive and systematic study of multiple streams in terms of both *streaming necessity* and *how-to*. To summarize, we make the following contributions:

- We build a statistical view of the data transfer fraction (R) with a large number of test cases and analyze its impacting factors (Sect. 3).
- We categorize the heterogeneous codes based on task dependency and present our approach to stream three types of applications (Sect. 4).
- We show a generic flow of using multiple streams for a given application: calculating R and performing code streaming (Sects. 3 and 4).
- We demonstrate the performance impact of using multiple streams on the CPU-MIC platform with 13 streamed benchmarks (Sect. 5).

2   Related Work

In this section, we list the related work on pipelining, multi-tasking, workload partitioning, multi-stream modeling, and offloading necessity.

---

[1] In the context, the streaming mechanism is synonymous with *multiple streams*, and thus we refer the *streamed code* as *code with multiple streams*.

Pipelinining is widely used in modern computer architectures [6]. Specifically, the pipeline stages of an instruction run on different functional units, e.g., arithmetic units or data loading units. In this way, the stages from different instructions can occupy the same functional unit in different time steps, thus improving the overall system throughput. Likewise, the execution of a heterogeneous application is divided into stages (H2D, KEX, D2H), and can exploit the idea of software pipelining on the heterogeneous platforms.

Multi-tasking provides concurrent execution of multiple applications on a single device. In [1], the authors propose and make the case for a GPU multitasking technique called *spatial multitasking*. The experimental results show that the proposed spatial multitasking can obtain a higher performance over cooperative multitasking. In [19], Wende et al. investigate the concurrent kernel execution mechanism that enables multiple small kernels to run concurrently on the Kepler GPUs. Also, the authors evaluate the Xeon Phi offload models with multi-threaded and multi-process host applications with concurrent coprocessor offloading [18]. Both multitasking and multiple streams share the idea of spatial resource sharing. Different from multi-tasking, using multiple streams needs to partition the workload of a single application (rather than multiple applications) into many tasks.

Workload Partitioning: There is a large body of workload partitioning techniques, which intelligently partition the workload between a CPU and a coprocessor at the level of algorithm [20,21] or during program execution [14,15]. Partitioning workloads aims to use unique architectural strength of processing units and improve resource utilization [11]. In this work, we focus on how to efficiently utilize the coprocessing device with multiple streams. Ultimately, we need to leverage both workload partitioning and multiple streams to minimize the end-to-end execution time.

Multiple Streams Modeling: In [4], Gomez-Luna et al. present performance models for asynchronous data transfers on different GPU architectures. The models permit programmers to estimate the optimal number of streams in which the computation on the GPU should be broken up. In [17], Werkhoven et al. present an analytical performance model to indicate when to apply which overlapping method on GPUs. The evaluation results show that the performance model are capable of correctly classifying the relative performance of the different implementations. In [9], Liu et al. carry out a systematic investigation into task partitioning to achieve maximum performance gain for AMD and NVIDIA GPUs. Unlike these works, we aim to evaluate the necessity of using multiple streams and investigate how to use streams systematically. Using a model on Phi to determine the number of streams will be investigated as our future work.

Offloading Necessity: Meswani et al. have developed a framework for predicting the performance of applications executing on accelerators [10]. Using automatically extracted application signatures and a machine profile based on benchmarks, they aim to predict the application running time before the application is ported. Evaluating offloading necessity is a former step of applying multiple streams. In this work, we evaluate the necessity of using multiple streams with a statistical approach.

3 A Statistical View

In this section, we give a statistical view of how many applications are worthwhile to be streamed on heterogeneous platforms, and analyze the factors that impact the streaming necessity.

3.1 Benchmarks and Datasets

As shown in Table 1, we use a large number of benchmarks that cover a broad range of interesting applications domains for heterogeneous computing. These benchmarks are from the Rodinia Benchmark Suite, the Parboil Benchmark Suite, the NVIDIA SDK, and the AMD APP SDK. In total, we employ 56 benchmarks and 223 configurations. The details about how applications are configured are summarized in Table 1. Note that we remove the redundant applications among the four benchmark suites when necessary.

Table 1. Applications, inputs and configurations

Suite	Applications	Input	Applications	Input
Rodinia (18)	backprop	$10 \times \{2^{16}, 2^{17}, 2^{18}, 2^{19}, 2^{20}\}$	bfs	graph$\{512K, 1M, 2M, 4M, 8M\}$
	b+tree	Kernel1, Kernel2	cfd	0.97K, 193K, 0.2M
	dwt2d,gaussian, lud	$2^{10}, 2^{11}, 2^{12}, 2^{13}, 2^{14}$	myocyte, srad	100, 200, 300, 400, 500
	hearwall, lavaMD, leukocyte	10, 20, 30, 40, 50	hotspot	$2^9, 2^{10}, 2^{11}, 2^{12}, 2^{13}$
	kmeans	$\{1, 3, 10, 30, 100\} \times 100000$	nn, nw	$2^{10}, 2^{11}, 2^{12}, 2^{13}, 2^{14}$
	pathfinder	$(\{1, 2, 4\} \times 10^5, \{100, 200, 400\})$	streamcluster	$100 \times \{2^{10}, 2^{11}, 2^{12}, 2^{13}, 2^{14}\}$
Parboil (9)	spmv	small, medium, large	stencil	small, default
	mri-gridding	small	cutcp	small, large
	tpacf	small, medium, large	bfs	1M, NY, SF, UT
	sgemm	small, medium	mri-q	small, large
	lbm	short, long		
NVIDIA SDK (17)	BlackScholes	$10^6 \times \{4, 8, 12, 16, 20\}$	ConvolutionSeparable	$2^{10} \times \{1, 2, 3, 4, 8\}$
	DCT8x8	$2^{10} \times \{1, 2, 3, 4, 8\}$	DotProduct	$2^{10} \times 10^3 \times \{1, 2, 3, 4, 8\}$
	DXTCompression	lena	FDTD3d	10, 20,30, 40, 50
	Histogram	1, 2, 3, 4, 5	MatrixMul	6, 7, 8, 9, 10
	MatVecMul	256, 128, 64, 32, 16	QuansiRandomGenerator	$2^{10} \times 10^3 \times \{1, 2, 3, 4, 8\}$
	Reduction	$2^{10} \times 10^3 \times \{1, 2, 3, 4, 8\}$	Reduction-2	$2^{10} \times 10^3 \times \{1, 2, 3, 4, 8\}$
	Transpose	$2^{10} \times \{1, 2, 3, 4, 8\}$	Tridiagonal	32, 64, 128, 256, 512
	VectorAdd	$2^{10} \times \{1, 2, 4, 8, 16\}$	FastWalshTransform	8M
			ConvolutionFFT2D	62500k
AMD SDK (12)	BinomialOption	$2^{10} \times \{1, 2, 4, 8, 16\}$	BitonicSort	$2^{20} \times \{1, 2, 4, 8, 16\}$
	BoxFilter	BoxFilter_Input	DwtHaar1D	$2^{10} \times 10^3 \times \{1, 2, 3, 4, 8\}$
	FloydWarshall	$2^{10} \times \{1, 2, 3, 4, 5\}$	MonteCarloAsian	$2^{10} \times \{1, 2, 3, 4, 5\}$
	RadixSort	$2^{12} \times \{12, 13, 14, 15, 16\}$	RecursiveGaussian	default
	ScanLargeArrays	$2^{10} \times \{1, 2, 4, 8, 16\}$	StringSearch	1, 2, 3, 4, 5
	URNG	1, 2, 3, 4, 5	PrefixSum	1024k

3.2 Experimental Platforms

The heterogeneous platform used in this work includes a dual-socket Intel Xeon CPU (12 cores for each socket) and an Intel Xeon 31SP Phi (57 cores for each card). The host CPUs and the cards are connected by a PCIe connection. As for the software, the host CPU runs Redhat Linux v7.0 (the kernel version is 3.10.0-123.el7.x86_64), while the coprocessor runs a customized uOS (v2.6.38.8). Intel's MPSS (v3.6) is used as the driver and the communication backbone between the host and the coprocessor. Also, we use Intel's multi-stream implementation hStreams (v3.5.2) and Intel's OpenCL SDK (v14.2). Note that the applications in Table 1 are in OpenCL, while the pipelined versions are in hStreams.

3.3   Measurement Methodology

A typical heterogeneous code has three parts: (1) transferring data from host
to device (H2D), (2) kernel execution (KEX), and (3) moving data from device
back (D2H). To measure the percentage of each stage, we run the codes in a
strictly stage-by-stage manner. Moreover, we perform 11 runs and calculate the
median value. Before uploading datasets, buffer allocation on the device side is
required. Due to the usage of the *lazy allocation policy*, the allocation overhead
is often counted into H2D. Thus, we argue that H2D might be larger than the
actual host-to-device data transferring time.

3.4   Results and Analysis

We define *data transfer ratio (R)* as the fraction of the data transfer time to the
total execution time, and take this metric (R) as an indicator of whether it is
necessary to use multiple streams. Figure 1 shows the CDF distribution of the
H2D and D2H duration versus the overall execution time $(R_{H2D}$ and $R_{D2H})$. We
observe that the CDF is over 50 % when $R_{H2D} = 0.1$. That is, the H2D transfer
time takes less than 10 % for more than 50 % configurations. Meanwhile, the
number is even larger (around 70 %) for the D2H part. In the remaining contents,
we will focus on R_{H2D} and use R (instead of R_{H2D}) for clarity.

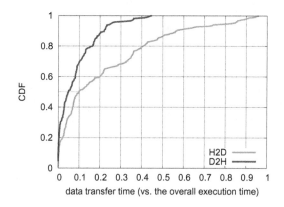

Fig. 1. The CDF curve for data transfers between the host and the accelerator.

The Impact of Input Datasets. Typically, the H2D ratio will remain when
changing the input datasets. This is because the computation often changes
linearly over the data amount. But this is not necessarily the case. Figure 2
shows how R changes with the input datasets for lbm and FDTD3d, respectively.
We note that, for lbm, using the short configuration takes a decent amount of
time to move data from host to device, while the data amount takes a much
smaller proportion for the long configuration. For FDTD3d, users have to specify

the number of time steps according to their needs. We note that the kernel execution time increases over time steps. When streaming such applications, it is necessary to focus on the commonly used datasets.

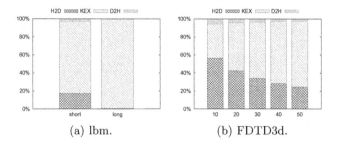

(a) lbm.   (b) FDTD3d.

Fig. 2. R changes over datasets for lbm and FDTD3d.

The Impact of Code Variants. Figure 3 shows how data transfers change with the two code variants for Reduction. Reduction v1 performs the whole reduction work on the accelerator, thus significantly reducing the data-moving overheads. Meanwhile, Reduction v2 performs the final reduction on the host side, and thus needs to transfer the intermediate results back to host. Therefore, different code variants will generate different data transferring requirements, which is to be taken into account when streaming such code variants.

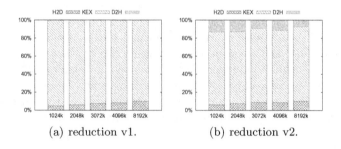

(a) reduction v1.   (b) reduction v2.

Fig. 3. R changes over code variants of NVIDIA Reduction.

The Impact of Platform Divergence. Figure 4 shows how R changes on MIC and a K80 GPU [2]. We see that the kernel execution time (of nn) on the MIC occupies 33 % on average while the number is only around 2 % on the GPU. This is due to the huge processing power from NVIDIA K80, which reduces the KEX fraction significantly. Ideally, using the streaming mechanism can improve the overall performance by 2 % on the GPU. In this case, we argue that it is unnecessary to use multiple streams on GPU.

---

[2] Note that the only difference lies in devices (Intel Xeon 31SP Phi versus NVIDIA K80 GPU) and all the other configurations are the same.

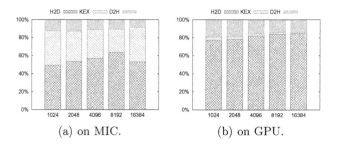

(a) on MIC.   (b) on GPU.

Fig. 4. R changes over platforms of `Rodinia nn`.

To summarize, we observe that R varies over platforms, benchmarks, code variants, and input configurations. Each benchmark has a unique balance between computation and memory accesses. Different code variants lead to the differences in transferred data amounts and kernel execution time. Also, input configurations can incur changes in transferred data amounts and/or kernel execution time. Furthermore, R depends on hardware capabilities (e.g., the PCIe interconnect and the accelerator).

We use R as an indicator of deciding whether the target application is worthwhile to be streamed. Figure 1 shows that H2D takes only 10 % of the total execution time for over 50 % test cases. We argue that, on the one hand, the applications are not worthwhile to be streamed when R is small. This is due to two factors: (1) code streaming introduces overheads for filling and emptying the pipeline, and (2) streaming an application requires extra programming efforts from reconstructing data structures and managing streams. Thus, streaming such applications might lead to a performance degradation compared with the non-streamed code. On the other hand, when R is too large (e.g., 90 %), it is equally not worthwhile to apply streams. When the fraction of H2D is too large, using accelerators may lead to a performance drop (when comparing to the case of only using CPUs), not to mention using streams. In real-world cases, users need make the streaming decision based on the value of R and the coding effort.

4   Our Streaming Approach

4.1   Categorization

After determining the necessity to apply the pipelining/streaming mechanism, we further investigate *how-to*. Generally, we divide applications into tasks which are mapped onto different processing cores. As we have mentioned above, each task includes the subtasks of data transfers and kernel execution. To pipeline codes, we should guarantee that *there exist independent tasks* running concurrently. Once discovering independent tasks, we are able to overlap the execution of H2D from one task and KEX from another (Fig. 5(a)). For a single task, H2D is dependent on KEX.

In practice, more than one H2D may depend on a single kernel execution (Fig. 5(b)). Thus, we need to analyze each H2D–KEX dependency to determine whether each pair can be overlapped. Moreover, an application often has more than one kernel. Implicitly, each kernel is synchronized at the end of its execution. Therefore, the kernel execution order is strictly respected within a single task. Figure 5(c) shows that H2D(1) is depended by KEX(1), but the data is not used til the execution of KEX(2). Thus, this data transfer can be delayed right before KEX(2) when analyzing dependency and/or streaming the code.

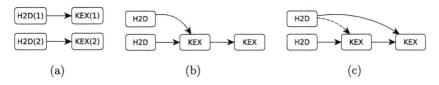

Fig. 5. The dependent relationship between H2D and KEX (The number in the parenthesis represents stages from different tasks).

Based on the dependency analysis, we categorize the codes listed in Table 1 as *streamable codes* (Sect. 4.2) and *non-streamable codes*. The first pattern (SYNC) of *non-streamed codes* is when the H2D data is shared by all the tasks of an application. In this case, the whole data transfer has to be finished before kernel execution. The second non-streamable pattern is characterized as Iterative, for which KEX will be invoked in an iterative manner once the data is located on device. Although such cases can be streamed by overlapping the data transfer and the first iteration of kernel execution, we argue that the overlapping brings no performance benefit for a large number of iterations.

We analyze the heterogeneous codes listed in Table 1 and categorize them in Table 2. Each nonstreamable code is labeled with SYNC or Iterative. We note that the kernel of hearwall has such a large number of lines of codes and complex structures that its execution takes a major proportion of the end-to-end execution time. It is unnecessary to stream such code on any platform. Due to the multiple H2D–KEX dependency pairs, an application might fall into more than one category (e.g., streamcluster). Also, the kernel of myocyte runs sequentially and thus there are no concurrent tasks for the purpose of pipelining. For the streamable codes, we group them into three categories, which are detailed in Sect. 4.2.

4.2   Code Streaming

We divide the streamable/overlappable applications into three categories based on task dependency: (1) embarrassingly independent, (2) false dependent, and (3) true dependent. Tasks are generated based on input or output data partitioning, and thus task dependency shows as a form of data dependency. We will explain them one by one.

Table 2. Application categorization.

	Nonstreamable		Streamable		
	SYNC	Iterative	Independent	False-dependent	True-dependent
Rodinia	backprop, bfs, b+tree, Kmeans, streamcluster	hotspot, pathfinder	backprop, dwt2d, nn, srad, streamcluster	lavaMD, leukocyte	gaussian, lud, nw
Parboil	spmv, tpacf, bfs, mri-q	mri-gridding, cutcp	sgemm	stencil, lbm	
NVIDIA SDK	Reduction-2,	FDTD3d, DXTCompression	BlackScholes, DCT8x8, DotProduct, Histogram, MatrixMul, MatVecMul, QuansirandomGenerator, Reduction, Transpose, Tridiagonal, VectorAdd	ConvolutionSeparable FastWalshTransform ConvolutionFFT2D	
AMD SDK		BitonicSort, FloydWarshall, RadixSort	BinomialOption, MonteCarloAsian, RecursiveGaussian, ScanLargeArrays, URNG, PrefixSum	BoxFilter, DwtHaar1D, StringSearch	

Embarrassingly Independent. Tasks from such overlappable applications are completely independent. Thus, there is no data dependency between tasks. Taking nn (nearest neighbor) for example, it finds the k-nearest neighbors from an unstructured data set. The sequential nn algorithm reads in one record at a time, calculates the Euclidean distance from the target latitude and longitude, and evaluates the k nearest neighbors. By analyzing its code, we notice no dependency between the input data. Figure 6 shows how to partition the input data. Assuming 16 elements in the set, we divide them into 4 groups, which represent 4 tasks. Then we spawn streams to run the tasks. Due to no dependency, data transferring from one task can overlap kernel execution from another. More Embarrassingly Independent applications are shown in Table 2.

Fig. 6. Nearest neighbor data partition (16 elements and 4 groups).

False Dependent. There exist data dependencies in such overlappable applications, but the dependencies come from read-only data (i.e., RAR dependency). In this case, two tasks will share common data elements. A straightforward solution to this issue is that each task moves the shared data elements separately. For example, FWT (fast walsh transform) is a class of generalized Fourier transformations. By analyzing the code, we find that there are dependencies between the input data elements: As shown in Fig. 7(a), calculating element x is related to the 4 neighbors which are marked in red. The input elements are read-only, so we can eliminate the relationship by redundantly transferring boundary elements (Fig. 7(b)). We first divide the total elements into four blocks, corresponding to four tasks (in blue). Then, we additionally transfer the related boundary elements (in red) when dealing with each data block. More `False Dependent` applications are shown in Table 2.

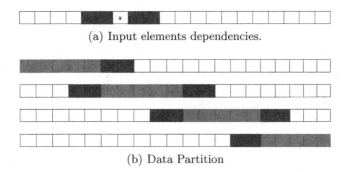

(a) Input elements dependencies.

(b) Data Partition

Fig. 7. Task dependency and data partition for `FWT`

True Dependent. The third category of overlappable applications is similar to the second one in that there exist data dependencies between tasks. The difference is that the dependency is true (i.e., RAW). This is complicated for programmers not only because there is a dependence between the input data elements, but because they need to update input data in the process of calculation. Thus, the output elements depend on the updated input data, and we must control the order of calculation. The key for this pattern is to discover concurrency while respecting the dependency.

NW, Needleman-Wunsch is a nonlinear global optimization method for DNA sequence alignments. The potential pairs of sequences are organized in a 2D matrix. In the first step, the algorithm fills the matrix from top left to bottom right, step-by-step. The optimum alignment is the pathway through the array with maximum score, where the score is the value of the maximum weighted path ending at that cell. Thus, the value of each data element depends on the values of its northwest-, north- and west-adjacent elements. In the second step, the maximum path is traced backward to deduce the optimal alignment. As shown in Fig. 8(a), calculating element x is related with three elements: 'n' (north-element), 'w' (west-element), and 'nw' (northwest-element). We must calculate output elements diagonal by diagonal (in the same color), and the elements on the same diagonal can be executed concurrently. Figure 8(b) shows how we divide the data: we number all blocks from the top-left diagonal to the bottom-right one (the first row and first column are the two DNA sequences, marked in number 0), and then change the storage location to let elements from the same block stored contiguously. Figure 8(c) shows the storage pattern, and the numbers represent the relative location. By controlling the execution in the order of diagonal from top-left to bottom-right, we can respect the dependencies between tasks.

Further, the tasks on the same diagonal can run concurrently with multiple streams. Note that the number of streams changes on different diagonals. More True Dependent applications can be found in Table 2.

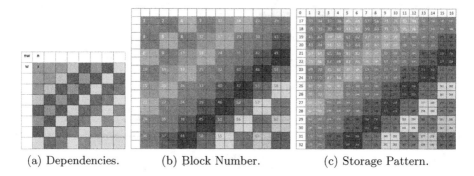

(a) Dependencies.   (b) Block Number.   (c) Storage Pattern.

Fig. 8. NW input elements dependencies and how to partition.

5   Experimental Results

In this section, we discuss the performance impact of using multiple streams. We use the CPU-MIC heterogeneous platform detailed in Sect. 3.2. Due to the limitation in time and space, we port 13 applications from Table 1 with hStreams. As shown in Table 2, these 13 benchmarks are characterized as different categories and thus we use the corresponding approach to stream them.

Figure 9 shows the overall performance comparison. We see that using multiple streams outperforms using a single stream, with a performance improvement of 8 %–90 %. In particular, for nn, FastWalshTransform, ConvolutionFFT2D, and nw, the improvement is around 85 %, 39 %, 38 %, and 52 %, respectively. However, for applications such as lavaMD, we cannot obtain the expected performance improvement with multiple streams, which will be discussed in the following.

Also, we notice that the performance increase of using multiple streams varies over benchmarks and datasets. This is due to the differences in data transfer ratio (R): a larger R leads to a greater performance improvement. For example, for ConvolutionSeparable and Transpose, the average performance improvement is 45 % and 11 %, with R being 19 % and 14 %, respectively. Further, when selecting two datasets (400M and 64M) for Transpose, we can achieve a performance increase of 14 % and 8 %, with R being 20 % and 10 %, respectively.

For the False Dependent applications, if the extra overhead of transferring boundary elements is nonnegligible, code streaming is not beneficial. For FWT, one element is related to 254 elements which is far less than the subtask data size of 1048576. Therefore, although having to transfer extra boundary values, the overall streaming performance impact is positive. However, when the boundary elements are almost equal to the subtask size, the overhead introduced by

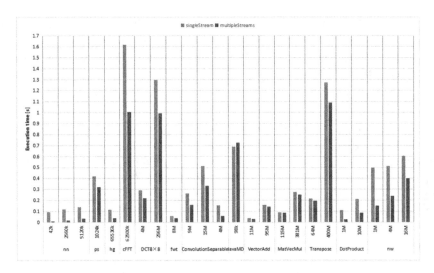

Fig. 9. A performance comparison between single stream and multiple streams. For each application, we employ different configuration, corresponding to different data size. Note that **ps**, **hg**, **cFFT** and **fwt** represents **PrefixSum**, **Histogram**, **ConvolutionFFT2D** and **FastWalshTransform**, respectively.

boundary transmission can not be ignored. **LavaMD** calculates particle potential and relocation due to mutual forces between particles within a large 3D space. In the experiment, one element for lavaMD depends on 222 elements, in which 111 elements are lying before the target element and the other half behind. The task data size is 250, which is close to the boundary element number. Thus, we cannot get the expected performance improvement, and the experimental results confirm our conclusion. Specifically, when the task is of 250 and remains unchanged, for single stream, the **H2D** and **KEX** time is 0.3476 s and 0.3380s, respectively. When using multiple streams, the overall execution time is 0.7242s. Therefore, it is not beneficial to stream the overlappable applications like **lavaMD**.

6   Conclusion

In this paper, we summarize a systematic approach to facilitate programmers to determine whether the application is required and worthwhile to use streaming mechanism, and how to stream the code. (1) obtaining the ratio R: run the codes in stage-by-stage manner, record the **H2D** and **KEX** time, and calculate R; (2) judging whether the application is overlappable; (3) streaming the codes by either eliminating or respecting data dependency. Our experimental results on 13 streamed benchmarks show a performance improvement of upto 90 %.

The process of analyzing whether a code is streamable and transforming the code is manually performed. Thus, we plan to develop a compiler analysis and tuning framework to automate this effort. Based on the streamed code, we will further investigate how to get optimal performance by setting a proper task and/or resource granularity. Ultimately, we plan to autotune these parameters leveraging machine learning techniques. Also, we want to investigate the streaming mechanism on more heterogeneous platforms, other than the CPU-MIC one.

Acknowledgment. We would like to thank the reviewers for their constructive comments. This work was partially funded by the National Natural Science Foundation of China under Grant No. 61402488, No. 61502514 and No. 61602501, the National High-tech R&D Program of China (863 Program) under Grant No. 2015AA01A301, the National Research Foundation for the Doctoral Program of Higher Education of China (RFDP) under Grant No. 20134307120035 and No. 20134307120031.

References

1. Adriaens, J.T., Compton, K., Kim, N.S., Schulte, M.J.: The case for GPGPU spatial multitasking. In: 2012 IEEE 18th International Symposium on High Performance Computer Architecture (HPCA), pp. 1–12. IEEE, February 2012
2. Boyer, M., Meng, J., Kumaran, K.: Improving GPU performance prediction with data transfer modeling. In: 2013 IEEE 27th International Symposium on Parallel and Distributed Processing Symposium Workshops and PhD Forum (IPDPSW), pp. 1097–1106. IEEE, May 2013
3. Che, S., Boyer, M., Meng, J., Tarjan, D., Sheaffer, J.W., Lee, S.-H., Skadron, K.: Rodinia: a benchmark suite for heterogeneous computing. In: IEEE International Symposium on Workload Characterization, 2009. IISWC 2009, pp. 44–54. IEEE, October 2009
4. Gómez-Luna, J., González-Linares, J.M., Benavides, J.I., Guil, N.: Performance models for asynchronous data transfers on consumer graphics processing units. J. Parallel Distrib. Comput. **72**(9), 1117–1126 (2012)
5. Gregg, C., Hazelwood, K.: Where is the data? Why you cannot debate CPU vs. GPU performance without the answer. In: 2011 IEEE International Symposium on Performance Analysis of Systems and Software (ISPASS), pp. 134–144. IEEE, April 2011
6. Hennessy, J.L., Patterson, D.A.: Computer Architecture: A Quantitative Approach, 4th edn. Morgan Kaufmann, Burlington (2006)
7. Ino, F., Nakagawa, S., Hagihara, K.: GPU-chariot: a programming framework for stream applicationsrunning on multi-GPU systems. IEICE Trans. **96-D**(12), 2604–2616 (2013)
8. Intel Inc. hStreams Architecture document for Intel MPSS 3.5, April 2015
9. Liu, B., Qiu, W., Jiang, L., Gong, Z.: Software pipelining for graphic processing unit acceleration: partition, scheduling and granularity. Int. J. High Perform. Comput. Appl. **30**(2), 169–185 (2015)
10. Meswani, M.R., Carrington, L., Unat, D., Snavely, A., Baden, S., Poole, S.: Modeling and predicting performance of high performance computing applications on hardware accelerators. Int. J. High Perform. Comput. Appl. **27**(2), 89–108 (2013)
11. Mittal, S., Vetter, J.S.: A survey of CPU-GPU heterogeneous computing techniques. ACM Comput. Surv. **47**(4), 36 (2015)
12. NVIDIA Inc. CUDA C Best Practices Guide Version 7.0, March 2015
13. Owens, J.D., Houston, M., Luebke, D., Green, S., Stone, J.E., Phillips, J.C.: GPU computing. Proc. IEEE **96**(5), 879–899 (2008)

14. Pienaar, J.A., Raghunathan, A., Chakradhar, S.: MDR: performance model driven runtime for heterogeneous parallel platforms. In: Proceedings of the International Conference on Supercomputing, ICS 2011, pp. 225–234. ACM, New York (2011)

15. Takizawa, H., Sato, K., Kobayashi, H.: SPRAT: runtime processor selection for energy-aware computing. In: 2008 IEEE International Conference on Cluster Computing, pp. 386–393. IEEE (2008)

16. The Khronos OpenCL Working Group. OpenCL - The open standard for parallel programming of heterogeneoussystems, January 2016. http://www.khronos.org/opencl/

17. Werkhoven, B.V., Maassen, J., Seinstra, F.J., Bal, H.E.: Performance models for CPU-GPU data transfers. In: 2014 14th IEEE/ACM International Symposium on Cluster, Cloud and Grid Computing (CCGrid), pp. 11–20. IEEE, May 2014

18. Wende, F., Steinke, T., Cordes, F.: Concurrent kernel execution on xeon phi within parallel heterogeneous workloads. In: Silva, F., Dutra, I., Santos Costa, V. (eds.) Euro-Par 2014. LNCS, vol. 8632, pp. 788–799. Springer, Heidelberg (2014). doi:10.1007/978-3-319-09873-9_66

19. Wende, F., Steinke, T., Cordes, F.: Multi-threaded kernel offloading to GPGPU using hyper-Q on kepler architecture. Technical report 14–19, ZIB, Takustr. 7, 14195 Berlin (2014)

20. Yang, C., Wang, F., Du, Y., Chen, J., Liu, J., Yi, H., Lu, K.: Adaptive optimization for petascale heterogeneous CPU/GPU computing. In: 2010 IEEE International Conference on Cluster Computing (CLUSTER), pp. 19–28. IEEE (2010)

21. Yang, C., Xue, W., Fu, H., Gan, L., Li, L., Xu, Y., Lu, Y., Sun, J., Yang, G., Zheng, W.: A peta-scalable CPU-GPU algorithm for global atmospheric simulations. In: Proceedings of the 18th ACM SIGPLAN Symposium on Principles and Practice of Parallel Programming, PPoPP 2013, pp. 1–12. ACM, New York (2013)

Data Processing and Big Data

DSS: A Scalable and Efficient Stratified Sampling Algorithm for Large-Scale Datasets

Minne Li[(✉)], Dongsheng Li, Siqi Shen, Zhaoning Zhang, and Xicheng Lu

National Laboratory for Parallel and Distributed Processing,
National University of Defense Technology, Changsha 410073, China
litoeknee@gmail.com, dsli@nudt.edu.cn

Abstract. Statistical analysis of aggregated records is widely used in various domains such as market research, sociological investigation and network analysis, etc. Stratified sampling (SS), which samples the population divided into distinct groups separately, is preferred in the practice for its high effectiveness and accuracy. In this paper, we propose a scalable and efficient algorithm named DSS, for SS to process large datasets. DSS executes all the sampling operations in parallel by calculating the exact subsample size for each partition according to the data distribution. We implement DSS on Spark, a big-data processing system, and we show through large-scale experiments that it can achieve lower data-transmission cost and higher efficiency than state-of-the-art methods with high sample representativeness.

Keywords: Stratified sampling · Aggregation · Distributed processing · Spark

1 Introduction

With the rapid advancement in the data collection and storage technology, burgeoning data size has brought both opportunities and challenges to driving business decisions. Valuable information and knowledge could be extracted from the ever-increasing datasets. To gain knowledge from the dataset, various computing techniques such as cloud computing [15,23] and big-data processing [5,22] have been proposed, which provide us the computing platform to process the data. However, it is time-consuming to process the ever-increasing and massive-scale data. Data sampling techniques can be used to gain statistical results, estimation and approximation of data in short time with slightly reduced accuracy. They are playing critical roles in areas such as social network analysis [8,18] and business market research [4]. In this work, we focus on stratified sampling (SS), a widely adopted sampling technique [20] with high efficiency and accuracy. We implement a Distributed Stratified Sampling (DSS) algorithm, and the experimental results show that our algorithm can be 65 % faster than a well-known distributed SS algorithm [14] with high-accuracy and high-scalability.

© IFIP International Federation for Information Processing 2016
Published by Springer International Publishing AG 2016. All Rights Reserved
G.R. Gao et al. (Eds.): NPC 2016, LNCS 9966, pp. 133–146, 2016.
DOI: 10.1007/978-3-319-47099-3_11

Basic steps of sampling consist of extracting a representative subset of the population, performing the estimation and experiment, and extrapolating the results back in order to understand characteristics of the overall population. Specifically, stratified sampling is a sampling method involving the division of a population into distinct groups known as *strata* (homogeneous subgroups, in which the inner items are similar to each other). It assigns individuals of the surveyed population to *strata*, and then applies normal sampling methods (e.g., simple random sampling (SRS) or systematic sampling) without replacement to each *stratum* independently. Compared to SRS, stratified sampling is able to get higher statistical precision because the variability within subgroups sharing the same properties is lower than that of the entire population [20]. Thus stratified sampling improves the representativeness by reducing sampling error. In addition, having a higher statistical precision enables stratified sampling to tolerate smaller sample size than other methods, which helps to save time and effort of researchers. Consequently, stratified sampling outperforms other sampling methods both in efficiency and accuracy. Traditional implementation of stratified sampling, e.g., *reservoir sampling*, is not designed for distributed computing environment. Although several distributed implementations [14,22] have been proposed, they are either not able to generate a statistical satisfied answer under certain conditions or not able to fully utilize the computing resources. We will further discuss this point in Sects. 2 and 4.

In this work, we propose a distributed algorithm for SS which is scalable and efficient. It has four main steps: (1) conducts a modified reservoir sampling with rough sampling size inside each data partition, (2) gathers the meta-data of intermediate results, (3) computes the exact sampling size for each partition and (4) performs a modified reservoir sampling in parallel to generate the final sampling results. Different from the method *Spark Single Query Evaluator* (Spark-SQE) proposed in [14], DSS reduces significantly the computational cost by conducting sampling process in a distributed manner. Moreover, the data transfer cost is reduced considerably because the computation phases are conducted in distributed nodes instead of in a master node, meaning that the volume of data transferred is much reduced.

The remainder of this paper is structured as follows. In Sect. 2, we compare our work with related research with a focus on scalable sampling techniques. In Sect. 3, we further discuss the definition and provide the syntax and semantics of stratified sampling queries, and present the sequential stand-alone algorithm of answering a single stratified sampling query. In Sect. 4, we describe the design of the algorithm. In Sect. 5, we show the experimental results, and in Sect. 6, we conclude this work.

2   Related Work

A lot of research effort has been made to design scalable algorithms for processing large-scale datasets. Boyd et al. [2] have investigated the alternating direction method of multipliers to solve distributed convex optimization problem, and Owen et al. [17] have introduced Mahout to apply machine learning algorithm against large datasets. However, many of these algorithms cannot generate results within an acceptable range of time without reducing data size [16].

In order to reduce the storage and computational cost as well as keep important statistical properties of the original data, researchers have proposed various data sampling algorithms. Gjoka et al. [7] have implemented a multi-graph sampling method for online social network datasets to generate representative samples for highly clustered individual social graphs. Kurant et al. [12] have utilized stratification to generate weighted graphs for efficient data crawling and metric estimation. However, these works are not designed for distributed computing environment [14].

In terms of stratified sampling, numbers of previous works have been proposed for the stand-alone environment. One of the many classical methods is the *reservoir sampling* algorithm [21], which requires a single pass over the whole dataset to generate representative results. However, the original *reservoir sampling* algorithm is not designed for distributed computing environments: data shuffling among clusters for a single query is required because the partition of data into clusters is mostly different to the partition of the population into strata. However, conducting data shuffling is unbearable in the big data environment. In order to design a scalable sampling algorithm and implement it on top of the data stored on distributed machines, the sampling process should be conducted in a parallel and distributed manner. Spark [22], a platform for large-scale datasets processing, provides the distributed stratified sampling API as one of its basic statistic functions, namely *sampleByKey* and *sampleByKeyExact*. These functions conduct sampling with given sampling probability. However, in order to draw a stratified sampling set by sample size in Spark, users need to provide the total count of records satisfied the stratum constraint, which is not possible in the practical, distributed computing environment. Even if the actual count is provided, the existing function could still fail the statistical requirement if the product of sampling fraction and total record count is not an integer. Levin et al. [14] have proposed a framework for stratified sampling queries, which will be further discussed in Sect. 3.

3   Stratified Sampling Queries

In this section we will provide the definition, syntax and semantics of stratified sampling queries, as well as present the sequential stand-alone algorithm (the *modified reservoir sampling algorithm*) of answering a single stratified sampling query. We will further discuss in Sect. 4 that our sequential algorithm can be conducted in a parallel and distributed manner effortlessly.

3.1   A Single Stratified Sampling Query

The notations used in this work is defined as follows. A single stratified sampling query in this paper is defined as a set of stratum constraints s_k, denoted by $Q = (s_1, s_2, \ldots, s_m)$. Each stratum constraint s_k is denoted by $s_k = (p_k, f_k)$, where p_k is a propositional formula and f_k is the required sample size. It is worth noting that for a qualified stratified sampling query, the strata must be non-overlapping, in other words every individual should be assigned to only one stratum. Joint strata will result in nonprobability sampling since some individuals may have greater chances of being chosen. For example, if we define two stratum constraints s_1 and s_2 for a group of students, where $p_1 = (male)$ and $p_2 = (age > 10)$, conducting two simple random sampling separately in stratum defined by s_1 and s_2 will give males over 10 years old greater chances of being selected.

3.2   Sequential Answering Process

A valid answer to a query $Q = (s_1, s_2, \ldots, s_m)$ is the union of m disjoint sample sets where (1) every single individual in subset k ($k = 1, 2, 3, \ldots, m$) satisfies the propositional formula p_k and (2) there are exactly f_k individuals in subset k. In addition, a statistically representative answer set should guarantee that each subset k is a simple random sample of all the individuals in the population that satisfy p_k. We will further discuss this point in Sects. 4 and 5.

Algorithm 1. Reservoir sampling for stratum constraint s_k

1: Store the first f_k individuals satisfied p_k into a reservoir R_k
2: **for** j from $f_k + 1$ to n **do**
3:     With probability f_k/j, randomly choose an individual from R_k and replace it with individual j
4: **end for**
5: **return** Individuals in R_k

After providing the definition of a single stratified sampling query, we present a sequential stand-alone algorithm for generating the subset satisfying a stratum constraint, which is listed in Algorithm 1. Algorithm 1 is derived from the *reservoir algorithm* [21] with almost the same procedure. The algorithm creates a *reservoir* array of size f_k with the first f_k items satisfied p_k from the population containing n individuals. Then the algorithm iterates through the remaining population. At the jth iteration, the algorithm randomly chooses an individual from the *reservoir* and replace it by individual j with probability f_k/j. It can be proved that at the end of the iteration, every individual has equal probability (i.e. f_k/n) of being chosen for the *reservoir*.

Thanks to the disjoint property of strata, answering a query $Q = (s_1, s_2, \ldots, s_m)$ requires only single pass over the population set sequentially if we maintain m *reservoirs* R_k and m element indexes j_k. Each *reservoir* contains f_k individuals satisfied p_k respectively and thus holds a simple random sample of the processed individuals at any step during the execution.

4   Distributed Sampling Design

This section commences by focusing on the detailed design of our algorithm *Distributed Stratified Sampling* DSS. We first present the algorithm which reduces significantly the data transmission cost among distributed nodes by sending the abstract of intermediate result rather than the result itself. In addition, DSS considerately reduces the computational cost compared to existing alternatives by conducting all the sampling phases in a distributed manner. The experimental comparison will be covered in Sect. 5.

4.1   Sampling Representativeness in Distributed Environment

We now give the definition of representativeness in distributed environment can be seen as a cluster of connected computers (the nodes) or virtual machines provided by cloud computing services including Amazon EC2, Microsoft Azure, etc. Note that in the production environment, data is already stored in the file system and distributed separately to nodes. We are required to answer the sampling query without changing the original position of data. To generate a statistically representative answer set to a single stratified sampling query, the sample result should be unbiased in the first place. Because the partition of the population into strata is always different to the partition of data into clusters, data shuffling is required to response a sampling query. However, this is unrealistic in industrial and practical environment. Consequently, the proportion of satisfied elements in each data partition must be taken into account.

For example, we are asked to generate a sample of 10 male students playing basketball from a population of 50 students. The satisfied population (all the male students playing basketball in the population) data is distributed among two separate nodes, 20 in node O_1 and 30 in node O_2. A simple solution is to generate an intermediate sample of 10 male students playing basketball for both of nodes, and then conduct a unification process to produce the final answer set. However, this approach will trigger a biased, statistically invalid sample. The above approach produces a male student playing basketball selected for intermediate a probability of $1/2$ and $1/3$, for O_1 and O_2 respectively. After conducting a simple random sampling to select 10 individuals among intermediate results, the probability of individuals from O_1 and O_2 appearing in the final answer set will be $1/4$ and $1/6$ respectively. This answer, however, is biased and statistically invalid since each individual should have a chance of $1/5$ to be selected for the query. Consequently, in order to have a uniform and unbiased sample, the proportion of satisfied elements in each data partition located in each node must be taken into account for deciding the selection ratio from each intermediate sample. In this case specifically, the intermediate results from O_1 and O_2 should be selected with probability of $1/2$ and $1/3$ respectively.

4.2   Distributed Algorithm Spark-SQE

In Sect. 3.2, we present the *modified reservoir algorithm* (Algorithm 1) for answering sequentially a single stratified sampling query. By combining this algorithm with the sampling method discussed in Sect. 4.1, we further describe a distributed version of Algorithm 1, namely *Spark Single Query Evaluator* (Spark-SQE), derived from the *Map Reduce Single Query Evaluator* provided by [14]. The procedure of Spark-SQE is depicted in Fig. 1.

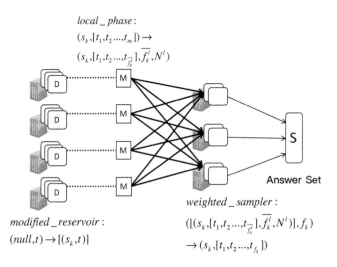

$local\_phase$:
$$(s_k,[t_1,t_2...t_m]) \rightarrow$$
$$(s_k,[t_1,t_2...t_{\overline{f_k^l}}],\overline{f_k^l},N^l)$$

Answer Set

$weighted\_sampler$:
$$([(s_k,[t_1,t_2...t_{\overline{f_k^l}}],\overline{f_k^l},N^l)],f_k)$$
$$\rightarrow (s_k,[t_1,t_2...t_{f_k}])$$

$modified\_reservoir$:
$$(null,t) \rightarrow [(s_k,t)]$$

Fig. 1. Process of Spark-SQE, including the map phase (Algorithm 1), the *local phase* and the *weighted sampler*. The symbolic tuples besides the arrow in each phase represents input and output for this phase respectively. The local transformation and computation between the raw data and the intermediate sample is connected by *dotted line*. Data transmission among clusters is represented by *solid lines*. *Thick lines* indicate large data-transmission while the *thin ones* indicate the opposite. Each D, M and S stands for data partition, intermediate sample, and final result respectively.

In each data partition, similar process as Algorithm 1 is conducted to generate local intermediate result, of the form $[(s_k,t)]$ which is a list of tuple (s_k,t) if individual t satisfies s_k. A parallel execution of Algorithm 1 can be seen as a *map* phase specified by Spark, which deals with key-value pairs to generate a set of intermediate key-value pairs of the form $[(s_k,t)]$.

To gather the intermediate results, one of the naive implementations will copy all the satisfied individuals from the whole cluster to the master node. However, this procedure cannot fully utilize the computing resources.

Instead of the naive method above, during the *local* phase of Spark-SQE, we can merely collect a certain amount of intermediate sample. For example, we can construct a simple random selection of $\overline{f_k^l}$ individuals for each data partition l before passing them to the *weighted sampler* ($\overline{f_k^l}$ could be less than f_k if not enough satisfied individuals exist in some certain data partitions). The *local* phase generates the local sample set satisfied s_k, the sampling size $\overline{f_k^l}$ and N^l, the total number of individuals satisfied s_k in this partition. This approach could considerably reduce the data sent over the network and increase concurrency.

Lastly, a *weighted sampler* merges all intermediate results, which are already shrunk by the *local* process in each data node, and conducts a weighted random selection of size f_k. This approach will generate a representative answer because the final sampling size is proportional to N^l of each intermediate result as we described in Sect. 4.1.

4.3   Improved Distributed Algorithm DSS

By sending the meta-data rather than original data to the *reduce* function after conducting the *local* phase in Spark-SQE, we can further reduce the amount of data transmitted over the network. Figure 2 illustrates the process of *Distributed Stratified Sampling* (DSS) which is an improved version of Spark-SQE.

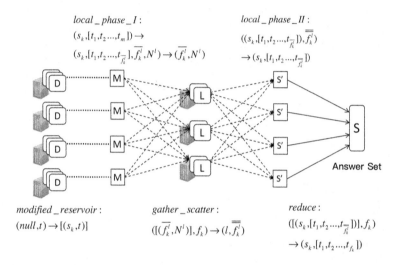

Fig. 2. Process of DSS, including the map phase (Algorithm 1), the *local phase I*, the *gather scatter* phase, the *local phase II* and the *reduce phase*. The *dotted lines* represent local transformation and computation between the raw data and the intermediate sample. In addition, the data and meta-data transmission among clusters are represented by *solid lines* and *dashed lines* respectively. Each D, M, L, S' and S stands for data partition, intermediate sample, required sampling frequency list, local weighted result and final result respectively.

The *map* phase of DSS is derived from Spark-SQE and generates the same result. In the *local phase I*, DSS has already generated an intermediate sample of $\overline{f_k^l}$ from N^l individuals satisfied p_k in data partition l as the Spark-SQE. To reduce the data transfer cost, we can simply send $\overline{f_k^l}$ and N^l instead of the whole intermediate result to the master node which will execute the *gather-scatter* function. Then in the *gather-scatter* phase, DSS computes the required sampling frequency $\overline{\overline{f_k^l}}$ of s_k for each data partition using weighted sampling.

These required sampling frequency $\overline{\overline{f_k^l}}$ of each partition is delivered to each data node separately. Thirdly, a local simple random selection shown as the *local phase II* in DSS is conducted to generate local parts of the final answer set. Compared to Spark-SQE, the computational cost is reduced considerably as well since we conduct the weighted sampling phase in different nodes separately rather than running a sequential process in a single reduce node. Finally, the *reduce* phase in DSS gathers every part of the final result from each data node together to compose a correct, unbiased and uniform answer to the single stratified sampling query.

The *gather-scatter algorithm* listed in Algorithm 2 receives L meta-data tuples of intermediate samples for s_k from L data partitions. Each tuple consists of the actual intermediate sample size $\overline{f_k^l}$ and N^l, the total number of satisfied individuals in data partition l. At first, the algorithm checks if the sum of intermediate sample size is enough for the required sample size f_k (Line 1). If not, the algorithm simply returns $\overline{f_k^l}$ as the weighted sample size for each data partition l to generate the final answer (Line 2). Otherwise, the algorithm continues by iterating over 1 through L to compute an index list for determining the exact sample size of each data partition (Line 8 to 13). Because the index list is constructed based on the count of satisfied individuals N^l in data partition l, it is thus probabilistically proportional to N^l.

Algorithm 2. Gather-scatter $([(\overline{f_k^l}, N^l)], f_k) \rightarrow [(l, \overline{\overline{f_k^l}})]$

1: **if** $\sum_{l=1}^{L} \overline{f_k^l} < f_k$ **then**
2:     **return** $[(l, \overline{f_k^l})], l \in [1, L]$
3: **end if**
4: $N \leftarrow \sum_{l=1}^{L} N^l$
5: $I \leftarrow$ *Randomly select n indexes from* $[0, N]$
6: *low_bound* $\leftarrow 0$
7: *up_bound* $\leftarrow N^1$

8: $\overline{\overline{f_k^l}} \leftarrow 0, l \in [1, L]$
9: **for** l from 1 to L **do**
10:     $\overline{\overline{f_k^l}} \leftarrow |I \cap [low\_bound, up\_bound]|$
11:     *low_bound* $\leftarrow$ *low_bound* $+ N^l$
12:     **if** $l < L$ **then**
13:         *up_bound* $\leftarrow$ *up_bound* $+ N^{l+1}$
14:     **end if**
15: **end for**
16: **return** $[(l, \overline{\overline{f_k^l}})], l \in [1, L]$

The *weighted sampler* phase in Spark-SQE is similar as the *gather-scatter algorithm*. Instead of the meta-data, it receives the intermediate sample and then generates the final result, thus it requires significantly larger amount of data transfer compared to the *gather-scatter algorithm*.

It is trivial to prove the correctness (a simple random sample) of the *gather-scatter algorithm* by induction. The proof can be drawn inductively over the size n of the final sample. Basically, we need to prove that every subset of the population of size n has equal probability of selection, for every n.

5   Experimental Evaluation

In this section, we conduct large-scale and systematic experiments to evaluate the proposed DSS and compare it with Spark-SQE, which is the Spark implementation of a well-known stratified method provided in [14]. We describe the experimental setup in Sect. 5.1, and demonstrate the efficiency and scalability of the algorithms by examining the running times and transmitted data size. We also discuss how the sampled data generated by DSS precisely represent the original data.

5.1   Experimental Setup

Dataset. In this experiment, we use two real-world datasets and one synthetic dataset shown in Table 1. The two real-world datasets are the LiveJournal social network dataset [13] and the Twitter-2010 social network dataset [1]. These datasets are natural graphs following the *power-law* [6] distribution, where only a few vertices have large numbers of neighbors while most of the vertices have relatively few neighbors. We pre-process the datasets by changing the graph storage structure from edge list to adjacency list. The synthetic graph dataset is generated through Power Graph API [9]. By adjusting the *power-law* exponent constant α we can control the skewness of the degree distribution, where a lower α implies a higher graph density and larger number of high-degree vertices. Because the adjacency list stores all neighbors of a vertex in a single record, a lower α will result in a larger storage size of high degree vertices records.

Stratified Sampling Query. We generate the sampling query by considering the out-degree of vertices. The strata are created by partitioning the out-degree of vertices into sub-ranges, which are represented by propositional formulas, e.g., (*out-degree* < 20). We generate valid sampling query by randomly selecting non-overlapping degree ranges. For example, $Q = (s_1, s_2)$ where $s_1 = (out\text{-}degree < 20, 2000)$ and $s_2 = (out\text{-}degree > 50, 1000)$ represents a query with two distinct strata where the out-degree of vertices is lower than 20 and higher than 50.

Environment. We have implemented the algorithms in Apache Spark framework. The Spark environment is built on top of a cluster consisting four nodes, with one serving as the master and three as worker. Each node is configured with Ubuntu 14.04 LTS, 47 GB RAM, 8 Intel Xeon E5-1620 CPUs, and 2.7 TB storage. All the data is stored in HDFS.

Table 1. Properties of the dataset.

Dataset	$|V|$	$|E|$	Size
LiveJournal	4,847,571	68,993,773	514M
alpha1.8	9,999,999	641,383,778	4.6G
Twitter-2010	41,652,230	1,468,365,182	13G

5.2   Results

In the experiment, we evaluate the efficiency and scalability of the algorithms in terms of the runtime and transmitted data size, respectively. The runtime is counted from receiving a query to generating a final result. The transmitted data size is measured by calculating the data received in *weighted sampler* phase for Spark-SQE and *gather-scatter* phase for DSS. The result has eliminated the time of loading the raw data into memory from HDFS. Moreover, we perform experiments to evaluate the representativeness and quality of the stratified sampled data generated by DSS. For the social network datasets, we calculate their degree distributions and check if the sampled data have the same degree distribution as the original data.

Efficiency. Figure 3 illustrates the relative runtime of the algorithms grouped by different datasets. The type of query has been classified by different scales, which is the total number of records satisfied the stratum constraint. We generate the query by defining the large group as $p_{large} = (out\text{-}degree < 50)$ and the small group as $p_{small} = (out\text{-}degree > 200)$ and use the same sampling frequency as 2000. The small group indicates the "long tail" of the *power-law* graph, which represents vertices with many neighbors. On the contrary, vertices with few neighbors comprise the large group. According to the *power-law* we discussed in Sect. 5.1, the number of records in large group is significantly bigger than the small group.

 As is shown in Fig. 3, the runtime of DSS can be only 35 % of Spark-SQE in the best case. Even in the worst case, the runtime of DSS is about 65 % of that of Spark-SQE. This achievement is mostly attributed to our distributed sampling process in the *weighted sampling* phase. The enhancement is not directly related to the data size. The most time-consuming phases of the two algorithms are the *local* phase and the *reduce* phase (*weighted sampler* phase for Spark-SQE). For the *local* and *map* phase both algorithms are totally conducted in parallel. For the *reduce* phase, only DSS runs in parallel and the time used in this phase is directly related to the sampling frequency. Because we use the same sampling frequency and a growing data size, according to the result shown in Fig. 3, we can conclude that the *local* and *map* phase contributes more to the running time. This conclusion is theoretically explainable as the *local* and *map* phase needs to conduct an iteration over all records while the *reduce* phase only needs an iteration of 2000 records in our experiment.

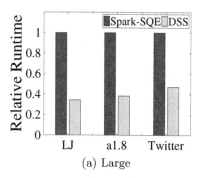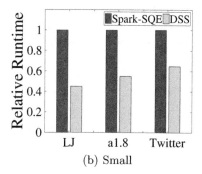

(a) Large   (b) Small

Fig. 3. The running time of DSS divided by Spark-SQE for different query group: (left) large group and (right) small group.

Scalability. As we mentioned above, the enhancement of our algorithm is directly related to the sampling frequency. To evaluate the scalability of our algorithm, we create a group of stratum constraints, which ask for sampling sizes ranging from 1000 to 4000. The running time for these groups of stratum constraints is shown in Fig. 4.

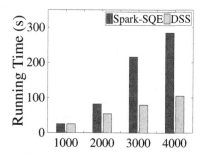

Fig. 4. The running time of Spark-SQE and DSS under different sampling frequencies for the LiveJournal dataset.

Figure 4 illustrates the runtime of DSS under different sampling frequencies can reach a linear improvement. Compared to Spark-SQE, a relative enhancement of 65 % is drawn in the best case. Note that we almost touch the upper bound of optimization in our experiment environment since we have only three executors.

Transmission Cost. Table 2 shows the comparison of network transmission cost for the two algorithms. We focus on the intermediate data collection phase and use the LiveJournal dataset. As is depicted in Table 2, the size of the transmitted data of DSS is much smaller than that of Spark-SQE. The reason is that

Table 2. The size of data transmitted in bytes during the intermediate data collection phase of the algorithms using LiveJournal dataset under different workloads, which represents by a stratum constraint $s_k = (p_k, f_k)$ as described in Sect. 3.1.

Workload	Spark-SQE	DSS
$s_1 = (out\text{-}degree < 10, 1000)$	2,017,416	112
$s_2 = (out\text{-}degree < 10, 2000)$	4,028,816	112
$s_3 = (out\text{-}degree < 10, 3000)$	6,048,232	112
$s_4 = (out\text{-}degree < 10, 4000)$	8,064,840	112

the data transfer cost of Spark-SQE is proportional to sampling frequency, while that of DSS remains the same across different frequencies. This is due to the fact that DSS only transmits the metadata (a tuple of two integers per partition), whose size increases linearly with the number of partitions in clusters. In contrast to DSS, Spark-SQE sends an array of all intermediate records for each partition, thus performs poorly when the sampling size increases.

Sample Representativeness. Degree distribution is an important property of social network and has frequently been analyzed in much social network research [3,10]. We evaluate the representativeness of the sampled datasets through evaluating the difference between the degree distributions of the stratified sampled datasets and that of the original datasets using *Kolmogorov–Smirnov test* (K–S test) [11,19]. The K–S test works as follows. It firstly generates cumulative probability plots for the two data and calculate each vertical distance for a given x values between the two curves. Then the maximum distance (called K–S statistic) is searched from all the vertical distances. In the end, the *probability value* (p-value) is calculated by plugging this maximum distance into K–S probability function. The closer to 1 the p-value is the more likely the two distributions are similar, and vice versa.

Table 3. The K–S statistic and p-values of K–S tests for the three datasets used in this work. The stratum constraint is defined as $s_k = (out\text{-}degree < 50, 1000)$.

Dataset	K–S statistic	p-value
LiveJournal	0.020336	0.798941
alpha1.8	0.017253	0.925117
Twitter-2010	0.016218	0.953649

As is shown in Table 3, the p-values of all the datasets are high (79.9%, 92.5%, 95.4%), thus we cannot reject the null hypothesis that the degree distributions of stratified sampled data by DSS and that of original data are the same.

In other words, the degree distributions of sampled data and original data share great similarities, which means the sampled data precisely represent the original data.

6   Conclusion

This paper proposed a distributed algorithm DSS for applying stratified sampling to large-scale, distributed datasets. DSS significantly reduces the computational cost of selecting stratified sample by implementing a *modified reservoir algorithm* inside each stratum in a distributed manner. Moreover, the data transfer cost is reduced significantly as well, by transmitting the meta-data instead of the data records. We implement DSS on Spark, a big-data processing platform, and evaluate the algorithm using two large-scale real-world datasets. The experiment results show that DSS performs well in terms of efficiency, scalability and representativity. Compared to Spark-SQE, which is a Spark implementation of state-of-the-art method, DSS reaches a relative enhancement of 65 %. In addition, DSS requires extremely smaller amount (less than 0.05 % in our experiment) of network resources in clusters than that of Spark-SQE.

Acknowledgments. This work is sponsored in part by the National Basic Research Program of China (973) under Grant No. 2014CB340303, the National Natural Science Foundation of China under Grant No. 61222205, the Program for New Century Excellent Talents in University, and the Fok Ying-Tong Education Foundation under Grant No. 141066.

References

1. Boldi, P., Vigna, S.: The webgraph framework I: compression techniques. In: Proceedings of the 13th International Conference on World Wide Web, pp. 595–602. ACM (2004)
2. Boyd, S., Parikh, N., Chu, E., Peleato, B., Eckstein, J.: Distributed optimization and statistical learning via the alternating direction method of multipliers. Found. Trends® Mach. Learn. **3**(1), 1–122 (2011)
3. Clauset, A., Shalizi, C.R., Newman, M.E.J.: Power-law distributions in empirical data. SIAM Rev. **51**(4), 661–703 (2009). http://dx.doi.org/10.1137/070710111
4. Cooper, D.R., Schindler, P.S., Sun, J.: Business Research Methods (2006)
5. Dean, J., Ghemawat, S.: MapReduce: simplified data processing on large clusters. Commun. ACM **51**(1), 107–113 (2008)
6. Faloutsos, M., Faloutsos, P., Faloutsos, C.: On power-law relationships of the internet topology. ACM SIGCOMM Comput. Commun. Rev. **29**, 251–262 (1999). ACM
7. Gjoka, M., Butts, C.T., Kurant, M., Markopoulou, A.: Multigraph sampling of online social networks. IEEE J. Sel. Areas Commun. **29**(9), 1893–1905 (2011)
8. Gjoka, M., Kurant, M., Butts, C.T., Markopoulou, A.: A walk in facebook: uniform sampling of users in online social networks. arXiv preprint arXiv:0906.0060 (2009)
9. Gonzalez, J.E., Low, Y., Gu, H., Bickson, D., Guestrin, C.: Powergraph: distributed graph-parallel computation on natural graphs. Presented as Ppart of the 10th USENIX Symposium on Operating Systems Design and Implementation (OSDI 2012), pp. 17–30 (2012)

10. Jia, A.L., Shen, S., van de Bovenkamp, R., Iosup, A., Kuipers, F.A., Epema, D.H.J.: Socializing by gaming: revealing social relationships in multiplayer online games. TKDD **10**(2), 11 (2015). http://doi.acm.org/10.1145/2736698
11. Kolmogorov, A.N.: Sulla determinazione empirica di una legge di distribuzione. na (1933)
12. Kurant, M., Gjoka, M., Butts, C.T., Markopoulou, A.: Walking on a graph with a magnifying glass: stratified sampling via weighted random walks. In: Proceedings of the ACM SIGMETRICS Joint International Conference on Measurement and Modeling of Computer Systems, pp. 281–292. ACM (2011)
13. Leskovec, J., Krevl, A.: SNAP datasets: Stanford large network dataset collection, June 2014. http://snap.stanford.edu/data
14. Levin, R., Kanza, Y.: Stratified-sampling over social networks using mapreduce. In: Proceedings of the 2014 ACM SIGMOD International Conference on Management of Data, pp. 863–874. ACM (2014)
15. Lu, X., Wang, H., Wang, J., Xu, J., Li, D.: Internet-based virtual computing environment: beyond the data center as a computer. Future Gener. Comput. Syst. **29**(1), 309–322 (2013)
16. Meng, X.: Scalable simple random sampling and stratified sampling. In: Proceedings of the 30th International Conference on Machine Learning (ICML-2013), pp. 531–539 (2013)
17. Owen, S., Anil, R., Dunning, T., Friedman, E.: Mahout in Action. Manning Publications Co., Greenwich (2011)
18. Papagelis, M., Das, G., Koudas, N.: Sampling online social networks. IEEE Trans. Knowl. Data Eng. **25**(3), 662–676 (2013)
19. Smirnov, N.: Table for estimating the goodness of fit of empirical distributions. Ann. Math. Stat. **19**(2), 279–281 (1948)
20. Thompson, S.K.: Stratified Sampling, pp. 139–156. Wiley (2012). http://dx.doi.org/10.1002/9781118162934.ch11
21. Vitter, J.S.: Random sampling with a reservoir. ACM Trans. Math. Softw. (TOMS) **11**(1), 37–57 (1985)
22. Zaharia, M., Chowdhury, M., Das, T., Dave, A., Ma, J., McCauley, M., Franklin, M.J., Shenker, S., Stoica, I.: Resilient distributed datasets: a fault-tolerant abstraction for in-memory cluster computing. In: Proceedings of the 9th USENIX Conference on Networked Systems Design and Implementation, p. 2. USENIX Association (2012)
23. Zhang, Z., Li, D., Wu, K.: Large-scale virtual machines provisioning in clouds: challenges and approaches. Front. Comput. Sci. **10**(1), 2–18 (2016)

A Fast and Better Hybrid Recommender System Based on Spark

Jiali Wang[✉], Hang Zhuang, Changlong Li, Hang Chen, Bo Xu,
Zhuocheng He, and Xuehai Zhou

University of Science and Technology of China, No. 96 Jinzhai Road,
Hefei, Anhui, China
{ustcwjl,zhuangh,liclong,hangc,xubo245,orcking}@mail.ustc.edu.cn,
xhzhou@ustc.edu.cn

Abstract. With the rapid development of information technology, recommender systems have become critical components to solve information overload. As an important branch, weighted hybrid recommender systems are widely used in electronic commerce sites, social networks and video websites such as Amazon, Facebook and Netflix. In practice, developers typically set a weight for each recommendation algorithm by repeating experiments until obtaining better accuracy. Despite the method could improve accuracy, it overly depends on experience of developers and the improvements are poor. What worse, workload will be heavy if the number of algorithms rises. To further improve performance of recommender systems, we design an optimal hybrid recommender system on Spark. Experimental results show that the system can improve accuracy, reduce execution time and handle large-scale datasets. Accordingly, the hybrid recommender system balances accuracy and execution time.

Keywords: Recommender system · Hybrid · Weight · Spark

1 Introduction

Along with the popularization of the Internet, a sharp increase in the amount of data leads to information overload [1]. Thus, recommender systems [2] were proposed to relieve the stress of massive data. To improve recommender systems performance, researchers put forward the weighted hybrid method. Despite performance boost has been brought by the method, there are still several problems affecting performance, including weight setting and computation load. Hence, we implement a weighted hybrid recommender system on Spark. In the system, we design a new method to compute weights, using cluster analysis and user similarity. Besides, the execution time can be reduced by deploying the system on Spark.

© IFIP International Federation for Information Processing 2016
Published by Springer International Publishing AG 2016. All Rights Reserved
G.R. Gao et al. (Eds.): NPC 2016, LNCS 9966, pp. 147–159, 2016.
DOI: 10.1007/978-3-319-47099-3_12

1.1 Hybrid Recommender Systems

Hybrid recommender systems combine two or more recommendation algorithms to overcome weaknesses of each algorithm. It is generally classified as Switching, Mixed, Feature Combination, Meta-Level, and Weighted [3].

The weighted hybrid technique combines different algorithms with different weights [3]. The main idea is that the algorithm with better accuracy has a higher weight. At present, developers always set a weight for an algorithm manually and repeat experiments until achieving superior accuracy. Thus, the method depends on developers' experience to determine accuracy of an algorithm in different datasets. Due to large-scale datasets, sparsity of rating data and the number of algorithms, it's generally hard to obtain appropriate weights. Eventually the improvements of accuracy are poor.

In addition, to improve user experience, the system should return recommendation results efficiently. In other words, it has to quickly locate information which can appeal users in massive data. Thus, execution time is another evaluation standard of performance. However, the weighted hybrid technique needs to execute two or more algorithms and compute hybrid results, it's tough to reduce execution time.

Apart from accuracy and execution time of the system, scalability is also an important consideration. With the increasing of data scale and the algorithm complexity, the system requires more storage space and computing resources. It's difficult to meet the actual demand by only optimizing algorithms.

To address the above-mentioned issues, we design a hybrid recommender system on Spark. In the system, we propose an optimized method to improve accuracy. It computes weights and hybrid results based on cluster analysis and user similarity. Meanwhile, we deploy the system on Spark which is a fast and general engine for large-scale data processing [4] to accelerate the training process and improve scalability.

1.2 Work of Paper

The rest of this paper is organized as five sections. Section 2 reviews recommendation algorithms and introduces the Spark. Section 3 describes the design of the optimized method. Section 4 shows how we implement the system on Spark. Section 5 gives experimental results and our analysis. Section 6 presents our conclusions and future work.

2 Related Work

In this section, we first review and compare recommendation algorithms and recommender systems. Then, we briefly analyze predicting ratings of algorithms. Finally, we introduce the distributed computing platform Spark and compare Hadoop and Spark.

2.1   Recommender Systems

Recommendation algorithms are the basis of recommender systems. In this section, we first introduce several representative algorithms.

Collaborative recommendation is almost the most popular algorithm. Based on overlapped ratings, it computes similarities among users. And then, it uses similarities to predict the rating that the current user on an item [5]. Tapestry [6], Ringo [7] and GroupLens [8] are typical systems with the algorithm.

Content-based recommendation pays attention to connections between items. It analyses descriptions of items that have been rated by users [9] and calculates similarities between items. The representation of an item's feature and the way to classify a new item are two important sub-problems [9].

Demographic-based recommendation [9] is a simple algorithm. It focuses on types of users that like a certain item. The technique identifies features of users such as age, gender, nationality, education, etc. It measures user similarity by taking those features into consideration. Table 1 shows strengths and weaknesses of each algorithm [5,9].

Table 1. Strengths and weaknesses of recommendation algorithms

Algorithm	Strength	Weakness
Collaborative	Field independence. Not necessary to understand descriptions of items. Support users to discover potential interests	New user problem. New item problem. Sparsity.
Content	Improve accuracy by increasing dimensions of item features	Cold start problem. Similarity measurement is one-sided.
Demographic	Historical data are not necessary. Wide range of applications. No cold start problem	The algorithm is rough and imprecise

As the simple and effective technique, the weighted hybrid recommender system has been widely used in numerous fields. P-Tango and Pazzani are two typical systems. P-Tango is an online news system. It combines collaborative and content-based recommendation algorithms. The system adjusts weights of algorithms in the process of operation. Until the system obtains the expected accuracy, it determines weights. Pazzani is the other weighted hybrid recommender system. It combines collaborative, content-based and demographic-based recommendation algorithms. The system uses voting to determine recommendation results.

2.2 Weight Analysis

As previously described in Sect. 1, we give the formalized representation of the weighted hybrid technique as follows:

$$\widetilde{R_{ui}} = \sum_{j=1}^{n} \alpha_j r_{ui}^j \tag{1}$$

where j represents the j'th algorithm, it ranges from 1 to n. α_j corresponds to the weight of the j'th algorithm. r_{ui}^j is the predicting rating of user u on item i by the j'th algorithm. $\widetilde{R_{ui}}$ indicates the final hybrid result. From the formula (1), we can recognize that each algorithm just has a certain weight. That means the technique presupposes that predicting ratings of an algorithm are all greater or less than their ratings. However, this condition evaluates to false. Here we give some empirical evidence. We implement the User-based Collaborative Filtering (User-CF) and the Alternating Least Squares (ALS) in Python2.7, and use MovieLens-100K as observed data.

Table 2. The results of statistic analysis on predicting ratings

Algorithm	countH	countL	countE
User-CF	9181	10752	11
ALS	6992	12952	0

In the Table 2, countH is the number of predicting ratings which are greater than real ratings. The countL is less than real ratings and countE is equivalent amounts. From the empirical results, we know that:

(1) In these algorithms, there are little predicting ratings that equal to ratings.
(2) A part of predicting ratings are greater than ratings, and another are less than ratings.
(3) Only a weight for an algorithm may affect accuracy.

Thus, it is essential to optimize weights.

2.3 Spark

Spark is a fast and general-purpose cluster computing platforms for large-scale data processing [4] which is developed by UC Berkeley. In the environment of Spark, it includes Spark SQL [10], Spark Streaming [11], Mllib [12], GraphX [13], etc. Based on resilient distributed dataset (RDD) [14], it achieves memory-based computing, fault tolerance and scalability. Currently, Spark is deployed in Amazon, ebay and Yahoo! to process large-scale datasets.

For a hybrid recommender system, performance is affected by data scale, the number of algorithms and the complexity of algorithms. Deploy the system on Spark can mitigate above affects.

(1) In the system, large-scale datasets could be stored in distributed storage.
(2) Algorithms are independent with each other, they are supposed to be performed in parallel.
(3) Intermediate values can be cached in memory to decrease execution time.

Therefore, in this paper, we design an optimized hybrid recommender system on Spark.

3   Design Overview

The empirical evidence from Sect. 2 suggests that accuracy still has chance to be improved. The predicting ratings are higher or lower than corresponding ratings. Thus, we use cluster analysis to obtain more accurate weights. The principle of cluster analysis is that according to the properties of samples, using mathematical methods to determine relationship between samples, and according to the relationship to cluster samples. Based on cluster analysis, we present an optimized method for calculating personalized weights. Now let us discuss the method in detail.

3.1   Objective Function

In this section, we first give explanations of several concepts. In the following statement:

(1) Assume that there are n algorithms in the system and j is the j'th algorithm.
(2) u for user, i for item and (u,i) represents the data item of u and i.
(3) R_{ui} is the rating of u on i, r_{ui}^j is the predicting rating of u on i which is computed by the j'th algorithm.
(4) For the j'th algorithm, the error between the rating and the predicting rating is: $D_{ui}^j = R_{ui} - r_{ui}^j$. In order to reduce $\sum_{j=1}^n \sum_{u,i} D_{ui}^j$, similar errors are expected to get same weights. Based on errors, we divide (u,i) into k clusters and design $C_{ui} = (c_1, c_2, \cdots, c_k)$ to reflect the cluster of (u,i). For the j'th algorithm, $\alpha_j = (\alpha_{j1}, \alpha_{j2}, \cdots, \alpha_{jk})$ represents k weights of the algorithm. $\alpha_j C_{ui}^T$ finally determines the weight for r_{ui}^j.

According to our analysis, we define the objective function as formula (2):

$$F(\alpha) = \sum_{u,i} (R_{ui} - \alpha_1 C_{ui}{}^T r_{ui}{}^1 - \alpha_2 C_{ui}{}^T r_{ui}{}^2 - \cdots - \alpha_n C_{ui}{}^T r_{ui}^n)^2 \qquad (2)$$

$$s.t. \sum_{j=1}^n \alpha_j C_{ui}^T = 1 \qquad (3)$$

3.2 Weight Calculation

According to D_{ui}^j, the optimized method classifies all (u,i) into k clusters. For each (u,i), it has a vector $\boldsymbol{C_{ui}} = (c_1, c_2, \cdots, c_k)$ and is initialized to $\boldsymbol{C_{ui}} = (0, 0, \cdots, 0)$. The value which corresponds to (u,i)'s cluster is set to 1. For instance, if (u,i) belongs to the cluster 2, $\boldsymbol{C_{ui}} = (0, 1, 0, \cdots, 0)$. The weight for r_{ui}^j is α_{j2} which is computed by $\boldsymbol{\alpha_j C_{ui}}^T$. Therefore, $\boldsymbol{C}$ could map weights to predicting ratings and achieve multiple weights for an algorithm. Figure 1 shows the pipeline of the method.

After calculating $\boldsymbol{C}$, the optimized method requires to compute α_j. For the purpose of minimizing the objective function, we make use of the Lagrange theory and minimum theory [15,16]. Based on formula (2), the method constructs the Lagrange function $L(\boldsymbol{\alpha})$.

$$L(\boldsymbol{\alpha}) = F(\boldsymbol{\alpha}) + \lambda \sum_{u,i} \phi(\alpha) \tag{4}$$

$$\phi(\alpha) = \sum_{j=1}^{n} \alpha_j \boldsymbol{C_{ui}}^T - 1 \tag{5}$$

For each j, let $\frac{\partial L}{\partial (\alpha_j \boldsymbol{C_{ui}}^T)} = 0$. We can get an equation:

$$2 * \sum_{u,i} (\alpha_1 \boldsymbol{C_{ui}}^T r_{ui}^1 r_{ui}^j + \alpha_2 \boldsymbol{C_{ui}}^T r_{ui}^2 r_{ui}^j + \cdots \tag{6}$$

$$+ \alpha_n \boldsymbol{C_{ui}}^T r_{ui}^n r_{ui}^j) + \lambda = 2 * \sum_{u,i} R_{ui} r_{ui}^j$$

The Eq. (6) can be represented by matrix:

$$XY = 2 * \begin{pmatrix} \alpha_1 & \alpha_2 & \cdots & \alpha_n & \lambda \end{pmatrix}$$

$$* \begin{pmatrix} \sum_{u,i} \boldsymbol{C_{ui}}^T r_{ui}^1 r_{ui}^1 & \sum_{u,i} \boldsymbol{C_{ui}}^T r_{ui}^1 r_{ui}^2 & \cdots & \sum_{u,i} \boldsymbol{C_{ui}}^T r_{ui}^1 r_{ui}^n & \sum_{u,i} \boldsymbol{C_{ui}}^T \\ \sum_{u,i} \boldsymbol{C_{ui}}^T r_{ui}^2 r_{ui}^1 & \sum_{u,i} \boldsymbol{C_{ui}}^T r_{ui}^2 r_{ui}^2 & \cdots & \sum_{u,i} \boldsymbol{C_{ui}}^T r_{ui}^2 r_{ui}^n & \sum_{u,i} \boldsymbol{C_{ui}}^T \\ \vdots & \vdots & \ddots & \vdots & \vdots \\ \sum_{u,i} \boldsymbol{C_{ui}}^T r_{ui}^n r_{ui}^1 & \sum_{u,i} \boldsymbol{C_{ui}}^T r_{ui}^n r_{ui}^2 & \cdots & \sum_{u,i} \boldsymbol{C_{ui}}^T r_{ui}^n r_{ui}^n & \sum_{u,i} \boldsymbol{C_{ui}}^T \\ 1 & 1 & \cdots & 1 & 0 \end{pmatrix}$$

$$= 2 * \begin{pmatrix} \sum_{u,i} R_{ui} r_{ui}^1 \\ \sum_{u,i} R_{ui} r_{ui}^2 \\ \vdots \\ \sum_{u,i} R_{ui} r_{ui}^n \\ \sum_{u,i} 1 \end{pmatrix} = R \tag{7}$$

Thus the weight matrix X can be calculated by

$$X = R * Y^{-1} \tag{8}$$

The optimized method uses ratings which have already stored in the system to compute weights. However, these weights aren't entirely appropriate for a new (u,i). We further introduce user similarity to compute weights. The user similarity is computed by cosine similarity:

$$sim_{u,v} = \frac{|N_{(u)} \cap N_{(v)}|}{\sqrt{|N_{(u)}||N_{(v)}|}} \tag{9}$$

where $sim_{u,v}$ is the similarity between u and v. $N_{(u)}$ means the number of items that u have rated. $N_{(v)}$ is the same as $N_{(u)}$. For the (u',I'), the optimized method calculates the hybrid result as:

$$r_{\hat{u'}I'} = \frac{\sum_v sim_{u',v} * (\alpha_1 C_{vI'}{}^T r^1_{u'I'} + \alpha_2 C_{vI'}{}^T r^2_{u'I'} + \cdots + \alpha_n C_{vI'}{}^T r^n_{u'I'})}{\sum_v sim_{u'v}} \tag{10}$$

The Eq. (10) is able to filter the interference of non similar weights and get a personalized weight for the (u',I').

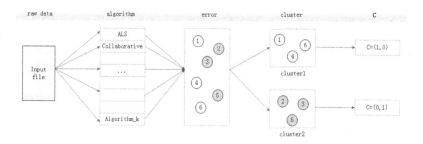

Fig. 1. The pipeline of the optimized method. The input file consists of ratings. Algorithms read the input file and output predicting ratings. Then the system computes errors and cluster data items. Finally the system gives the C.

4   Implementation

According to the design overview, we deploy the hybrid recommender system on Spark. The system contains data storage, prediction, cluster, weight, model fusion and recommendation, totally 6 modules. Figure 2 shows the architecture of the system.

4.1   Modules

Data storage module is the basis of the system. It stores input data, including historical data and ratings. We use HDFS which is a distributed file system to store raw data [17]. The pre-processed data are put in the database such as HBase, Redis, Hive, etc. [18–20]. Topside modules read data from the database. Prediction module is used to compute predicting ratings. It performs recommendation algorithms in parallel. Outputs are predicting ratings.

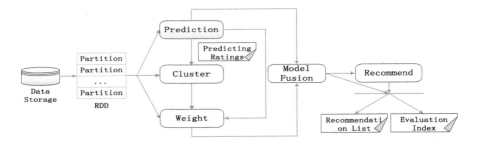

Fig. 2. The architecture of the hybrid recommender system. The system reads ratings and output recommendation lists. Besides, it also provides an evaluation index.

The cluster module concentrates on errors of (u,i). It exploits k-means to classify (u,i). Output of the module is C. The weight module accepts C to compute weights. With C and α, the module can get a weight for each r_{ui}^j. Output of it is α.

The model fusion calculates hybrid results based on predicting ratings, C, α and user similarity. According to these parameters, it determines hybrid results by logistic regression [21]. Recommendation is used to recommend items for users. Based on hybrid results, it generates recommendation lists. Besides, it also outputs an evaluation for results.

4.2 Discussion

In the hybrid recommender system on Spark, data are translated into RDDs. Because of the characteristics of memory-based computing and parallel operations, RDDs can be processed in parallel to reduce execution time. The read-only and fault tolerance of RDD make the system more reliable. Besides, due to the distributed storage of Spark, the system is able to handle large-scale datasets. It improves scalability of the system. Therefore, deploy the hybrid recommender system on Spark could decrease execution time and further improve scalability.

5 Performance

5.1 Evaluation Index

Accuracy. The system accuracy is measured by root mean square error (RMSE) [22]. It is defined as:

$$RMSE = \sqrt{\frac{\sum_{u,i \in T}(R_{ui} - \hat{r_{ui}})^2}{|T|}} \qquad (11)$$

where R_{ui} and $\hat{r_{ui}}$ is the rating and the hytbrid result that u on i respectively. $|T|$ denotes the number of $\hat{r_{ui}}$.

Execution Time. The execution time includes time of algorithms, clustering, calculating weights and hybrid results. It is measured in minutes.

5.2 Experimental Setup

In this experiment, we choose Spark as our platform. All experiments were performed using a local cluster with 7 nodes (1 master and 6 worker nodes): each node has Xeon(R) dual-core 2.53 GHz processor and 6 GB memory.

Dataset. In Table 3, we list datasets that were used in the experiment. For each dataset, we divide it into 2 training sets and a test set randomly.

Table 3. Datasets in the experiment

Dataset	Users	Items	Ratings
MovieLens-100K	1000	1700	100000
MovieLens-200K	1371	10153	200000
MovieLens-300K	2004	10850	300000
MovieLens-400K	2661	11634	400000
MovieLens-500K	3462	13257	500000
MovieLens-600K	4073	13488	600000
MovieLens-700K	4753	14154	700000
MovieLens-800K	5543	14230	800000
MovieLens-900K	6207	14963	900000
MovieLens-1M	6000	4000	1 million
BookCrossing	71212	176272	400000

Algorithms. We implement 3 recommendation algorithms: User-CF, Item-based Collaborative Filtering (Item-CF) and ALS. We perform them in training sets and test sets to compute predicting ratings, weights and hybrid results.

Nodes. We compare execution time of the stand-alone system and the distributed system. For the former, we use the server with Xeon(R) dual-core 2.53 GHz processor and 6 GB memory. For the latter, we use a local cluster with 7 nodes (1 master and 6 worker nodes): each node has Xeon(R) dual-core 2.53 GHz processor and 6 GB memory.

5.3 Performance Comparision

In this section, we evaluate performance of the hybrid recommender system on Spark, including accuracy and execution time.

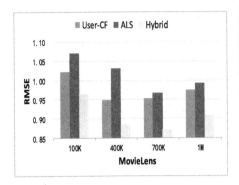
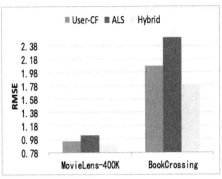

Fig. 3. The RMSE of different scale MovieLens. The x-axis indicates datasets, and the y-axis describes the RMSE.

Fig. 4. The RMSE of different types of datasets. The x-axis indicates datasets, and the y-axis describes the RMSE.

Figure 3 shows impacts of data scales on accuracy. In the experiment, we perform the combination of User-CF and ALS on four MovieLens datasets. In the Fig. 3, with the increasing of data scale, RMSE generally decreases. Due to the sparsity of MovieLens-700K, the hybrid recommender system obtains the best result. Compare with User-CF and ALS, the system improves accuracy of 8.21

Figure 4 gives the RMSE of different types of datasets. In the experiment, we perform the combination of User-CF and ALS on MovieLens-400K and BookCrossing. The Fig. 4 shows that the hybrid recommender system can improve accuracy of different types of datasets. And there are significant improvements on BookCrossing. The improvements demonstrate that the system is available for sparse datasets.

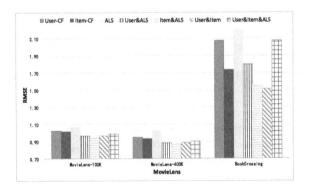

Fig. 5. The RMSE of different combinations of algorithms. The x-axis indicates the dataset, and the y-axis describes the RMSE.

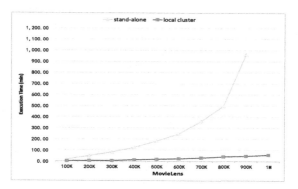

Fig. 6. The execution time of 2 modes. The x-axis indicates datasets and the y-axis describes execution time.

Figure 5 shows correlations between accuracy and combinations of algorithms. In the experiment, four combinations of algorithms are performed on MovieLens-100K, MovieLens-400K and BookCrossing respectively. In Fig. 5, the hybrid recommender system obtains better accuracy than single algorithm. When accuracy of single algorithm is favorable, the hybrid recommender system also obtains better accuracy.

Figure 6 compares execution time of stand-alone mode and local cluster mode. The experiment performs the combination of User-CF and ALS on MovieLens-100K to MovieLens-1M. For the stand-alone system, execution time increases sharply with the expansion of data scale. However, execution time of local cluster mode remains relatively constant. When the data scale is larger than MovieLens-900K, the stand-alone mode couldn't handle it. The local cluster mode could handle MovieLens-10M or larger datasets. From Fig. 6, we can recognize that memory-based computing, parallel operations and distributed storage of Spark are helpful to decrease execution time and improve scalability.

6 Conclusion and Future Work

Improving performance of recommender systems is a crucial solution for information overload. This paper designs a new weighted hybrid recommender system to solve this problem. We are the first to compute weights by using cluster analysis, user similarity and minimum theory. Besides, we deploy the hybrid recommender system on Spark. The system improves accuracy by optimizing weights and reduces execution time by memory-based computing and parallel operations. And distributed storage of the system is helpful to improve scalability. The experiment results demonstrate the performance of our hybrid recommender system.

In future work, we will consider to improve and extend the system: expansion of algorithm to process more complex scenes. Further research on factors influencing weights to improve accuracy. Meanwhile, optimize the implementation of the system on Spark.

References

1. Eppler, M.J., Mengis, J.: The concept of information overload: a review of literature from organization science, accounting, marketing, mis, and related disciplines. Inf. Soc. **20**(5), 325–344 (2004)
2. Cosley, D., Lam, S.K., Albert, I., Konstan, J.A., Riedl, J.: Is seeing believing?: how recommender system interfaces affect users' opinions. In: Proceedings of the SIGCHI Conference on Human Factors in Computing Systems, pp. 585–592. ACM (2003)
3. Burke, R.: Hybrid recommender systems: survey and experiments. User Model. User-Adap. Inter. **12**(4), 331–370 (2002)
4. Zaharia, M., Chowdhury, M., Franklin, M.J., Shenker, S., Stoica, I.: Spark: cluster computing with working sets. HotCloud **10**, 10 (2010)
5. Burke, R.: Hybrid systems for personalized recommendations. In: Mobasher, B., Anand, S.S. (eds.) ITWP 2003. LNCS (LNAI), vol. 3169, pp. 133–152. Springer, Heidelberg (2005)
6. Goldberg, D., Nichols, D., Oki, B.M., Terry, D.: Using collaborative filtering to weave an information tapestry. Commun. ACM **35**(12), 61–70 (1992)
7. Shardanand, U., Maes, P.: Social information filtering: algorithms for automating word of mouth. In: Proceedings of the SIGCHI Conference on Human Factors in Computing Systems, pp. 210–217. ACM Press/Addison-Wesley Publishing Co. (1995)
8. Resnick, P., Iacovou, N., Suchak, M., Bergstrom, P., Riedl, J.: Grouplens: an open architecture for collaborative filtering of netnews. In: Proceedings of the 1994 ACM Conference on Computer Supported Cooperative Work, pp. 175–186. ACM (1994)
9. Pazzani, M.J.: A framework for collaborative, content-based and demographic filtering. Artif. Intell. Rev. **13**(5–6), 393–408 (1999)
10. Armbrust, M., Xin, R.S., Lian, C., Huai, Y., Liu, D., Bradley, J.K., Meng, X., Kaftan, T., Franklin, M.J., Ghodsi, A., et al.: Spark SQL: relational data processing in spark. In: Proceedings of the 2015 ACM SIGMOD International Conference on Management of Data, pp. 1383–1394. ACM (2015)
11. Zaharia, M., Das, T., Li, H., Shenker, S., Stoica, I.: Discretized streams: an efficient and fault-tolerant model for stream processing on large clusters. Presented as Part of the (2012)
12. Meng, X., Bradley, J., Yavuz, B., Sparks, E., Venkataraman, S., Liu, D., Freeman, J., Tsai, D., Amde, M., Owen, S., et al.: MLlib: machine learning in apache spark. arXiv preprint arXiv:1505.06807 (2015)
13. Xin, R.S., Gonzalez, J.E., Franklin, M.J., Stoica, I.: GraphX: a resilient distributed graph system on spark. In: First International Workshop on Graph Data Management Experiences and Systems, p. 2. ACM (2013)
14. Zaharia, M., Chowdhury, M., Das, T., Dave, A., Ma, J., McCauley, M., Franklin, M.J., Shenker, S., Stoica, I.: Resilient distributed datasets: a fault-tolerant abstraction for in-memory cluster computing. In: Proceedings of the 9th USENIX Conference on Networked Systems Design and Implementation, p. 2. USENIX Association (2012)
15. Borneas, M.: On a generalization of the lagrange function. Am. J. Phys. **27**(4), 265–267 (1959)
16. Mitra, N.J., Nguyen, A.: Estimating surface normals in noisy point cloud data. In: Proceedings of the Nineteenth Annual Symposium on Computational Geometry, pp. 322–328. ACM (2003)

17. Borthakur, D.: The hadoop distributed file system: architecture and design. Hadoop Project Website **11**(2007), 21 (2007)
18. Zhang, D.W., Sun, F.Q., Cheng, X., Liu, C.: Research on hadoop-based enterprise file cloud storage system. In: 2011 3rd International Conference on Awareness Science and Technology (iCAST), pp. 434–437. IEEE (2011)
19. Han, J., Haihong, E., Le, G., Du, J.: Survey on NoSQL database. In: 2011 6th International Conference on Pervasive Computing and Applications (ICPCA), pp. 363–366. IEEE (2011)
20. Thusoo, A., Sarma, J.S., Jain, N., Shao, Z., Chakka, P., Anthony, S., Liu, H., Wyckoff, P., Murthy, R.: Hive: a warehousing solution over a map-reduce framework. Proc. VLDB Endow. **2**(2), 1626–1629 (2009)
21. Tsukimoto, H.: Logical regression analysis: from mathematical formulas to linguistic rules. In: Chu, W., Lin, T.Y. (eds.) Foundations and Advances in Data Mining. SFSC, vol. 180, pp. 21–61. Springer, Heidelberg (2005)
22. Willmott, C.J., Matsuura, K.: Advantages of the mean absolute error (MAE) over the root mean square error (RMSE) in assessing average model performance. Climate Res. **30**(1), 79 (2005)

Discovering Trip Patterns from Incomplete Passenger Trajectories for Inter-zonal Bus Line Planning

Zhaoyang Wang[1,2(✉)], Beihong Jin[1,2], Fusang Zhang[1,2],
Ruiyang Yang[1,2], and Qiang Ji[1,2]

[1] State Key Laboratory of Computer Sciences, Institute of Software,
Chinese Academy of Sciences, Beijing, China
jbh@octaix.iscas.ac.cn
[2] University of Chinese Academy of Sciences, Beijing, China

Abstract. Collecting the trajectories occurring in the city and mining the patterns implied in the trajectories can support the ITS (Intelligent Transportation System) applications and foster the development of smart cities. For improving the operations of inter-zonal buses in the cities, we define a new trip pattern, i.e., frequent bus passenger trip patterns for bus lines (FBPT4BL patterns in short). We utilize the passenger trajectories from bus smart card data and propose a two-phase approach to mine FBPT4BL patterns and then recommend inter-zonal bus lines. We conduct extensive experiments on the real data from the Beijing Public Transport Group. By comparing the experimental results with the actual operation of inter-zonal buses at the Beijing Public Transport Group, we verify the validity of our proposed method.

1 Introduction

With the popularity of smart devices and wireless networks, a large number of digital trajectories in everyday life from different objects (such as persons or vehicles) can be collected. Mining these trajectories gives us the opportunities to discover new knowledge or create new value.

Trip patterns are a kind of frequent sequence pattern. They can be loosely defined as a class of frequently-occurring trajectories that appear in the same spatial positions at the same periods. In real life, trip patterns can be found almost everywhere. For example, a student's behaviors in a university often follow some pattern: he or she often moves in the morning from the dormitory to the classroom, and then gets to the canteen; in the afternoon departs for the playground from the library and then heads for the canteen. Similarly, tourists often follow one of several kinds of travelling routes. As we know, office workers often take the buses of the same line to go to their companies or go home during the weekdays. The vehicles in logistics companies often deliver the goods together. Their trajectories also contain the trip patterns. Further, discovering trip patterns is a constituent part of many applications, which include transportation planning, logistics optimization, friend recommendation, etc.

G.R. Gao et al. (Eds.): NPC 2016, LNCS 9966, pp. 160–171, 2016.
DOI: 10.1007/978-3-319-47099-3_13

We note that while mining the trip patterns, the key step is to determine whether a trajectory contains a trip pattern. A variety of criteria can be made, depending on the definition of inclusion relation of the spatial and temporal attributes. However, the inclusion relation on these two dimensions will be completely different in various applications. It leads to the high diversity and complexity in mining trip patterns. Meanwhile, these trajectory data that have been obtained may suffer the problem of incomplete information. For example, the data from bus smart cards which are a specific kind of public transportation card, only recording the bus trajectories, belong to incomplete trajectories. Because we only know the boarding and disembarking times of these trajectories, and do not know the exact times that the passengers pass the intermediate bus stations along the trajectories.

At present, the data from bus smart cards are often used to analyze travel behaviors of individuals or crowds. As far as we know, they have not been used for inter-zonal bus planning and real-time bus scheduling. We think that the data from bus smart cards reflect the public's travel needs and they are an important basis for bus scheduling. Because of this, this paper attempts to mine a specific trip pattern from the data of bus smart cards and then suggests some inter-zonal bus lines.

The main contribution of this paper is that we propose a solution which utilizes the data of public smart cards for planning inter-zonal buses. In the proposed solution, we first distinguish the commuters by clustering bus passengers. Then, we mine frequent bus passenger trip patterns for bus lines (FBPT4BL patterns in short) and determine some inter-zonal bus lines. We also conduct extensive experiments based on the public smart card data from the Beijing Public Transport Group. By comparing the experimental results with the actual operation of inter-zonal bus at the Beijing Public Transport Group, we verify the validity of our proposed method.

The rest of this paper is organized as follows. First, we review the related work in Sect. 2. Then, we define the problem formally in Sect. 3. Next, we describe the process of mining FBPT4BL patterns from the public smart card data in Sect. 4. In Sect. 5, we give the experimental evaluation with real data as input. Finally, we conclude our paper in Sect. 6.

2   Related Work

We first review the previous methods of mining trip patterns. Next, we investigate the existing work on public transportation card data. Finally, we discuss the ways of optimizing bus lines and public transport scheduling with different data sources.

Trip Pattern Mining. A trip pattern denotes in essence a frequent path. The kernel issue in mining trip patterns is how to organize and search the trajectory information in an effective and efficient way [1, 2]. For example, [1] adopts a sequence instead of a single scalar to describe the frequency of a path so as to avoid the influences of infrequent edges and the number of constituent edges of a path, and construct the footmark graph and the corresponding footmark indexes. Next, [1] proposes a dynamic programming algorithm for path selection and applies an improved Bellman-Ford algorithm for mining frequent paths.

On the other hand, different application requirements derive new variants of trip patterns [3–5]. For example, the T pattern is proposed in [3] for obtaining the classification of persons. Moreover, [3] adopts a density-based clustering method to mine ROIs (Regions-of-Interest) from history trajectories, then mines T patterns in an incremental way from ROI sequences, and finally obtains the classification of persons on the basis of T patterns. For another example, the gathering pattern is proposed in [4] whose goal is to identify various group events, such as celebrations, parades, protests, traffic jams and so on. In [4], objects' trajectories are clustered into several crowds. Next, the Hausdorff distance is used for measuring the distance between crowds, and neighboring crowds comprise the group. And then, the lower bounds for the number of crowds in one group and the number of moving objects appearing in a group are given for mining gathering patterns.

Smart Card Data Analysis. The existing work on smart card data mainly includes the analyses of individual travel behaviors and collective behaviors.

As an example of mining individual behaviors, [6] adopts the bag-of-words model to build a passenger profile by his or her trip information in the smart card data, and employs the hierarchical clustering to get groups of passengers. [6] uses the results of clustering as input of a three-layer back-propagation neural network to generate the predictions. The results show that passengers have their inner mobility patterns and usually hold the same patterns as the ones in the same group. However, for mining the patterns implied in the collective behaviors, the starting point is in general to classify the passengers according to the smart card data. [7] divides passengers into two groups: extreme travelers and non-extreme travelers, and then employs different methods to analyze the mobility and stability of two kinds of travelers. [7] concludes that the stability of extreme traveler's travel pattern cannot last for a long time and the non-extreme shows high regularity. [8] classifies passengers into four types and then conducts the statistical analyses for each passenger type.

Bus Line Planning and Scheduling. Planning bus lines and scheduling buses on the basis of big data is an emerging topic in intelligent transportation systems.

[9] utilizes smart card data and GPS data of buses to calculate the passenger density of a bus service, so as to verify the validity of time arrangements and assess the selections of bus scheduling schemes. [10] focuses on performing the bus scheduling of urban bus lines and proposes an improved multi-objective genetic algorithm and obtains multiple Pareto solutions. In order to meet individual travel needs, [11] proposes a flexible mini-shuttle like transportation system called flexi, to establish a flexible bus scheduling by exploring the taxi trajectories. The authors first adopt a hierarchical clustering algorithm to get the frequent taxi trajectory clustering, named hot line. Then, they construct a directed acyclic graph of hot lines, and mine bus lines and bus schedule strategies depending on the connectivity between hot lines.

Compared with the existing work, our work has a different goal, that is, inter-zonal bus line planning. For this goal, we propose a new variant of the trip pattern named the FBPT4BL pattern, and design a two-phase appraoch to mining this pattern from the smart card data.

3   Problem Definition

Generally, a trajectory of an object refers to a sequence of time-stamped locations, representing the traces collected by some mobile wireless devices. As far as a bus trip is concerned, the following information can be obtained from bus smart card data, i.e., the bus card ID, the bus ID, the bus line ID, the boarding time of a passenger, the disembarking time of a passenger, the GPS data of the boarding station, and the GPS data of the disembarking station. These data reflect the spatio-temporal characteristics of the boarding and disembarking behaviors. With the aid of bus line details, the station information which a bus passenger passes can be supplemented, but the times of reaching these passing stations are still unknown. So the trajectories from smart card data are incomplete ones.

For clearly defining the problem to be solved, the concepts below are given at first.

Definition 1 (Bus Trajectory): A bus trajectory is a pair $(T, A) = <(b_0, t_0), b_1, ..., (b_n, t_1)>$. Here, T denotes a sequential sequence of bus stations, that is, $T = <b_0, b_1, ..., b_n>$, where b_0 stands for the boarding station, b_n is the disembarking station, and the rest are the stations a passenger passes through. However, $A = [t_0, t_1]$, where t_0 and t_1 stand for the boarding and disembarking times, respectively.

Definition 2 (Bus Passenger Trip pattern, BPT pattern): A trip pattern, called BPT pattern, is a pair (P, τ), where $P = <b'_0, b'_1, \cdots, b'_n>$ denotes a sequential sequence of bus stations which a bus trajectory, in whole or part, passes through, and τ is the time interval that P goes through.

For deciding whether a trajectory is included in a BPT pattern, we have to define a binary relation between a trajectory and a BPT pattern.

Definition 3 (the inclusion between a bus trajectory and a BPT pattern, $\subseteq$): For any bus trajectory $(T, A) = <(b_0, t_0), b_1, ..., (b_m, t_1)>$ and a BPT pattern (P, τ), where $P = <b'_0, b'_1, \cdots, b'_n>$. We say that (T, A) is included in (P, τ), denoted as $(T, A) \subseteq (P, \tau)$, if and only if the following conditions are satisfied:

1. $m \leq n$ and $t_0 \in \tau$;
2. if $m = n$, then $T = P$;
3. if $m < n$, then $\exists x \geq 0$, s.t. $<b_0, b_1, ..., b_m> = <b'_x, b'_{x+1}, ..., b'_{x+m}>$, where $0 \leq x, x + m \leq n$.

Definition 4 (Frequent Bus Passenger Trip pattern, FBPT pattern): Given a bus trajectory set D, the minimum support threshold s_{min}, and the time interval $\tau_{interval}$, mining a FBPT pattern is to find a BPT pattern (P, τ) that includes at least s_{min} trajectories and whose τ is within $\tau_{interval}$. That is, for any BPT pattern (P, τ), such that $support_D((P, \tau)) \geq s_{min}$, where $support_D((P,\tau))$ stands for the number of trajectories $(T_k, A_k) \in D$, $k = 1, 2, 3 \cdots$, that satisfy $(T_k, A_k) \subseteq (P, \tau)$ and τ is within $\tau_{interval}$.

Note that in *Definition 4*, different $support_D((P,\tau))$ will lead to the different definitions of the frequent trip pattern.

In the paper, we explore bus smart card data to discover the commuters and mine one kind of specific frequent BPT pattern, named FBPT4BL patterns: i.e., frequent BPT patterns for bus lines. Now, we give the definition of mining FBPT4BL patterns.

Definition 5 (Frequent Bus Passenger Trip pattern for Bus Lines, FBPT4BL pattern): Given the bus trajectory set of commuters $D_{commuter}$, the minimum busload threshold between adjacent stations ps_{min}, the minimum trip length r, and the time interval $\tau_{interzonal}$, mining a FBPT4BL pattern is to find a BPT pattern $(P, \tau_{commuter})$ in $\tau_{interzonal}$ whose trip length is longer than r and *score* is higher than ps_{min}. That is, for any BPT pattern $(P, \tau_{commuter})$, such that $Score_{D_{Commuter}}((P, \tau_{commuter})) \geq ps_{min}$ and $length(P) \geq r$, where $length(P)$ is the total length of P, $\tau_{commuter}$ is within $\tau_{interzonal}$, and $Score_{D_{Commuter}}$ stands for the score of $(P, \tau_{commuter})$, which is computed as follows:

$$Score_{D_{Commuter}}((P, \tau_{commuter})) = ITFQ_{D_{Commuter}}(P, \tau_{commuter})/(length(P) - 1) \quad (1)$$

$$ITFQ_{D_{Commuter}}((P, \tau_{commuter})) = \{count((T, A))|(T, A) \\ \in D_{commuter} \land (T, A) \subseteq (P, \tau_{commuter})\} \quad (2)$$

where *ITFQ* denotes the busload of $(P, \tau_{commuter})$.

4   Mining Frequent Trip Patterns for Inter-zonal Bus Lines

In this section, we propose an approach to mining commuter-based frequent trip pattern (the MCFTP approach in short) for recommending inter-zonal bus lines. The MCFTP approach consists of two phases: commuter recognition and inter-zonal bus mining. In the first phase, the DBSCAN algorithm is applied for passenger classification. In the second phase, with the support of a forest structure, an incremental data mining algorithm is designed for mining FBPT4BL patterns from the commuter trajectories. As a result, top-k inter-zonal bus lines can be obtained.

4.1   Mining Commuters

For the perspective of bus line planning, inter-zonal bus lines should satisfy the travel needs from commuters. Thus, we employ the DBSCAN algorithm and identify commuters by clustering the trajectories on spatial and temporal features. In spatial aspect, we cluster on boarding and disembarking stations respectively to discover frequent OD (Origin-Destination) pairs and then find frequent trajectories. In temporal aspect, we also use the density clustering algorithm DBSCAN to get the habitual time feature.

Mining Frequent OD Pairs. For mining a passenger's frequent boarding stations, we adopt the DBSCAN algorithm to cluster for each bus station in geographical position. Let $Neib_\varepsilon(i)$ represent the collection of neighbor stations of station i, that is, $Neib_\varepsilon(i) = \{i'|dis(i', i) \leq \varepsilon\}$, where ε is the upper bound on distance and $dis(\cdot)$ is the Euclidean distance. Let *MinPts* be the lower bound on the number of neighbors. The following four steps describe how to cluster.

Step 1: for a station i in the collection of boarding stations, if i has not been marked (which means that i is not marked as "processed" or "noise"), then check its neighborhood. If $|Neib_\varepsilon(i)| \geq MinPts$, then create a new cluster h, add i into h, and add all its neighbors to the candidate set N.

Step 2: for the neighborhood of station i' that has not been marked in N, if $|Neib_\varepsilon(i')| \geq MinPts$, then add $Neib_\varepsilon(i')$ into N, add i' into h, and mark i' as "processed", else mark i' as "noise".

Step 3: repeat *Step* 2, until all stations in N have been processed.

Step 4: repeat *Step* 1 to *Step* 3, until each station has been marked.

Note that the clustering steps in this paper are a bit different from the ones in original DBSCAN algorithm. Now, these isolated points in the result of clustering are not noise. Each isolated point indicates that only one bus station is found nearby. Thus, it should form a distinct cluster. We store the clustering attributes of each boarding station in $H_{boarding}$.

For a passenger p, by matching all boarding stations of smart card records with $H_{boarding}$, we can get arrival times for each cluster. Finally, the high frequency clustering is supposed to be frequent boarding stations, and the others are general boarding stations.

While mining frequent disembarking stations, we also employ the DBSCAN algorithm. The specific mining steps are the same as the ones in mining boarding stations. We store all clustering attributes of disembarking stations in $H_{disembarking}$. Then, by matching all disembarking stations in smart card records with $H_{disembarking}$, we can get frequent disembarking stations.

For a passenger p, if the boarding station (O) and the disembarking station (D) of a record belong to different high frequency clustering respectively, then this record is a frequent OD record. If the proportion of the frequent OD records in p's records (denoted as $\rho_{p,OD}$) is greater than 50 % (which is $\rho_{p,OD} \geq 50\%$), then p is frequent in terms of OD.

Fig. 1. The result of mining frequent OD pairs. (Color figure online)

Figure 1 shows the result of mining frequent OD pairs for a passenger. The yellow bubbles represent the results of clustering of frequent boarding stations. And the purple bubbles represent the results of clustering of frequent disembarking stations. The number in each bubble is the frequency of boarding or disembarking for a passenger. If the frequency in a bubble is more than 6, then the station is regarded as a frequent boarding station or disembarking station. Following this rule, clusters $BC2$ and $DC2$ are frequent stations, while $BC1$ and $DC1$ are normal ones. So only $(BC2, DC2)$ is a frequent OD pair. From Fig. 1, we know that the proportion of frequent trajectories is greater than 50 % (10/15 = 67 %), so this passenger is frequent in terms of OD pairs.

Mining the Habit of Travel Time. For a passenger p, if he or she takes buses within a certain time interval frequently, this time interval is referred to as the habit of travel time for p. Once again, we adopt the DBSCAN algorithm to cluster the boarding times of p in the bus smart card records for getting all the habits of travel time of p. In particular, the object i in the DBSCAN algorithm corresponds to the boarding time. The distance between objects corresponds to the time interval expressed in milliseconds. *MinPts* is the lower bound on i's neighbors. The resultant clusters signify frequent times, and isolated points signify noise. If the proportion of p's records with frequent times in all p's records (denoted as $\rho_{p,Habitual}$) is greater than 50 %, then we say that p has habitual time.

Recognizing Commuters. Having the above clustering analysis results, we can further make passenger classification. First, different kinds of passengers are defined as follows:

- OD passengers: the passengers are frequent in terms of OD pairs, but have no habitual time.
- Habitual time passengers: the passengers have habitual times, but are infrequent in terms of OD pairs.
- Commuters: the passengers are both frequent in spatial and temporal aspects.
- Casual passengers: they have none in spatio-temporal features.

Next, for each passenger p, the following rules are given to distinguish commuters:
Rule 1: if both $\rho_{p,OD}$ and $\rho_{p,Habitual}$ are small enough, p is a casual passenger.
Rule 2: if $\rho_{p,Habitual} < 50\%$, $\rho_{p,OD} > \rho_{p,Habitual}$, and $\rho_{p,OD}$, $\rho_{p,Habitual}$ are not too small, p is an OD passenger.
Rule 3: if $\rho_{p,OD} < 50\%$, $\rho_{p,Habitual} > \rho_{p,OD}$ and $\rho_{p,OD}$, $\rho_{p,Habitual}$ are not too small, p is a habitual time passenger.
Rule 4: if $\rho_{p,OD} \geq 50\%$ and $\rho_{p,Habitual} \geq 50\%$, p is a commuter.

4.2   Mining FBPT4BL Patterns

For reducing the overheads of trajectory retrieval, we design a forest structure which can organize trajectories with the same boarding station into a tree.

Establishing a Tree Structure. Each tree in the forest is used to store the trajectories with the same boarding station. Specifically, the same boarding station is stored in the root node, the disembarking station and these stations which passengers pass through are stored in the children nodes. Each node stores a triple, i.e., (*item, count, children*), where *item* stores the name of current station; *count* is the number of commuters' trips whose boarding station is the root node of this tree and the disembarking station is current node; and *children* contains the children of this node which are stored in a hash table.

Creating a Forest. The forest is established by these trees above and stored in a hash table. For a trajectory that has not been visited, if the tree whose root node is the boarding station of the trajectory does not exist, then we create the tree, otherwise we search the tree for the branch that matches with the trajectory. If the matched branch exists, then we increment count, where the count belongs to the node that matches with the disembarking station. Otherwise, we create a new branch and set count of the leaf node to 1.

Executing FBPT4BL Patterns Mining. The mining steps in the form of the pseudo code are shown in Fig. 2.

```
Input: forest forest, trip length bound r
Output: top-k result
Function GetFrequencyPattern(forest)
   Foreach tree in forest
      Foreach tp_c in tree whose count > 0
         If tp_pc exist in TP
            tp_c.ITFQ = tp_pc.ITFQ
            Add c.count of branch from each node o in tp_pc to c
            into tp_c.ITFQ;
         Else
            tp_c.ITFQ = GetPassengerCountP(tp_c);
         End If
         Save tp_c into TP, and count the score of tp_c;
      End Foreach
   End Foreach
   Sort TP by score and return top-k result from TP whose
   length is more than r;
End Function;
Function GetPassengerCountP(trip)
   If(trip is null)
      Return 0;
   End If
   ITFQ = Sum(count of all the nodes in trip);
   Remove root node in trip;
   ITFQ += GetPassengerCountP(trip);
   Return ITFQ;
End Function;
```

Fig. 2. Mining FBPT4BL patterns

Step 1: traverse the tree in a depth-first order. Let c be the current visiting node. If $c.count > 0$, then mark the branch from root node to c as a BPT pattern tp_c, and store tp_c into a set of BPT pattern TP.

Step 2: let pc be the father node of c. If BPT pattern tp_{pc} exists in TP, then set $tp_c.ITFQ$ to $tp_{pc}.ITFQ$. Then, for each node o in tp_{pc}, find the tree whose root node is o, search for the branch that matches with the sub-trip in tp_c from o to c, and add the *count* of end node in the matched branch to $tp_c.ITFQ$, and then get to *Step* 5. If tp_{pc} is not in TP, then continue *Step* 3.

Step 3: sum all count values in tp_c to $tp_c.ITFQ$.

Step 4: delete the first node of tp_c to get the new pattern tp_c'. If tp_c' is empty, then continue *Step* 5, else match tp_c' against the forest. If the matched branch is found, then turn to *Step* 3. If not, then turn to *Step* 4. Here, the meaning of match is to get a branch whose root node is the first node of tp_c', and each node of the branch is the same as the bus station in tp_c' in order.

Step 5: select BPT patterns in TP whose lengths are larger than r, and compute the commuters' *score* values of these patterns by Eq. 1. Then, sort the selected patterns by *score* to get top-k results which are the trips of BPT4BL patterns. By matching these trips to bus lines, the inter-zonal bus lines and bus intervals can be gotten.

4.3   Time Complexity Analysis

Let w be the number of bus stations, g be the number of commuters, and u be the trajectory number. The analysis of the MCFTP approach consists of three parts: commuter mining, forest creation, and FBPT4BL pattern mining.

In the commuter mining part, since the DBSCAN algorithm has the complexity of $O(w \cdot \log w)$, the complexity of mining frequent ODs is $O(2 g \cdot u)$, and the complexity of mining habitual time is $O(g \cdot u \log u)$, the total complexity is $O(w \cdot \log w + 2 g \cdot u + g \cdot u \log u)$.

In the second part, creating a forest needs to traverse all trajectories, which will make the complexity of this process $O(u \cdot w)$.

In the third part, we use an incremental method to mine FBPT4BL patterns. A new BPT pattern's *ITFQ* is calculated by the existing pattern's *IFTQ* via a traverse from the root node to its father node. From *Step* 2, we see that the complexity is $1 + 2 + 3 + \ldots + d = O(d^2)$, where d is the station number in a branch. Let e be the number of leaf nodes in the forest. The complexity of mining process is $O(d^2 \cdot e)$. Considering that each branch in a tree is a sub-trajectory of passengers and the total station number of one bus line in Beijing is no more than 50, which means that the maximum length of branches cannot be larger than 50, the complexity of mining process is $O(2500 \cdot e)$.

5   Evaluation

In order to show availability of the MCFTP approach, we need to fix following questions:

- How do we set the distance upper bound ε and the minimum number of neighbors *MinPts* in the commuter identification phase?
- Does only commuter data result in better experimental results than all passengers or other types of passengers?
- Does the MCFTP approach is appropriate to a real-time bus scheduling?

To answer the above questions, we first conduct experiments to analyze the sensitivities of ε and *MinPts*. Then we evaluate effectiveness and efficiency of the MCFTP approach. In experiments, we use the real data from Beijing Public Transport Group, including 6,507,837 passengers and 48,427,884 items of bus smart card data from Aug. 3, 2015 to Aug. 9, 2015, as well as 5,622 bus stations and 707 bus lines.

5.1   Sensitivity Analysis of *MinPts* and ε

The application of the DBSCAN algorithm requires two important parameters: the distance upper bound ε and the minimum number of neighbors *MinPts*.

While the DBSCAN algorithm is applied to clustering by the spatial information, ε denotes the upper bound of spatial distance. A small ε may result in a big error since some stations which belong to the same destination may be clustered into different classes, whereas a too large ε also performs poorly since the stations falling into different destinations may be clustered into one class.

In Beijing, the distance between neighbor bus stations ranges from 500 m to 1200 m. Considering that an acceptable walking distance is 1000 m or so, we increase ε from 500 m to 1000 m to evaluate clustering results. However, $MinPts$ is used to set a regular cluster density. In the downtown, bus stations within ε should not be very congested. Thus, in experiments, we increase $MinPts$ from 1 to 10.

While the DBSCAN algorithm is applied to temporal information, ε denotes the upper bound of the temporal distance. ε is set to 20 min, since in general commuters will arrive at stations at a relatively fixed time points, varying within a very narrow interval. $MinPts$ is set to 3. That means a passenger is regarded as frequent in temporal aspect if the passenger takes a bus at same station at least three times one week.

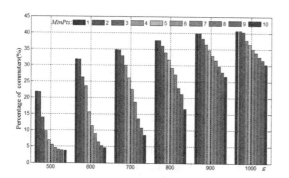

Fig. 3. The percentages of commuters.

Figure 3 shows percentages of commuters under different ε and $MinPts$ (in spatial clusters). From Fig. 3, we can see that for the same ε, commuter number decreases with the increase of $MinPts$. It is because a large $MinPts$ will generate a large number of clusters and those trips which should be in a same cluster will be departed into different clusters. In particular, we find when setting ε to 500 or 600 and $MinPts$ to a value greater than 5, the percentages of commuters will be less than 5 %, which cannot be true in Beijing. We deem that the percentages of commuters ranging from 20 % to 35 % is rational, so we set ε to 600 and $MinPts$ to 4 for the experiments in Sect. 5.2.

5.2 Effective and Efficient Analysis of MCFTP Approach

We collect the real inter-zonal bus lines in Beijing as the ground truth. So far, about 3,851 inter-zonal bus lines have been operated, covering 282 bus lines.

In experiments, we set r to 15, and then run our MCFTP approach using the smart card data of different days as input. We choose different percentages (denoted as γ, from 1 % to 20 %) of recommended inter-zonal bus lines as the results of our MCFTP approach, and calculate the matching ratio of our results to the ground truth. We also employ the methods in Sect. 4.2 to mine FBPT4BL patterns from all passengers, OD

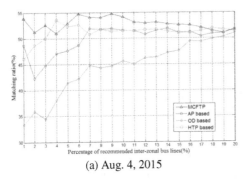

(a) Aug. 4, 2015

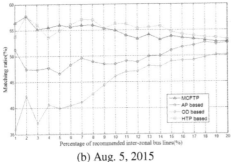

(b) Aug. 5, 2015

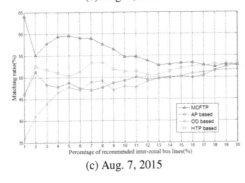

(c) Aug. 7, 2015

Fig. 4. The experiment results of inter-zonal bus recommendation.

passengers and habitual time passengers. The corresponding methods are called the AP based method, the OD based method and the HTP based method, respectively. The results are showed in Fig. 4.

From Fig. 4, we can see that the MCFTP approach performs better than other three methods. The highest matching ratio of our approach is 62 %, and the lowest matching ratio is 51 %. For the data on Aug. 7, our MCFTP approach is 28 % higher than the OD based method, 18 % higher than the HTP based method, and 18 % higher than the AP based method while γ is set to 1 %. On average, the HTP based method is mostly close to our method. The reason behind is that these habitual time passengers have regular boarding habits and inter-zonal bus lines in morning rush hours can greatly benefit these passengers.

We find that the OD based method performs worst in four methods. However, from the above experiments, we know that the sum of all passengers is 6,507,837. Among them, the number of OD passengers is 4,661,267, the number of habitual time passengers is 243,370, and the number of commuters is 1,536,927. OD passenger's number is about 3 times of commuter's number. That means that the inter-zonal bus lines planning should rely on the contributory passenger factor instead of passenger number.

As regard to the time complexity, for the data of one day, we need 65 s to build the forest and 5.852 s to mine inter-zonal bus lines. Our method has the low time complexity, and can be used for scheduling inter-zonal buses in real-time.

6 Conclusion

In the paper, we focus on mining patterns in the trajectories. We propose a two-phase approach to mine FBPT4BL patterns from the bus smart card data and obtain inter-zonal bus lines. The resulting inter-zonal bus lines can be used for evaluating the rationality of existing inter-zonal bus lines or guiding the opening of inter-zonal bus lines.

Acknowledgments. This work is supported by the National Natural Science Foundation of China under Grant No. 61472408.

References

1. Luo, W.M., Tan, H.Y., Chen, L., Lionel, M.N.: Finding time period-based most frequent path in big trajectory data. In: Proceedings of the 2013 ACM SIGMOD International Conference on Management of Data, pp. 713–724 (2013)
2. Lee, A.J.T., Chen, Y.A., Ip, W.C.: Mining frequent trajectory patterns in spatial–temporal databases. Inf. Sci. **179**, 2218–2231 (2009)
3. Fosca, G., Mirco, N., Fabio, P., Dino, P.: Trajectory Pattern Mining. In: KDD 2007 Proceedings of the 13th ACM SIGKDD International Conference on Knowledge Discovery and Data Mining, pp. 330–339 (2007)
4. Kai, Z., Yu, Z., Nicholas, J.Y., Shuo, S.: On discovery of gathering patterns from trajectories. In: IEEE 29th International Conference on Data Engineering, pp. 242–253 (2013)
5. Li, Z.-H., Bolin, D., Han, J.-W., Roland, K.: Swarm: mining relaxed temporal moving object clusters. J. Proc. VLDB Endowment **3**(1), 723–734 (2010)
6. Dou, M., He, T., Yin, H., Zhou, X., Chen, Z., Luo, B.: Predicting passengers in public transportation using smart card data. In: Sharaf, M.A., Cheema, M.A., Qi, J. (eds.) ADC 2015. LNCS, vol. 9093, pp. 28–40. Springer, Heidelberg (2015)
7. Cui, Z.Y., Long, Y.: Perspectives on stability and mobility of passenger's travel behavior through smart card data. In: UrbComp in Conjunction with ACM SIGKDD (2015)
8. Le, M.K., A.B., Edward C.: Passenger segmentation using smart card data. IEEE Trans. Intell. Transp. Syst., 1537–1548 (2015)
9. Zhang, J., Yu, X., Tian, C., Zhang, F., Tu, L., Xu, C.Z.: Analyzing passenger density for public bus: inference of crowdedness and evaluation of scheduling choices. In: Proceedings of IEEE International Conference on Intelligent Transportation Systems, ITSC (2014)
10. Zuo, X.Q., Chen, C., Tan, W., Zhou, M.C.: Vehicle scheduling of an urban bus line via an improved multiobjective genetic algorithm. IEEE Trans. Intel. Transp. Syst. **16**(2), 1030–1041 (2015)
11. Favyen, B., Huang, Y., Xie, X., Powell, J.W.: A greener transportation mode: flexible routes discovery from GPS trajectory data. In: GIS 2011 Proceedings of the 19th ACM SIGSPATIAL International Conference on Advances in Geographic Information Systems, pp. 405–408 (2011)

FCM: A Fine-Grained Crowdsourcing Model Based on Ontology in Crowd-Sensing

Jian An[1,2(✉)], Ruobiao Wu[1], Lele Xiang[1], Xiaolin Gui[1,3], and Zhenlong Peng[1,3]

[1] School of Electronics and Information Engineering, Xi'an Jiaotong University,
No.28, Xianning West Road, Xi'an 710049, People's Republic of China
{wuruobiao,xianglele,pengzl}@stu.xjtu.edu.cn,
{anjian,xlgui}@mail.xjtu.edu.cn
[2] Shaanxi Province Key Laboratory of Computer Network, No.28, Xianning West Road,
Xi'an 710049, People's Republic of China
[3] School of Business and Information Technology, Quanzhou Normal University,
Donghai, Quanzhou 362000, People's Republic of China

Abstract. Crowd sensing between users with smart mobile devices is a new trend of development in Internet. In order to recommend the suitable service providers for crowd sensing requests, this paper presents a Fine-grained Crowdsourcing Model (FCM) based on Ontology theory that helps users to select appropriate service providers. First, the characteristic properties which extracted from the service request will be compared with the service provider based on ontology triple. Second, recommendation index of each service provider is calculated through similarity analysis and cluster analysis. Finally, the service decision tree is proposed to predict and recommend appropriate candidate users to participate in crowd sensing service. Experimental results show that this method provides more accurate recommendation than present recommendation systems and consumes less time to find the service provider through clustering algorithm.

1 Introduction

In the new trend of ubiquitous computing, Crowd Sensing (CS) has been proposed to efficiently collect information in the multiple-source and heterogeneous environment. Based on massive information, including users' behavior characteristics, context information and activities law, the user behavior model and the relationship between service attributes could be obtained.

However, there are still some problems needed to be solved in the crowd sensing scenario. To start with, present crowdsourcing models do not particularly classifying the service requests [1]. Furthermore, the internal relationship between service preference of customers and historical data has not been fully considered in the existing service recommending model [2]. Thus, finding an applicable model to utilize the historical data is an effective way to promote success rate of service assignment.

To solve the problems mentioned above, a fine-grained crowdsourcing model has been proposed in this paper to realize sensing task assignment, which could recommend

© IFIP International Federation for Information Processing 2016
Published by Springer International Publishing AG 2016. All Rights Reserved
G.R. Gao et al. (Eds.): NPC 2016, LNCS 9966, pp. 172–179, 2016.
DOI: 10.1007/978-3-319-47099-3_14

a set of appropriate service providers to the requesters. The whole system model is showed in the Fig. 1. The key contributions of this paper are listed as following.

- In order to realize the reasonable distribution of sensing tasks, ontology theory is used in this paper to describe various attributes of users. Based on the ontology method, all service providers and requesters could be accurately differentiate.
- According to the fine granularity description of sensing requests, recommendation index of each service provider is calculated through similarity analysis.
- In addition, as a method to obtain approximate discrete valued target function, decision tree is also referred in the crowdsourcing model to predict potential attribute with the information entropy principle.

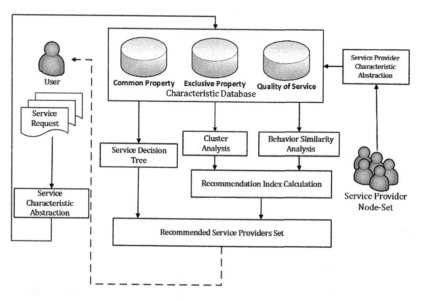

Fig. 1. Structure of service crowdsourcing model and whole process of recommending.

2   Characteristic Ontology Triple

The characteristic data should be defined in a unified form which could accurately describe the user behavior. Ontology, a concept data structure, could effectively show the user characteristic through concept sets and concept relationship set. In order to meticulously classify all service providers and customers, the characteristic is supposed to be defined as ontology triple $< CP, EP, QoS >$. The components in each type of property are listed as following.

Common Property. For a service provider or a customer, common property contains user ID, user name and additional information. Therefore, the common property is defined as a set,

$$CP = \{ID, Name, Additional\ Information\}$$

Particularly, all the elements of CP are text attributes, even though ID is the serial number of a service provider or a customer.

Exclusive Property The exclusive property contains the location, availability and the service type. The Exclusive Property is defined as following set,

$$EP = \{Location, Availability, Type\}$$

The element Location $\in$ EP is the GPS location of the service provider or the customer. The element Availability $\in$ EP describes whether the user could participate in the service. The type service providers specializing in or customers requesting for is selected from the type catalogue set which is determined subjectively in relation to the application scenarios.

QoS Property Although the exclusive properties will affect the decision of users, the Quality of Service properties are the determinant in service selection. The QoS property is defined as following set,

$$QoS = \{Vaulation, Success\ Rate\}$$

Both of Valuation $\in$ QoS and Success Rate $\in$ QoS are $N \times M$ matrixs, where N is the number of service providers and M is the number of customers. Every element in the Valuation matrix is valued in the range of [0, 10].

3   Recommendation Method

3.1   Recommendation Index

The recommendation index shows selection priority of a service provider. The higher recommendation index of a service provider, the more likely the user will enjoy the service.

Definition 1 (User Behavior Similarity) In the service selection method, the user behavior similarity between two users is calculated by valuation offered in the past service. The user behavior similarity between two users U_i and U_j could be calculated through following equation,

$$Sim_{user}(U_i, U_j) = \frac{\sum_{SP_x \in OS(U_i, U_j)} \left(Val(i, k) - \overline{Val_i} \right) \left(Val(j, k) - \overline{Val_j} \right)}{\sqrt{\sum_{SP_x \in OS(U_i, U_j)} \left(Val(i, k) = \overline{Val_i} \right)^2 \cdot \sum_{SP_x \in OS(U_i, U_j)} \left(Val(j, k) - \overline{Val_j} \right)^2}} \tag{1}$$

Where $OS(U_i, U_j)$ consists of the service providers which have both served users U_i and U_j, $Val(i, k) \in [0, 10]$ is the valuation that user U_i values on the service provider SP_k.

Except for User Behavior Similarity, the types of service the service providers specialize in will also impact the validity of the valuation. Concept Hierarchy Tree [3] is proposed to processing the service types.

According to the definition of the information content in the information theory [4], the present information content of service type $Type_x$ will be calculated through the method proposed by the Resnik, and the calculate method is mentioned as following,

$$IC(Type_x) = -\log p(Type_x) \tag{2}$$

Definition 2 (Type Similarity) After obtaining the information content of each type, the type similarity $Sim_{sp}(Type_i, Type_j)$ between $Type_i$ and $Type_j$ will use the following formula to calculate,

$$Sim_{sp}(Type_i, Type_j) = \frac{IC(A(Type_i, Type_j))}{IC(Type_i) + IC(Type_j)} + \frac{d(A(Type_i, Type_j))}{2(d(Type_i) + d(Type_j) - d(A(Type_i, Type_j)))} \tag{3}$$

Where $A(Type_i, Type_j)$ is the nearest common ancestor concept of $Type_i$ and $Type_j$. $d(Type_i), d(Type_j)$ and $d(A(Type_i, Type_j))$ are the depth of the $Type_i, Type_j$ and the nearest common ancestor concept of $Type_i$ and $Type_j$.

Recommendation Index Using user behavior similarity and type similarity, the recommendation index of service provider SP_j to user U_i is calculated as following,

$$RI(U_i, SP_j, Type_k) = Sim_{sp}(Type(SP_j), Type_k) \sum_{x=1}^{n} (Sim_{user}(U_i, U_x) \times Val(i, j)) \tag{4}$$

Where $Type(SP_j)$ is the Type property concluded in the exclusive property of SP_j, $Type_k$ is the service type which user requires, and n is the number of the users.

3.2 Service Decision Tree

Decision tree is an appropriate prediction model used in the process of selecting service provider. The attributes considered in the service decision tree conclude following data: Availability, Distance, Type and Success Rate.

After building the basis of the service decision tree by using the Ontology Triple, the rest of the service decision tree will be built through recursive process described as following step:

Step 1. Acquiring the data of node N_x which is going to build the its subtree, then defining the sample set remained as S_x, the attributes remained in the attribute list as $AttList_x$

Step 2. Check whether the attributes Valuation of samples in set S_x are the same. If the valuation attributes of samples in S_x are the same, this node should be marked as the leaves of the service decision tree. Conversely, if not all the valuation of samples is identical, turn to step 3.

Step 3. Check the attribute list. If the attribute list is empty, marking the major valuation attributes of the samples in S_x as the leaves of the service decision tree. Conversely, if the attribute list is not empty, turn to step 4.

Step 4. Find the most appropriate attribute Attribute$_x \in$ AttList$_x$ as the decision factor and divide the sample into different child nodes of N_x and remove Attribute$_x$ from AttList$_x$.

Step 5. Recur Step 1 with the child node $N_x^*(S_x^*,$ AttList$_x^*),$ S_x^* and AttList$_x^*$ are the sample set and attribute list in the node N_x^*.

4   Experiment

In the experiment, we have tested the fine-grained crowdsourcing model through data set collected from www.dianping.com. The data collects from 5000 customers and 100 service providers.

To show the recommendation process choosing the suitable service provider and improving the expect evaluation. In this experiment, Random Service Selection (RSS) and Convergent Population Diversity Handling Genetic Algorithm (CoDiGA) [5] are chosen to compare with Fine-grained Crowdsourcing Model (FCM). The experiment result shows in the Fig. 2.

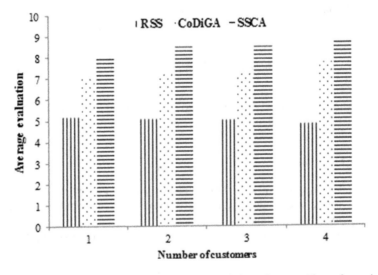

Fig. 2. Customers' average evaluation on recommended service providers after using RSS, CoDiGA and FCM in different sets of customers.

The recommendation effect of service decision tree should also be compared with recommendation index in the experiment. Hence, we choosing different numbers of service providers which have the highest prediction value gained from decision tree as the recommended service providers, in the meantime, choosing the same amount of service providers owns the highest recommendation index and choosing the same amount of service providers received the highest average valuation. The experiment result shows in the Fig. 3.

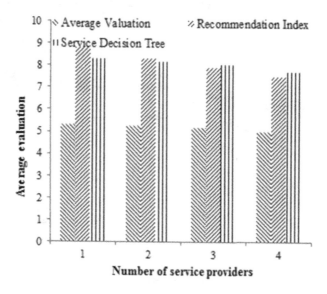

Fig. 3. The average scores valued by customers after accepting different number of recommended service providers through different recommendation methods.

In the fine-grained crowdsourcing model, different coefficient could lead to different results. The number of the customers, the number of the service providers and the number of clusters the server preparing to divide will impact the effectiveness of model. In order to affirm this model could be efficient in various environments. The experiment

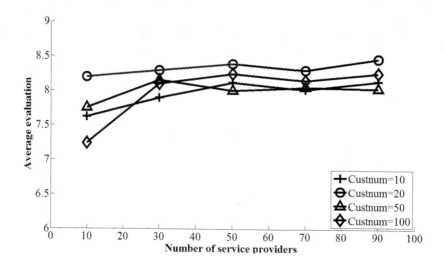

Fig. 4. The effect of model on different data scales (M = 2)

applies the fine-grained crowdsourcing model in different scales of customers and service providers, and gains the average valuation that customers score on the recommended service providers. The relationship between the scale of data and the average evaluation is showed in the Figs. 4 and 5.

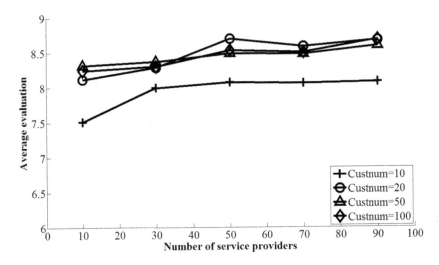

Fig. 5. The effect of model on different data scales (M = 5)

5   Conclusion

Taking the advantage of ontology theory and decision tree in the service recommendation could highly increase the customer satisfaction. The fine-grained crowdsourcing model discussed in this paper offering a good way to choose appropriate service providers.

In addition, we can find that if user needs a large amount of service provider, the service decision tree performs better, and if only a few service providers are needed, according to the recommendation index is a better choice. Both using service decision tree and recommendation index in the service recommendation could bring a perfect result to user.

Acknowledgments. This study was partly supported by NSFC under Grant (No.61502380, No. 61472316), Natural Science Basic Research Plan in Shaanxi Province of China (No.2014JQ8322), The Fundamental Research Funds for the Central Universities (No.XJJ2014049), and Shaanxi Science and Technology Innovation Project (2013SZS16-Z01/P01/K01), The Key projects of science and technology plan in Fujian province (No.2016H0029), Projects for Young Teacher in FuJian province (No.JA15401).

References

1. Doan, A., Ramakrishnan, R., Halevy, A.Y.: Crowdsourcing systems on the World-Wide Web. Commun. ACM **54**(4), 86–96 (2011)
2. Yang, W.S., Cheng, H.C., Dia, J.B.: A location-aware recommender system for mobile shopping environments. Expert Syst. Appl. **34**(1), 437–445 (2014)
3. Ye, F., Xiao, J.: Research on a data mining algorithm based on concept hierarchy tree and its application in CRM. In: Proceedings of the International Conference on Computer Supported Cooperative Work in Design, pp. 694–697 (2004)
4. Resnik, P.: Using information content to evaluate semantic similarity in a taxonomy. In: Proceedings of the International Conference on Artificial Intelligence, pp. 448–453 (2010)
5. Ma, Y., Zhang, C.W.: Quick convergence of genetic algorithm for QoS-driven web service selection. Comptu. Netw. **52**(5), 1093–1104 (2008)

QIM: Quantifying Hyperparameter Importance for Deep Learning

Dan Jia[1,2], Rui Wang[1], Chengzhong Xu[2], and Zhibin Yu[2(✉)]

[1] Beihang University, Beijing, China
[2] Shenzhen Institute of Advanced Technology, CAS, Shenzhen, China
zb.yu@siat.ac.cn

Abstract. Recently, Deep Learning (DL) has become super hot because it achieves breakthroughs in many areas such as image processing and face identification. The performance of DL models critically depend on hyperparameter settings. However, existing approaches that quantify the importance of these hyperparameters are time-consuming.

In this paper, we propose a fast approach to quantify the importance of the DL hyperparameters, called QIM. It leverages Plackett-Burman design to collect as few as possible data but can still correctly quantify the hyperparameter importance. We conducted experiments on the popular deep learning framework – Caffe – with different datasets to evaluate QIM. The results show that QIM can rank the importance of the DL hyperparameters correctly with very low cost.

Keywords: Deep learning · Plackett-burman design · Hyperparameter

1 Introduction

Deep learning (DL) is a sub-field of machine learning (ML) that focuses on extracting features from data through multiple layers of abstraction. While DL algorithms usually behave very differently with variant models such as deep belief networks [8], convolutional networks [13], and stacked denoising autoencoders [17], all of which have up to hundreds of hyperparameters which significantly affect the performance of DL algorithms.

Due to the inability for any one network to best generalize for all datasets, a necessary step before applying DL algorithm to a new dataset is to select an appropriate set of hyperparameters. To address this issue, a number of approaches are developed and the most popular three ones are (1) manual search, (2) grid search, and (3) random search [3]. These approaches have their respective advantages and disadvantages. However, how to optimize the hyperparameter settings for DL algorithms is still an open question.

There has been a recent surge of interest in more sophisticated hyperparameter optimization methods [1,3,9,15]. For example, [3] has applied Bayesian optimization techniques for designing convolutional vision architectures by learning

G.R. Gao et al. (Eds.): NPC 2016, LNCS 9966, pp. 180–188, 2016.
DOI: 10.1007/978-3-319-47099-3_15

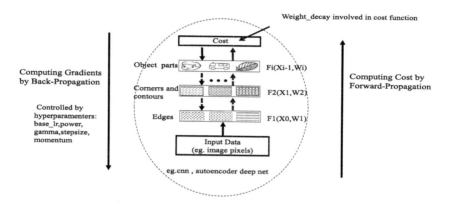

Fig. 1. Deep learning architecture

a probabilistic model over the hyperparameter search space. However, all these approaches have not provide scientists with answers to questions like the following: how important is each of the hyperparameters, and how do their values affect performance? The answer to such questions is the key to scientific discoveries. However, not much work has been done on quantifying the relative importance of the hyperparameters that does matter.

In this paper, we propose to quantify the importance of hyperparameters of DL using PB design [14], called QIM. To evaluate QIM, we employ Caffe [10] to implement the DL algorithm with the lenet [13] and auto-encoder [5] model. The results show that QIM is able to assess the importance of the five hyperparameters consistently with the assessments of ANOVA in both models. On the other hand, we demonstrate that QIM is 3× faster than ANOVA on average. In particular, we make the following contributions in this paper:

- We propose a PB design based approach to quantify the importance of hyperparameters of DL algorithms, called QIM.
- We leverage Cafe to implement two versions of the DL algorithm to evaluate QIM. The results show that QIM is able to correctly assess the importance of the hyperparameters of DL but is 3× faster than other approaches.

This paper is organized as follows. Section 2 describes the background of the DL and the PB design approach. Section 3 introduces our QIM. Section 4 describes the experimental setup for evaluating QIM. Section 5 presents the results and analysis. Section 6 describes the related work and Sect. 7 concludes the paper.

2 Background

2.1 Deep Learning (DL)

Generally, DL is a type of machine learning (ML) but is much more powerful than traditional ML. The great power of DL are obtained by learning to represent the world as a nested hierarchy of concepts, with each concept defined in

Table 1. The PB design matrix with 8 experiments.

Assembly	Parameters or factors						
	x1	x2	x3	x4	x5	x6	x7
1	+1	+1	+1	−1	+1	−1	−1
2	−1	+1	+1	+1	−1	+1	−1
3	−1	−1	+1	+1	+1	−1	+1
4	+1	−1	−1	+1	+1	+1	−1
5	−1	+1	−1	−1	+1	+1	+1
6	+1	−1	+1	−1	−1	+1	+1
7	+1	+1	−1	+1	−1	−1	+1
8	−1	−1	−1	−1	−1	−1	−1

relation to simpler concepts, as shown in Fig. 1. Each DL algorithm generally includes two sub-algorithms: *forward-propagation* and *back-propagation*. Most DL algorithms come with many hyperparameters that control many aspects of the learning algorithm behavior. Generally, properly setting the values of the hyperparameters is utter important but it is also difficult. The hyperparameters assessed in this paper include *learning rate, momentum, weight decay, gamma, power*, and *stepsize*.

Learning rate is a crucial hyperparameter for stochastic gradient descent(SGD) algorithm [2] which is used in the back-propagation algorithm. Momentum is designed to accelerate the learning process. Weight decay is designed to prevent the 'overfitting'. In other words, it governs the regularization term of the neural net which is added to the network's loss. The other hyperparameters, gamma, power, and stepsize are used to adjust the value of learning rate.

2.2   PB Design

The Plackett-Burman (PB) design [14] approach is one of the fractional factorial designs. PB design utilizes two values for each parameter: the high value is denoted as '+1' and the low value is denoted as '-1'. The '+1' and '-1' signs for the individual trial experiments are assigned in a cyclical manner. It involves $4k$ experiments, where $k = 1, 2, 3..., n$. In each case the maximum number of parameters that can be studied is $4k − 1$. For example, an 8-experiment PB design can study no more than 7 parameters.

We employ an example to describe how PB design works. Suppose that we want to quantify the parameter importance of a system with five parameters. The complete design is shown in Table 1. The importance of parameter x_1 is computed as:

$$m_1 = [r_1 + r_4 + r_6 + r_7 - r_2 - r_3 - r_5 - r_8] \tag{1}$$

where r_i is the performance measurement on experiment i. The importance of m_2, m_3, m_4, m_5 can be computed similarly.

Note that we want to quantify the importance of only 5 parameters but we construct a matrix with rows of 7 parameters; this is required by the PB design approach. However, we can use the quantities of the dummy parameters (m_6 and m_7) to represent experimental errors.

3   QIM

3.1   Overview

Figure 2 shows an overview of QIM. As can be seen, step 1 determines the value range of each hyperparameter by random search. The upper bound is used as the high value (+1) and the lower bound is used as the low value (-1) for each parameter. Step 2 employs the PB deign approach to quantify the importance of each hyperparameter of DL. This step contains several sub-steps which will be elaborated later. Step 3 validates whether the results obtained by QIM are correct or not. We use ANOVA in this paper because many studies use ANOVA as a golden reference. To demonstrate the efficacy of QIM, we employ two learning models: *lenet* and *auto-encoder*, each with two data sets: *CIFAR10* and *MNIST*. We form four types of experiments:*Lenet-cifar10, Lenet-mnist, Auto-cifar10* and *Auto-mnist*.

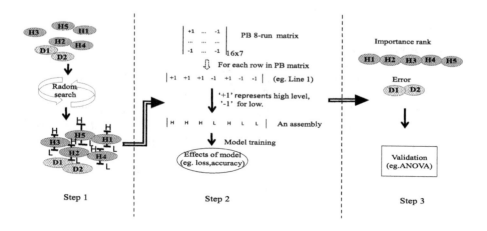

Fig. 2. Overview of QIM

3.2   Identifying the Value Range for Each Hyperparameter

In order to use QIM correctly, we need to know the value range of each hyperparameter for a certain DL algorithm. We propose a way named tentatively search(TS) to decide the value ranges of the hyperparameters. As shown in

Fig. 3, we iteratively decrease or increase the value of a parameter by a certain step-size while keep the values of all other parameters fixed and measure the performance. When we increase the value of the hyperparameter again and again until the gradient between the last two points achieves zero like CD shows, we choose the value of the hyperparameter corresponds to point C as the upper bound of the parameter. Another case is that DL algorithm fails to run successfully when we increase or decrease the value of the parameter further. It indicates that we already find the upper or lower bound of the hyperparameter in the previous try. In summary, we can find the bounds of the hyperparameters in either case.

3.3   QIM

We now turn to describe QIM in detail. We first describe the hyperparameters used in this study. The common hyperparameters used for all four types experiments include *base_lr*, *momentum*, *weight_decay* and *gamma*. The hyperparameter *power* is only used for *lenet-cifar10* and *lenet-mnist*, and *stepsize* only for *auto-cifar10* and *auto-mnist*. Since $4 \times 1 < 5 < 4 \times 2$, we use the $N = 8$ PB design as showed in Table 1 and we have two dummy parameters. To improve the confidence of QIM, we design 16-run trails instead of the 8-run one proposed by PB design. This is achieved by adding a mirroring line for each line in Table 1. For each type of experiment, we run 16 trails with different hyperparamenters settings corresponding to PB matrix. Then the importance of each hyperparameter is computed by using Eq. (1).

4   Experimental Setup

We conduct our experiments on two Intel 8-core Xeon(R) E5-2650, 2.60 GHz CPUs equipped with one Nvidia Tesla K20Xm GPU card. Caffe is used to implement the deep learning networks in our experiment. We use two versions of deep learning networks which are *Lenet* and *Auto-encoder*. The datasets used for these learning algorithms are *mnist* and *CIFAR10* respectively. The *mnist* [12] has 28×28 pixel grey-scale images of digits, each belonging to one of ten handwritten digit classes. The *CIFAR10* [11] consists of 60000 32×32 colour images in 10 classes, with 6000 images per class.

5   Evaluation

We first report the results with supervised learning and then with unsupervised learning algorithm.

5.1   Supervised Learning

The supervised learning algorithm used in this DL study is *lenet*. We feed lenet with data set CIFAR10 and MNIST respectively.

Results on CIFAR10 — Case 1. Figure 4 shows the importance obtained by QIM and ANOVA on CIFAR10. The importance rank given by QIM, from the most important to least important, is *base_lr*, *weight_decay*, *power*, *gamma* and *momentum*. On the other hand, ANOVA gives the similar rank except the

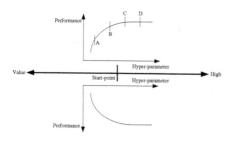

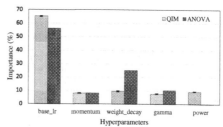

Fig. 3. Determining the value range of each hyperparameter.

Fig. 4. Comparison of hyperparameter importance evaluated by QIM and ANOVA with *lenet* on data set CIFAR10.

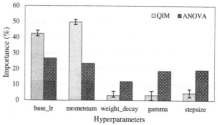

Fig. 5. Comparison of hyperparameter importance evaluated by QIM and ANOVA with *lenet* on data set MNIST.

Fig. 6. Comparison of hyperparameters importance evaluated by QIM and ANOVA with *Auto − encoder* on data set CIFAR10.

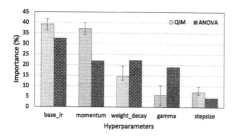

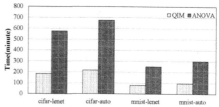

Fig. 7. Comparison of hyperparameter importance evaluated by QIM and ANOVA with Auto-encoder on data set MNIST.

Fig. 8. Comparison of time used by QIM and ANOVA to rank the hyperparameter importance.

importance of the hyperparameter power. In this experiment, QIM introduces an error of 10.52 %. This indicates that the importance rank obtained by QIM is generally correct and we can use it in practice. Moreover, we find the importance of *base_lr* is much higher than those of other hyperparameters, which implies that the *base_lr* dominates the performance of DL with *lenet* on CIFAR10 (Fig. 6).

Results on MNIST — Case 2. The task is to classify the images into 10 digit classes. Figure 5 compares the results of hyperparameter importance with QIM and ANOVA. As can be seen, both methods rank the *weight_decay* as the most important parameter and the *power* as the least important one. QIM treats the *base_lr* less important than ANOVA does while the two approaches give the similar importance for both *momentum* and *gamma*. In this experiment, QIM introduces an error of 5.12 %, which is smaller than the error obtained in the first case. This indicates that the the importance rank of the hyperparameters obtained by QIM is more convincible than the first case.

5.2 Unsupervised Pre-training

As a unsupervised pre-training model, deep auto-encoder [17] is trained on CIFAR10 and MNIST respectively.

Results on CIFAR10 — Case 3. QIM gives the top two importance to *base_lr* and *momentum*, which are consistent with the results of ANOVA. The error rate of QIM in this experiment is 5.4 %. For the less important hyperparameters such as *weight_decay, gamma, power, stepsize* assessed by ANOVA, QIM also gives the similar importance rank but with different absolute importance values. Comparing to the case 1,we find that the learning algorithm used in DL significantly affects the importance of its hyperparameters as well.

Results on MNIST — Case 4. QIM and ANOVA rank the same top three important hyperparameters including *base_lr, momentum,* and *weight_decay* as shown in Fig. 7. In this experiment, the error of QIM is 14.32 % which seems high. However, QIM assesses the importance of hyperparameters consistently with ANOVA but with less iterations.

5.3 Time Cost

Figure 8 compares the time used by QIM and ANOVA to rank the importance of hyperparameters of DL. As can be seen, the time used by QIM is 3× less than that used by ANOVA on average. As evaluated above, QIM can correctly rank the hyperparameter importance. This indicates that QIM is indeed a fast and efficient approach for quantifying the importance of hyperparameters.

6 Related Work

There are a lot of studies focusing on optimizing hyperparameters of DL algorithm [1,3,4,9]. In low-dimensional problems with numerical hyperparameters, the best available hyperparameter optimization methods use Bayesian optimization [6] based on Gaussian process models, whereas in high-dimensional and discrete spaces, tree-based models [4], and in particular random forests [9,16], are more successful [7]. Such modern hyperparameter optimization methods have achieved considerable recent success. For example, Bayesian optimization found a better instantiation of nine convolutional network hyperparameters than a domain expert, thereby achieving the lowest error reported on the CIFAR-10 benchmark at the time [15]. However, these studies do not quantify the importance of the hyperparameters while QIM does.

7 Conclusion

In this work, we propose an efficient PB design based approach to quantify the importance of the hyperparameters of DL algorithms named QIM. With 5–15 % of error, QIM can effectively assesses the importance of each hyperparameter with much smaller number of computation iterations. We empirically validate QIM with two deep models on two data sets. The results show that QIM can rank the importance of hyperparameters of DL algorithms correctly in four cases.

Acknowledgements. We thank the reviewers for their thoughtful comments and suggestions. This work is supported by national key research and development program under No.2016YFB1000204, the major scientific and technological project of Guangdong province (2014B010115003), Shenzhen Technology Research Project (JSGG20160510154636747), Shenzhen Peacock Project (KQCX20140521115045448), outstanding technical talent program of CAS, and NSFC under grant no U1401258.

References

1. Bardenet, R., Brendel, M., Kégl, B., Sebag, M.: Collaborative hyperparameter tuning. In: 30th International Conference on Machine Learning (ICML 2013), vol. 28, pp. 199–207. ACM Press (2013)
2. Bengio, Y., Goodfellow, I.J., Courville, A.: Deep learning. An MIT Press book in preparation (2015). Draft chapters available at http://www.iro.umontreal.ca/~bengioy/dlbook
3. Bergstra, J., Bengio, Y.: Random search for hyper-parameter optimization. J. Mach. Learn. Res. **13**(1), 281–305 (2012)
4. Bergstra, J.S., Bardenet, R., Bengio, Y., Kégl, B.: Algorithms for hyper-parameter optimization. In: Advances in Neural Information Processing Systems, pp. 2546–2554 (2011)
5. Bourlard, H., Kamp, Y.: Auto-association by multilayer perceptrons and singular value decomposition. Biol. Cybern. **59**(4–5), 291–294 (1988)

6. Brochu, E., Cora, V.M., De Freitas, N.: A tutorial on bayesian optimization of expensive cost functions, with application to active user modeling, hierarchical reinforcement learning. arXiv preprint arXiv:1012.2599 (2010)

7. Eggensperger, K., Feurer, M., Hutter, F., Bergstra, J., Snoek, J., Hoos, H., Leyton-Brown, K.: Towards an empirical foundation for assessing bayesian optimization of hyperparameters. In: NIPS Workshop on Bayesian Optimization in Theory and Practice (2013)

8. Hinton, G.E., Osindero, S., Teh, Y.-W.: A fast learning algorithm for deep belief nets. Neural Comput. **18**(7), 1527–1554 (2006)

9. Hutter, F., Hoos, H.H., Leyton-Brown, K.: Sequential model-based optimization for general algorithm configuration. In: Coello, C.A.C. (ed.) LION 2011. LNCS, vol. 6683, pp. 507–523. Springer, Heidelberg (2011). doi:10.1007/978-3-642-25566-3_40

10. Jia, Y., Shelhamer, E., Donahue, J., Karayev, S., Long, J., Girshick, R., Guadarrama, S., Darrell, T.: Caffe: convolutional architecture for fast feature embedding. In: Proceedings of the ACM International Conference on Multimedia, pp. 675–678. ACM (2014)

11. Krizhevsky, A., Hinton, G.: Learning multiple layers of features from tiny images (2009)

12. LeCun, Y., Boser, B., Denker, J.S., Henderson, D., Howard, R.E., Hubbard, W., Jackel, L.D.: Backpropagation applied to handwritten zip code recognition. Neural comput. **1**(4), 541–551 (1989)

13. LeCun, Y., Bottou, L., Bengio, Y., Haffner, P.: Gradient-based learning applied to document recognition. Proc. IEEE **86**(11), 2278–2324 (1998)

14. Plackett, R.L., Burman, J.P.: The design of optimum multifactorial experiments. Biometrika **33**(4), 305–325 (1946)

15. Snoek, J., Larochelle, H., Adams, R.P.: Practical bayesian optimization of machine learning algorithms. In: Advances in Neural Information Processing Systems, pp. 2951–2959 (2012)

16. Thornton, C., Hutter, F., Hoos, H.H., Leyton-Brown, K., Auto-weka: combined selection and hyperparameter optimization of classification algorithms. In: Proceedings of the 19th ACM SIGKDD International Conference on Knowledge Discovery and Data Mining, pp. 847–855. ACM (2013)

17. Vincent, P., Larochelle, H., Lajoie, I., Bengio, Y., Manzagol, P.-A.: Stacked denoising autoencoders: learning useful representations in a deep network with a local denoising criterion. J. Mach. Learn. Res. **11**, 3371–3408 (2010)

Algorithms and Computational Models

Toward a Parallel Turing Machine Model

Peng Qu[1](✉), Jin Yan[2], and Guang R. Gao[2]

[1] Tsinghua University, Haidian, Beijing, China
shen_yhx@163.com
[2] University of Delaware, Newark, DE 19716, USA

Abstract. In the field of parallel computing, the late leader Ken Kennedy, has raised a concern in early 1990s: "Is Parallel Computing Dead?" Now, we have witnessed the tremendous momentum of the "second spring" of parallel computing in recent years. But, what lesson should we learn from the history of parallel computing when we are walking out from the bottom state of the field?

To this end, this paper examines the disappointing state of the work in parallel Turing machine models in the past 50 years of parallel computing research. Lacking a solid yet intuitive parallel Turing machine model will continue to be a serious challenge. Our paper presents an attempt to address this challenge — by presenting a proposal of a parallel Turing machine model — the PTM model. We also discuss why we start our work in this paper from a parallel Turing machine model instead of other choices.

Keywords: Parallel Turing machine · Codelet · Abstract architecture · Parallel computing

1 Introduction and Motivation

Parallel computing is a type of computation in which many calculations are carried out simultaneously, operating on the principle that large problems can often be divided into multiple smaller ones such that teamwork by multiple processors can deliver the computational result sooner.

Historically, we have witnessed significant progress in parallel computing from 1960 s to 1980s. Notable advances in parallel computer architecture have been made ranging from the R&D on massive SIMD parallel computers [3] to the vector processing computers. However, in the early 1990s, the once bright looking future of the parallel and high-performance computing field had encountered serious challenge — so serious that had prompted a well known speech entitled

---

Peng Qu is pursuing his Ph.D. thesis study supervised by Prof. Youhui Zhang at Tsinghua University.

G.R. Gao et al. (Eds.): NPC 2016, LNCS 9966, pp. 191–204, 2016.
DOI: 10.1007/978-3-319-47099-3_16

"Is Parallel Computing Dead?" [30] given by late Ken Kennedy — an influential world leader of parallel computer field in 1994.

In the meantime, the world has witnessed the fantastically successful history of sequential computer systems based on so-called von Neumann model. The first von Neumann machine EDVAC [16] based on von Neumann architecture [39] was proposed in 1946 and soon found significant commercialization opportunities. Why does von Neumann architecture (the sequential computer architecture as it has been known) have such a robust history for over the past 60 plus years and continue to flourish in many ways into the new millennium? why does sequential approach continue more successfully than the parallel, given the advantages of the parallel approach?

One of such pillars is a robust sequential programming model whose foundation is based on the Turing machine model and the von Neumann architecture model that specifies an abstract machine architecture to efficiently support the Turing machine model. What should be the equivalent pillar to support parallel computation?

Unfortunately, there is no commonly accepted parallel Turing machine model and a corresponding parallel abstract architecture model for its realization. However, much good work on parallel models of computation exist, such as Leslie G. Valiant's work, proposing the Bulk Synchronous Parallelism (BSP) model as a bridging model of parallel computation between hardware and software [38], and David Culler's work on the LogP model as a practical model of parallel computation which focuses on performance characterization of parallel algorithms [6] — both served as significant milestones in the path searching for good models of parallel computation.

Most of the popular work on parallel models of computation have their basis on the concept of **threads**. Threads are a seemingly straightforward adaption of the dominate sequential model of computation in concurrent systems. However, as Ed. Lee stated in his paper "The Problem with Threads", "*they discard the most essential and appealing properties of sequential computation: understandability, predictability and determinism.*" [33]

Consequently, in this paper, we choose to begin our work from a Turing machine model — in a path that is not actively pursued in prior research of parallel models of computation. We believe that there is a need to clearly identify the two corner stones of a parallel Turing machine model: a parallel program execution model (PXM) and an abstract architecture model. The sound properties of parallel programs should be specified in a clean and simple program execution model (PXM), *which is not based on threads*, while the realization of PXM should be the role of the design of an efficient abstract architecture model — and there may well be more than one design choice.

A summary of main contributions of this paper is outlined as follows:

- A survey reveals a disappointing status of the field of parallel Turing machine model studies.
- A Parallel Turing machine (short named PTM) model is proposed. The formulation of the proposed PTM consists of two interrelated parts: (a) a parallel

program execution model; (b) an associated abstract architecture model serving as a guideline to individual physical machine implementations.

- We highlight how our PTM addresses some of the weaknesses of the existing parallel Turing machine models. The program execution model of our PTM is based on the concept of **codelets** (not **threads**), that preserve good properties, like determinacy, which are keys to the realization of modular (parallel) software construction principles by a parallel abstract architecture model.
- We conclude by presenting certain topics as future work on parallel Turing machine models.

The rest of this paper is organized as follows. In Sect. 2, we describe the existing parallel Turing machine model in detail and suggest possible areas for improvement. Section 3 presents our proposal: a parallel Turing machine model called PTM based on the concept of codelets and codelet graphs. A PTM consists of a codelet graph and a memory. The program of our PTM is represented by a codelet graph (CDG), and the corresponding abstract architecture model is called CAM (codelet abstract architecture). An example is included to illustrate how a parallel program is executed under our PTM. Section 4 briefly reviews related work. Section 5 gives the conclusion of our work and raises some open questions for future study.

2 Existing Work on Parallel Turing Machine — A Disappointing Status Report

2.1 Existing Parallel Turing Machine Proposals

In 1936, Alan Turing invented an idealized computing device [37], named Turing machine (TM). Dr. Turing's model for sequential program execution influenced the programming model of sequential computers. Hemmerling [24] first tried to propose a parallel computing Turing model in 1979. His model consists of a number of finite state machines working on a shared Turing tape.

Wiederman generalized Hemmerling's model [40] in an article published in 1984. Wiederman's parallel Turing machine has one infinite tape, as does a sequential Turing machine, but it may have multiple processing units (PUs), namely multiple read/write heads. Each processing unit, working in a similar fashion as a single sequential Turing machine, can read the input from the tape and write the output back to the tape independently. Figure 1a illustrates Wiederman's model.

The behavior of a "program", namely the corresponding FSM of a parallel Turing machine, is quite different from that of sequential Turing machine. Consider a state S of a FSM that has several successor states $\{S1, S2,...\}$ all corresponding to the same input. Under a sequential Turing machine, the transition from S will non-determistically select one of the states from the set $\{S1, S2,...\}$ to be next state and make a transition accordingly. Under Wiederman's Turing machine model, state S makes transitions to a set of states $\{S1,S2,...\}$ *simultaneously*, as shown in Fig. 1b.

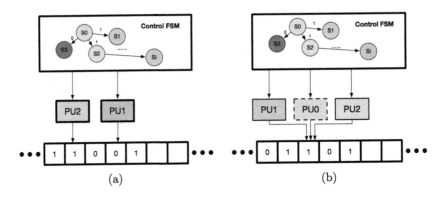

Fig. 1. (a) Wiederman's model: multiple processing units share a common tape; (b) Generating the new processing units: PU0 copies itself yielding PU1 and PU2, each with its own event in the shared FSM control. (Color figure online)

Wiederman's model starts with a single processing unit; as soon as the computation begins, when a running processing unit (PU) encounters any state with multiple succeeding states labelled with the same input, the FSM will begin to exploit the power of parallelism dynamically, i.e., the processing unit (PU) will produce copies of itself, so that there is one PU for each of the possible transitions, and carries out the operations.

Figure 1b and a illustrate this situation. In Fig. 1b, PU0 whose state is in $S0$ meets symbol '1'. Sharing the contol FSM, it provides for two processing units (PU1 and PU2) with events for state $S1$ and $S2$ respectively. After the multiplication, each of these processing units works as a separate Turing machine. However, all the new processing units in Wiederman's parallel Turing machine will still share the same FSM which is the same with the FSM before multiplying, as shown in Fig. 1a. The only difference between these PUs is that they are in different states of the FSM — the green PU1 is in state $S1$ and the brown PU2 is in state $S2$.

From our reading, in Wiederman's model, it appears to follow an assumption that all PUs run synchronously, which means they all finish a step in the same time. Thus additional wait states may be used to avoid serious conflicts (i.e., two memory operations happen concurrently and at least one of them is a write). However, if we allow the PUs to operate asynchronously, serious conflict, such as reordering writes to be after VS. before reads, may occur.

2.2 The Disappointing Status on Parallel Turing Machine Studies

There is little published work on parallel Turing machine. The few parallel Turing machine proposals we are aware of still use tapes as the model of storage in the corresponding architecture description. There seems to be little enthusiasm for or interest in searching for a commonly accepted parallel Turing machine model and corresponding abstract architecture model in the field of parallel computing. This is true even during the past 10+ years of the second spring of parallel computing.

Forty years have passed since Hemmerling's attempt to propose a parallel Turing machine model in 1979. In Computer Science, the field of *concurrency* — which covers both parallel computing and distributed computing — has advanced significantly since its infancy in 1960s and early 70s [31]. With the experience and lessons of the serious down turn of parallel computing in the 1990s, we also learned the importance of developing a standard, robust interface between software and hardware as a basis of machine independent parallel programming.

Today, any serious attempts on parallel Turing machine must have a solid model of memory beyond Turing's tape storage. As described in previous section on Wiederman's model, after the multiplication, those replicated processing units will operate in parallel but they still work on the same tape. So they will communicate with each other by reading and writing a shared memory location. However, concurrent access of the shared memory location may cause a *conflict*. The resolution of such memory conflicts must deal with the so-called memory consistency model of the underlied architecture model — a field pioneered by Leslie Lamport in 1978 [31] — at about the same time as the first parallel Turing machine work by Hemmerling was published.

3   A Parallel Turing Machine Model — Our Proposal

Like we have mentioned earlier, we choose to start our work on a parallel Turing machine model, instead of following the research of parallel models of computation. Section 3.1 gives a definition and description of concepts of codelets and codelet graphs. Section 3.2 demonstrates our proposed PTM, consisting of a PXM and an abstract architecture, while Sect. 3.3 shows an example of how the PTM works. Finally, in Sect. 3.4, we have a short discussion of determinacy property of our proposed PTM.

3.1   The Concept of Codelets and Codelet Graphs (CDGs)

Codelets. A codelet is a unit of computation that can be scheduled *atomically* for execution and it is the *principal scheduling quantum* (PSU) in codelet based execution model. A codelet may be made up of a group of (many) machine level instructions and organized with various control structures including loops. Once become **enabled** (i.e. ready to be scheduled for execution), a codelet may be scheduled to an **execution unit** (or EU) and be executed *non-preemptively* as an atomic PSU — keeping the EU usefully busy until its termination. The effectiveness of the non-preemptive model has been demonstrated through the mapping of a number of applications onto a many-core chip architecture with 160 cores [22].

Codelet Graphs. A program can be organized by a composition of multiple codelets into a graph called a **codelet graph**. A CDG is a directed graph $G(V, E)$, where V is a set of nodes and E is a set of directed arcs. In a CDG, nodes in V may be connected by arcs in E. Every node in G denotes a codelet. An arc (V_1, V_2) in the CDG is a representation of a precedence relation between nodes V_1 and V_2. Such a relation may be due to a data dependence between codelet V_1 and V_2.

The concept of a codelet graph (CDG) has its origin in *dataflow graphs* [13]. In particular, it leverages the dataflow program graphs proposed in the McGill Dataflow Architecture Model [17]. Consequently, a unique feature of CDGs is that they employ the *"argument–fetching"* dataflow model proposed by Dennis and Gao [10, 19].

Firing Rules. The execution model of a codelet graph is specified by its operational semantics — called **firing rules**: A codelet that has received all the required events[1] — "signal tokens" on the corresponding input arcs of the codelet — will become *enabled*. Any enabled codelet can be scheduled for execution (or called "firing", a term used in dataflow models of computation). Firing of an enabled codelet will consume all the input events (remove the signal tokens), perform the *computation* as specified by the codelet and produce results, and generate output events.

3.2   The Parallel Turing Machine Model

Program execution model (PXM) of the PTM. In our model, a PTM consists of a codelet graph (CDG) and a *memory*. The CDG can execute a program, which has been described in Sect. 3.1. It serves as the function of a "program" just like the finite state machine (FSM) in sequential Turing machine. A memory consists of a set of locations. The content of each location is addressable by an addressing mechanism, and manipulated through a set of memory operations like load and store operations. For the purpose of this paper, the memory can be considered organized and operated as a RAM (random access memory). The memory organization itself is left to be defined by a specific abstract architecture model and will be discussed later. A *state* of a PTM consists of the state of the CDG and memory. At a particular time, a state of a CDG is its configuration at that time, while the state of memory is the content of the memory at that time. A configuration of CDG is the assignment of events on the arcs of the CDG. An initial state of the PTM is the initial configuraton of the CDG and the initial contents of the memory. The computation of a PTM is carried out by the *state transitions* defined as follows.

Assume the CDG is currently at a particular state. Based on the current configuration, there may be a set of codelets which are *enabled* (or in enable

---

[1] The term *token*, is from a familiar terminology of dataflow literature. In the rest of this paper, we use the term *events* to denote signal tokens (or event tokens) present on certain arcs.

state) and a subset of which is selected to fire. Firing of an enabled codelet consists of the following three steps: firstly, it consumes all the input events; then the processing unit will read the input data from memory, perform the computation as specified by the codelet; finally, it stores results into memory, and generates output events. When the computation (firing) of the codelet is completed, some new events will be produced, and placed on its corresponding output arcs according to the specific firing rule of it. Also, upon completion, the memory state will be updated. Upon the completion of the firing of all selected codelets, a new state of the PTM is reached — consisting of a new configuration and a new memory state. This will complete the state transition process.

An abstract architecture model of the PTM. Now, we present the abstract architecture model of our proposed PTM which we named as CAM — i.e., *codelet abstract machine*, as shown in Fig. 2.

A CAM consists of (1) a collection of codelet processing units (CPUs) and memory units (MUs), (2) a collection of codelet scheduling units (CSUs), (3) a hierarchy of interconnection network (HIN). The CPUs and MUs can be grouped together by connecting through the HIN and form nodes of the CAM. A number of nodes can be connected into a cluster through the HIN. These clusters can be further connected and organized into higher-level hierarchy such as a hierarchy of trees, meshes, etc. The MUs in CAM are organized to share a single shared address space. Consequently, the design decision on the memory consistency model is critical. Our PTM and its CAM will follow a specific memory consistency model.

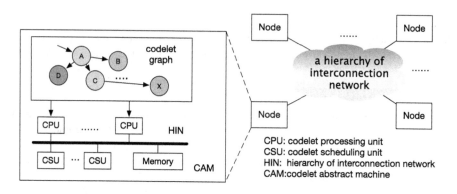

Fig. 2. CAM: codelet abstract machine

However, the details of the memory consistency model (MCM) and the structure of clusters connected by HIN are left as a design decision for any particular physical architecture that realizes the CAM. That is, we assume any physical architecture that implements the CAM will make the choice of a specific MCM and cluster structure that best apply to the underlying programming environment, hardware technology and other trade-offs so that a physical architecture and related machines may be built. Note that our CAM follows the stored-program principle as described by John von Neumann in the description of the EDVAC machine [39]. However, our CAM design may eliminate one-word-at-a-time between CPU and memory by permitting multiple data words be communicated concurrently between memory (made of multiple memory units) and CPUs.

3.3   An Example to Illustrate How the PTM Works

In Fig. 3 we illustrate a simple but informative CDG example of the proposed Parallel Turing machine. This "program" will first invert the tape contents and then change all the contents to '0'. If there are many execution units to do the work, which means each processing unit does the invert operation or changes the symbol to '0' at a specific memory location, the total excution time should be much less.

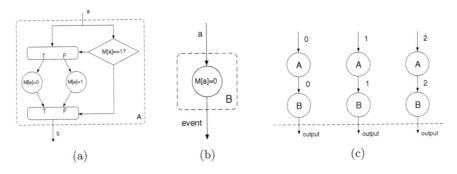

(a)   (b)   (c)

Fig. 3. A CDG example. (a) Codelet A: inverting the content of memory location a. (b) Codelet B: changing the content of memory location b to 0 (c) A non-conflict CDG

Codelet A (Fig. 3a) is a compound codelet which does the invert operation. It is defined as a conditional schema consisting of a decider, two codelets and a conditional merge. Codelet A is enabled once the input event (a) is available on the input arc. When fired, it will invert the content of memory location a. Also, an output event will be generated. Codelet B (Fig. 3b) is a simple codelet. It is enabled whenever the input event (a) arrives. When fired, it changes the content of memory location a to '0' and generates the output event.

Figure 3c illustrates a non-conflict CDG, which does exactly what we need and exploits as much parallelism as is presented in the problem to be solved. The three codelet As in Fig. 3c are first enabled by inputs and their outputs will carry the value of memory locations to be accessed and enable three codelet Bs. The numbers 0, 1 and 2 on codelet As' input arcs, act as the values of memory locations to be accessed. It means that when the input events arrive, the left codelet A, the middle codelet A and the right codelet A will invert the content of memory location 0, 1, 2 separately. So the contents of all the involved memory locations will be first inverted and then changed to '0'.

Figure 4 gives a detailed description about how the CDG is executed. A CDG could be executed on a CAM with arbitrary number of CPUs. Take Fig. 4 as an example. If there are more than three CPUs, three codelet As could be executed by any three of them. If there are fewer than three CPUs, the parallelism can not be fully exploited, only some of the enabled codelets (usually the same number as there are idle CPUs) are chosen by the CSUs and are executed first, then the CSUs continuously choose enabled codelets to execute until there are no more enabled codelets. Without losing generalization, we use a CAM with three CPUs to explain how this CDG is executed.

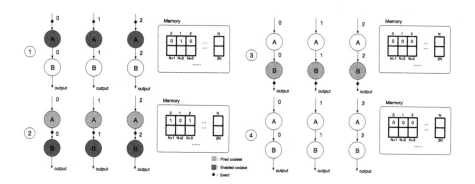

Fig. 4. The execution steps of non–conflict example

Figure 4 describes the detailed execution steps of the non-conflict CDG:

1. Step 1, the input events reach the corresponding input arcs of codelet As, thus all the codelet As are enabled.
2. Step 2, as there are three CPUs, the same number with enabled codelets, all these enabled codelet As are fired. They consume all the input events, invert the content of memory locations 0, 1 and 2, and then generate output events respectively. These output events further reach codelet Bs' input arcs, thus all three codelet Bs are enabled.
3. Step 3, all the enabled codelet Bs are fired. They consume all the input events, change the content of memory locations 0, 1 and 2 to '0' and then generate output events respectively.
4. Step 4, all those enabled codelets are fired and no more enabled codelets left, now the computation is finished.

If there are enough units (say, six), we can change the CDG to let all these six codelets enabled at the same time to achieve significant speedup. Although this may cause conflicts when several codelets which have data dependence are scheduled at the same time, we could use a weak memory consistency model to avoid it.

From the previous examples, we can see that our proposed PTM has advantages over Wiederman's model: using event-driven CDG, we can illustrate a parallel algorithm more explicitly. What's more, since necessary data dependence is explicitly satisfied by the "events", our PTM could execute a CDG correctly regardless of the number of CPUs or whether they are synchronous or not. Meanwhile, using memory model to replace Turing tape, as well as CAM instead of read/write head, we make it more suitable to realize our PTM in modern parallel hardware design. Thus, we still leave enough design space for system architecture and physical architecture design. For example, we don't limit the design choices of the detailed memory consistency model and cluster structure, because these design choices may differ according to the specific application or hardware.

3.4   Determinacy Property of Our Proposed PTM

Jack Dennis has proposed a set of principles for modular software construction and described a parallel program execution model based on functional programming that satisfied these principles [9]. The target architecture — the Fresh Breeze architecture [12] — will ensure a correct and efficient realization of the program execution model.

Several principles of modular software construction, like Information-Hiding, Invariant Behavior, Secure Argument and Recursive Construction principle are associated with the concept of determinacy [14]. Consequently, the execution model of our proposed PTM laid the foundation to construct well-behaved codelet graphs which preserve the determinacy property. A more detailed discussion of the well-behaved property and how to derive a well-behaved codelet graph (CDG) from a set of well-structured construction rules have been outlined in [21], where the property of determinacy for such a CDG is also discussed.

4   Related Work

4.1   Parallel Turing Machine

There seems to be little enthusiasm for or interest in searching for a commonly accepted parallel Turing machine model. This is true even during the past 10+ years of the second spring of parallel computing.

In Sect. 2, we have already introduced the early work on parallel Turing machine models proposed by Hemmerling and Wiederman. Wiederman showed that his parallel Turing machine was neither in the "first" machine class [2], which is polynomial-time and linear-space equivalent to a sequential Turing machine, nor in the "second" machine class, which cannot be simulated by STM in polynomial time.

Since the publication of early work on parallel Turing machine models, some researchers have investigated different versions of these parallel Turing machine models. Ito [28] and Okinakaz [36] analyzed two and three-dimensional parallel Turing machine models. Ito [29] also proposed a four-dimensional parallel Turing machine model and analyzed its properties. However, these works focused on extending the dimension of parallel Turing machine model of Wiederman's work, but ignore its inherent weaknesses outlined at the end of Sect. 2.

4.2   Memory Consistency Models

The most commonly used memory consistency model is Leslie Lamport's sequential consistency (SC) model proposed in 1978 [31]. Since then, numerous work have been conducted in the past several decades trying to improve SC model — in particular to overcome its limitation in exploitation of parallelism. Several weak memory consistency models have been introduced, including weak consistency (WC, also called weak ordering or WO) [15] and release consistency (RC) [23] models.

Existing memory models and cache consistency protocols assume *memory coherence* property which requires that all processors observe the same order of write operations to the same location [23]. Gao and Sarkar have proposed a new memory model which does not rely on the memory coherence assumption, called Location Consistency (LC) [20]. They also described a new multiprocessor cache consistency protocol based on the LC memory model. The performance potential of LC-based cache protocols has been demonstrated through software-controlled cache implementation on some real world parallel architectures [5].

4.3   The Codelet Model

The codelet execution model [21] is a hybrid model that incorporates the advantages of macro-dataflow [18,27] and von Neumann model. The codelet execution model can be used to describe programs in massive parallel systems, including hierarchical or heterogeneous systems.

The work on codelet based program execution models has its root in early work of dataflow models at MIT [8] and elsewhere in 1960–70s. It was inspired by the MIT dynamic dataflow projects based on the tagged-token dataflow model [1] and the MIT CILK project [4] of Prof. Leiserson and his group. The codelet execution model extends traditional macro-dataflow models by adapting the "argument-fetching" dataflow model of Dennis and Gao [10]. The term "codelet" was chosen by Gao and his associates to describe the concepts presented earlier in Sect. 3.1. It derives from the concept of "fiber" proposed in early 1990s in EARTH project [26] which has been influenced strongly by the MIT Static Dataflow Architecture model [11]. As a result, we can employ a popular RISC architecture as a codelet execution unit (PU) [25].

The terminology of codelet under the context of this paper was first suggested by Gao, and appeared in a sequence of project notes in 2009–2010, that finally appeared in [21]. It has been adopted by a number of researchers and practitioners in the parallel computing field. For example, the work at MIT led by Jack Dennis — the Fresh Breeze project, the DART project at university of Delaware [21], and the SWift Adaptive Runtime Machine (SWARM) under the DOE Dynax project led by ETI [32]. The DOE Exascale TG Project led by Intel has been conducting research in OCR (Open Community Runtime) which is led by Rice University [34]. And the relation between OCR and the above codelet concept can be analysed from [43]. What also notable to this community is the recent R&D work pursued at DOE PNNL that has generated novel and promising results.

4.4 Work on Parallel Computation Models

In Sect. 1, we already include a discussion of related work on parallel computation models. For space reasons, we will not discuss these works further. However, we still wish to point out some seminal work following modular software engineering principles — Niklaus Wirth's programming language work of Pascal [41] and Modula [42], John McCarthy's work on LISP [35], and Jack Dennis's work of programming generality [7].

5   Conclusion and Future Work

This paper has outlined our proposal of a parallel Turing machine model called PTM. We hope that our work may encourage similar activities in studying parallel Turing machine model. We look forward to seeing significant impact of such studies which will eventually contribute to the success of parallel computing.

We suggest the following topics as future work. A simulator of our proposed PTM should be useful to show how the program execution model and the corresponding abstract architecture work. Two attributes of our PTM may by demonstrated through the simulation — practicability and generality. Since our PTM tries to establish a different model from the previous work, we will show how parallel computation can be effectively and productively represented, programed and efficiently computed under our PTM. Meanwhile, through simulation, we should be able to implement and evaluate extensions and revisions of our PTM. It may also provide a platform to evaluate other alternatives for abstract parallel architecture, such as those that utilize different memory models, or even an implementation that incorporates both shared memory and distributed memory models in the target parallel system.

Acknowledgements. The authors wish to show their profound gratitude to Prof. Jack B. Dennis at MIT whose pioneer work in computer systems and dataflow have greatly inspired this work. We are grateful to his selfless teaching to his students that served as a source of constant and profound inspiration. We also acknowledge support from University of Delaware and Tsinghua University which provided a wonderful environment for collaboration that led to the successful completion of this paper.

References

1. Arvind, K., Nikhil, R.S.: Executing a program on the MIT tagged-token dataflow architecture. IEEE Trans. Comput. **39**(3), 300–318 (1990)
2. van Boas, P.E.: Machine models and simulations. Handb. Theor. Comput. Sci. **A**, 1–66 (2014)
3. Bouknight, W.J., Denenberg, S.A., McIntyre, D.E., et al.: The Illiac IV system. Proc. IEEE **60**(4), 369–388 (1972)
4. Blumofe, R.D., Joerg, C.F., Kuszmaul, B.C., et al.: Cilk: an efficient multithreaded runtime system. J. Parallel Distrib. Comput. **37**(1), 55–69 (1996)

5. Chen, C., Manzano, J.B., Gan, G., Gao, G.R., Sarkar, V.: A study of a software cache implementation of the OpenMP memory model for multicore and many-core architectures. In: D'Ambra, P., Guarracino, M., Talia, D. (eds.) Euro-Par 2010. LNCS, vol. 6272, pp. 341–352. Springer, Heidelberg (2010). doi:10.1007/978-3-642-15291-7_31

6. Culler, D.E., Karp, R.M., Patterson, D., et al.: LogP: a practical model of parallel computation. Commun. ACM **39**(11), 78–85 (1996)

7. Dennis, J.B.: Programming generality, parallelism and computer architecture. Inf. Process. **68**, 484–492 (1969)

8. Dennis, J.B.: First version of a data flow procedure language. In: Robinet, B. (ed.) Programming Symposium. LNCS, vol. 19, pp. 362–376. Springer, Heidelberg (1974). doi:10.1007/3-540-06859-7_145

9. Dennis, J.B.: A parallel program execution model supporting modular software construction. In: Proceedings of the 1997 Working Conference on Massively Parallel Programming Models, MPPM 1997, pp. 50–60. IEEE, Los Alamitos (1997)

10. Dennis, J.B., Gao, G.R.: An efficient pipelined dataflow processor architecture. In: Proceedings of the 1988 ACM/IEEE Conference on Supercomputing, SC 1988, pp. 368–373. IEEE Computer Society Press, Florida (1988)

11. Dennis, J.B., Misunas, D.P.: A preliminary architecture for a basic data-flow computer. In: Proceedings of the 2nd Annual Symposium on Computer Architecture, pp. 126–132. IEEE Press, New York (1975)

12. Dennis, J.B.: Fresh breeze: a multiprocessor chip architecture guided by modular programming principles. ACM SIGARCH Comput. Archit. News **31**(1), 7–15 (2003)

13. Dennis, J.B., Fosseen, J.B., Linderman, J.P.: Data flow schemas. In: Ershov, A., Nepomniaschy, V.A. (eds.) International Symposium on Theoretical Programming. LNCS, vol. 5, pp. 187–216. Springer, Heidelberg (1974). doi:10.1007/3-540-06720-5_15

14. Dennis, J.B., Van Horn, E.C.: Programming semantics for multiprogrammed computations. Commun. ACM **9**(3), 143–155 (1966)

15. Dubois, M., Scheurich, C., Briggs, F.: Memory access buffering in multiprocessors. ACM SIGARCH Comput. Architect. News **14**(2), 434–442 (1986)

16. Eckert Jr., J.P., Mauchly, J.W.: Automatic high-speed computing: a progress report on the EDVAC. Report of Work under Contract No. W-670-ORD-4926, Supplement (1945)

17. Gao, G.R.: An efficient hybrid dataflow architecture model. J. Parallel Distrib. Comput. **19**(4), 293–307 (1993)

18. Gao, G.R., Hum, H.H.J., Monti, J.-M.: Towards an efficient hybrid dataflow architecture model. In: Aarts, E.H.L., Leeuwen, J., Rem, M. (eds.) PARLE 1991. LNCS, vol. 505, pp. 355–371. Springer, Heidelberg (1991). doi:10.1007/BFb0035115

19. Gao, G.R., Tio, R., Hum, H.H.: Design of an efficient dataflow architecture without data flow. In: Proceedings of the International Conference on Fifth Generation Computer Systems, FGCS 1988 (1988)

20. Gao, G.R., Sarkar, V.: Location consistency – a new memory model and cache consistency protocol. IEEE Trans. Comput. **49**(8), 798–813 (2000)

21. Gao, G.R., Suetterlein, J., Zuckerman, S.: Toward an execution model for extreme-scale systems-runnemede and beyond. CAPSL Technical Memo 104 (2011)

22. Garcia, E., Orozco, D., Gao, G.R.: Energy efficient tiling on a many-core architecture. In: Proceedings of 4th Workshop on Programmability Issues for Heterogeneous Multicores, MULTIPROG 2011; 6th International Conference on High-Performance and Embedded Architectures and Compilers, HiPEAC 2011, pp. 53–66, Heraklion (2011)

23. Gharachorloo, K., Lenoski, D., Laudon, J., et al.: Memory consistency and event ordering in scalable shared-memory multiprocessors. In: Proceedings of the 25th International Symposium on Computer Architecture, ISCA 1998, pp. 376–387. ACM, Barcelona (1998)

24. Hemmerling, A.: Systeme von Turing-Automaten und Zellularräume auf rahmbaren pseudomustermengen. Elektronische Informationsverarbeitung und Kybernetik **15**(1/2), 47–72 (1979)

25. Hennessy, J.L., Patterson, D.A.: Computer Architecture: A Quantitative Approach. Morgan Kaufmann Publishers, San Francisco (2011)

26. Humy, H.H., Maquelin, O., Theobald, K.B., et al.: A design study of the EARTH multiprocessor. In: Proceedings of the International Conference on Parallel Architectures and Compilation Techniques, PACT 1995, pp. 59–68, Limassol (1995)

27. Iannucci, R.A.: Toward a dataflow/von Neumann hybrid architecture. ACM SIGARCH Comput. Architect. News **16**(2), 131–140 (1988)

28. Ito, T.: Synchronized alternation and parallelism for three-dimensional automata. Ph.D. thesis. University of Miyazaki (2008)

29. Ito, T., Sakamoto, M., Taniue, A., et al.: Parallel Turing machines on four-dimensional input tapes. Artif. Life Rob. **15**(2), 212–215 (2010)

30. Kennedy, K.: Is parallel computing dead? http://www.crpc.rice.edu/newsletters/oct94/director.html

31. Lamport, L.: Time, clocks, and the ordering of events in a distributed system. Commun. ACM **21**(7), 558–565 (1978)

32. Lauderdale, C., Khan, R.: Position paper: towards a codelet-based runtime for exascale computing. In: Proceedings of the 2nd International Workshop on Adaptive Self-Tuning Computing Systems for the Exaflop Era, EXADAPT 2012, pp. 21–26. ACM, London (2012)

33. Lee, E.: The problem with threads. Computer **39**(5), 33–42 (2006)

34. Mattson, T., Cledat, R., Budimlic, Z., et al.: OCR: the open community runtime interface version 1.1.0 (2015)

35. McCarthy, J.: LISP 1.5 programmer's manual (1965)

36. Okinaka, K., Inoue, K., Ito, A.: A note on hardware-bounded parallel Turing machines. In: Proceedings of the 2nd International Conference on Information, pp. 90–100, Beijing (2002)

37. Turing, A.: On computable numbers, with an application to the Entscheidungsproblem. In: Proceedings of the London Mathematical Society, pp. 230–265, London (1936)

38. Valiant, L.G.: A bridging model for parallel computation. Commun. ACM **33**(8), 103–111 (1990)

39. Von Neumann, J., Godfrey, M.D.: First draft of a report on the EDVAC. IEEE Ann. Hist. Comput. **15**(4), 27–75 (1993)

40. Wiedermann, J.: Parallel Turing machines. Research Report (1984)

41. Wirth, N.: The programming language Pascal. Acta Informatica **1**(1), 35–63 (1971)

42. Wirth, N.: Modula: a language for modular multiprogramming. Softw. Pract. Experience **7**(1), 3–35 (1977)

43. Zuckerman, S., Suetterlein, J., Knauerhase, R., et al.: Using a codelet program execution model for exascale machines: position paper. In: Proceedings of the 1st International Workshop on Adaptive Self-Tuning Computing Systems for the Exaflop Era, EXADAPT 2011, pp. 64–69. ACM, San Jose (2011)

On Determination of Balance Ratio
for Some Tree Structures

Daxin Zhu[1], Tinran Wang[3], and Xiaodong Wang[2($\boxtimes$)]

[1] Quanzhou Normal University, Quanzhou 362000, China
[2] Fujian University of Technology, Fuzhou 350108, China
wangxd135@139.com
[3] School of Mathematical Science, Peking University, Beijing 100871, China

Abstract. In this paper, we studies the problem to find the maximal number of red nodes of a kind of balanced binary search tree. We have presented a dynamic programming formula for computing $r(n)$, the maximal number of red nodes of a red-black tree with n keys. The first dynamic programming algorithm uses $O(n^2 \log n)$ time and uses $O(n \log n)$ space. The basic algorithm is then improved to a more efficient $O(n)$ time algorithm. The time complexity of the new algorithm is finally reduced to $O(n)$ and the space is reduced to only $O(\log n)$.

1   Introduction

This paper studies the worst case balance ratio of the red-black tree structure. A red-black tree is a kind of self-balancing binary search tree. Each node of the binary tree has an extra bit, and that bit is often interpreted as the color (red or black) of the node. These color bits are used to ensure the tree remains approximately balanced during insertions and deletions. The data structure was originally presented by Rudolf Bayer in 1972 with its name 'symmetric binary B-tree' [2]. Guibas and Sedgewick named the data structure red-black tree in 1978, [4]. They introduced the red/black color convention and the properties of a red-black tree at length. A simpler-to-code variant of red-black trees was presented in [1,5]. This variant of red-black trees was called the variant AA-trees [8]. The left-leaning red-black tree [6] was introduced in 2008 by Sedgewick. It is a new version of red-black tree which eliminated a previously unspecified degree of freedom. Either 2–3 trees or 2–4 trees can also be made isometric to red-black trees for any sequence of operations [6].

2   The Basic Properties and Algorithms

A red-black tree of n keys is denoted by T in this paper. In a red-black tree T of n keys, $r(n)$ and $s(n)$, are defined as the maximal and the minimal number of red internal nodes respectively. It is readily seen that in this case of $n = 2^k - 1$, the number of red nodes of T achieves its maximum, if the node from the bottom

© IFIP International Federation for Information Processing 2016
Published by Springer International Publishing AG 2016. All Rights Reserved
G.R. Gao et al. (Eds.): NPC 2016, LNCS 9966, pp. 205–212, 2016.
DOI: 10.1007/978-3-319-47099-3_17

to the top are colored alternately red and black. the number of red nodes of T achieves its minimum, if the node from the bottom to the top are all colored black.

In the special case of $n = 2^k - 1$, we can conclude,

$$r(n) = r(2^k - 1) = \sum_{i=0}^{\lfloor (k-1)/2 \rfloor} 2^{k-2i-1}$$

$$= 2^{k-1} \sum_{i=0}^{\lfloor (k-1)/2 \rfloor} \frac{1}{4^i}$$

$$= \frac{2^{k-1}}{3} \left(4 - \frac{1}{4^{\lfloor (k-1)/2 \rfloor}} \right)$$

$$= \frac{2^{k+1} - 2^{k-1-2\lfloor (k-1)/2 \rfloor}}{3}$$

$$= \frac{2^{k+1} - 2^{(k-1) \bmod 2}}{3}$$

$$= \frac{2^{k+1} - 2 + k \bmod 2}{3}$$

$$= \frac{2(2^k - 1) + k \bmod 2}{3}$$

$$= \frac{2n + \log(n+1) \bmod 2}{3}$$

The number of black nodes $b(n)$ can then be,

$$b(n) = n - r(n)$$

$$= n - \frac{2n + \log(n+1) \bmod 2}{3}$$

$$= \frac{n - \log(n+1) \bmod 2}{3}$$

Therefore, in this case, the ratio of red nodes to black nodes is,

$$r(n)/b(n) = \frac{2n + \log(n+1) \bmod 2}{n - \log(n+1) \bmod 2}$$

In the general cases, the maximal number of red nodes of a red-black tree with n keys can be denoted by $\gamma(n, 0)$ if root is red, and by $\gamma(n, 1)$ if root is black. We then have,

$$r(n) = \max\{\gamma(n, 0), \gamma(n, 1)\}.$$

It can be proved by induction further that $\gamma(n, 0) \leq \frac{2n+1}{3}$ and $\gamma(n, 1) \leq \frac{2n}{3}$. Therefore,

$$r(n) \leq \max \left\{ \frac{2n+1}{3}, \frac{2n}{3} \right\} = \frac{2n+1}{3}$$

Thus, for $n \geq 7$, we have

$$0 \leq \frac{r(n)}{n - r(n)} \leq \frac{\frac{2n+1}{3}}{n - \frac{2n+1}{3}} = \frac{2n + 1}{n - 1} \leq 2.5$$

In the general cases, the maximal number of red nodes of a subtree of black-height j and size i can be denoted by $a(i, j, 0)$ if root is red and by $a(i, j, 1)$ if root is black. It follows from $\frac{1}{2} \log n \leq j \leq 2 \log n$ that

$$\gamma(n, k) = \max_{\frac{1}{2} \log n \leq j \leq 2 \log n} a(n, j, k) \tag{1}$$

Furthermore, we can denote for any $1 \leq i \leq n, \frac{1}{2} \log i \leq j \leq 2 \log i$ that

$$\begin{cases} \alpha_1(i, j) = \max_{0 \leq t \leq i/2} \{a(t, j, 1) + a(i - t - 1, j, 1)\} \\ \alpha_2(i, j) = \max_{0 \leq t \leq i/2} \{a(t, j, 0) + a(i - t - 1, j, 0)\} \\ \alpha_3(i, j) = \max_{0 \leq t \leq i/2} \{a(t, j, 1) + a(i - t - 1, j, 0)\} \\ \alpha_4(i, j) = \max_{0 \leq t \leq i/2} \{a(t, j, 0) + a(i - t - 1, j, 1)\} \end{cases} \tag{2}$$

Theorem 1. $a(i, j, 0)$ and $a(i, j, 1)$ can be formulated for each $1 \leq i \leq n, \frac{1}{2} \log(i + 1) \leq j \leq 2 \log(i + 1)$, as follows.

$$\begin{cases} a(i, j, 0) = 1 + \alpha_1(i, j) \\ a(i, j, 1) = \max\{\alpha_1(i, j - 1), \alpha_2(i, j - 1), \alpha_3(i, j - 1)\} \end{cases} \tag{3}$$

Proof. Let i, j be two indices such that $1 \leq i \leq n, \frac{1}{2} \log(i+1) \leq j \leq 2 \log(i+1)$. $T(i, j, 0)$ is defined to be a red-black tree of i keys and black-height j, and its root red. $T(i, j, 1)$ is defined similarly if its root black. The number of red nodes in $T(i, j, 0)$ and $T(i, j, 1)$ can be denoted respectively by $a(i, j, 0)$ and $a(i, j, 1)$.

(1) We consider $T(i, j, 0)$ first. The two children of $T(i, j, 0)$ must be black, since its root red. The two subtrees L and R must both have a black-height of j. The subtrees $T(t, j, 1)$ and $T(i - t - 1, j, 1)$ which connected to a red node must be a red-black tree of black-height j and i keys. The number of red nodes is thus $1 + a(t, j, 1) + a(i - t - 1, j, 1)$. $T(i, j, 0)$ have a maximal number of red nodes, and thus,

$$a(i, j, 0) \geq \max_{0 \leq t \leq i/2} \{1 + a(t, j, 1) + a(i - t - 1, j, 1)\} \tag{4}$$

On the other hand, If the number of red nodes of L and R are denoted by $r(L)$ and $r(R)$, and the sizes of L and R are t and $i - t - 1$, then we can conclude that $r(L) \leq a(t, j, 1)$ and $r(R) \leq a(i - t - 1, j, 1)$. Therefore we have,

$$a(i, j, 0) \leq 1 + \max_{0 \leq t \leq i/2} \{a(t, j, 1) + a(i - t - 1, j, 1)\} \tag{5}$$

It follows from (4) and (5) that,

$$a(i, j, 0) = 1 + \max_{0 \leq t \leq i/2} \{a(t, j, 1) + a(i - t - 1, j, 1)\} \tag{6}$$

(2) We now consider $T(i, j, 1)$. The two subtrees L and R must both have a black-heights $j - 1$.

If both L and R have a black root, then $T(t, j-1, 1)$ and $T(i-t-1, j-1, 1)$ must have black-height j and i keys. The number of red nodes must be $a(t, j - 1, 1) + a(i - t - 1, j - 1, 1)$. It follows that

$$a(i, j, 1) \geq \max_{0 \leq t \leq i/2} \{a(t, j - 1, 1) + a(i - t - 1, j - 1, 1)\} = \alpha_1(i, j - 1) \tag{7}$$

The other three cases, can be discussed similarly.

$$a(i, j, 1) \geq \max_{0 \leq t \leq i/2} \{a(t, j - 1, 0) + a(i - t - 1, j - 1, 0)\} = \alpha_2(i, j - 1) \tag{8}$$

$$a(i, j, 1) \geq \max_{0 \leq t \leq i/2} \{a(t, j - 1, 1) + a(i - t - 1, j - 1, 0)\} = \alpha_3(i, j - 1) \tag{9}$$

$$a(i, j, 1) \geq \max_{0 \leq t \leq i/2} \{a(t, j - 1, 0) + a(i - t - 1, j - 1, 1)\} = \alpha_4(i, j - 1) \tag{10}$$

Therefore, we can conclude,

$$a(i, j, 1) \geq \max\{\alpha_1(i, j - 1), \alpha_2(i, j - 1), \alpha_3(i, j - 1), \alpha_4(i, j - 1)\} \tag{11}$$

On the other hand, If the number of red nodes of L and R are denoted by $r(L)$ and $r(R)$, and the sizes of L and R are t and $i-t-1$, then we can conclude that $r(L) \leq a(t, j - 1, 1)$ and $r(R) \leq a(i - t - 1, j - 1, 1)$. Therefore we have,

$$a(i, j, 1) \leq \max_{0 \leq t \leq i/2} \{a(t, j - 1, 1) + a(i - t - 1, j - 1, 1)\} = \alpha_1(i, j - 1) \tag{12}$$

The other three cases can be discussed similarly that

$$a(i, j, 1) \leq \max_{0 \leq t \leq i/2} \{a(t, j - 1, 0) + a(i - t - 1, j - 1, 0)\} = \alpha_2(i, j - 1) \tag{13}$$

$$a(i, j, 1) \leq \max_{0 \leq t \leq i/2} \{a(t, j - 1, 1) + a(i - t - 1, j - 1, 0)\} = \alpha_3(i, j - 1) \tag{14}$$

$$a(i, j, 1) \leq \max_{0 \leq t \leq i/2} \{a(t, j - 1, 0) + a(i - t - 1, j - 1, 1)\} = \alpha_4(i, j - 1) \tag{15}$$

It follows that

$$a(i, j, 1) \leq \max\{\alpha_1(i, j - 1), \alpha_2(i, j - 1), \alpha_3(i, j - 1), \alpha_4(i, j - 1)\} \tag{16}$$

It follows from (11) and (16) that

$$a(i, j, 1) = \max\{\alpha_1(i, j - 1), \alpha_2(i, j - 1), \alpha_3(i, j - 1), \alpha_4(i, j - 1)\} \tag{17}$$

It is clear that $\alpha_4(i,j)$ achieves its maximum at t_0 $\alpha_4(i,j) = a(t_0,j,0)+a(i-t_0-1,j,1), 0 \le t_0 \le i/2$, then $\alpha_3(i,j)$ achieves its maximum at $t_1 = i-t_0-1$, $\alpha_3(i,j) = a(t_1,j,1) + a(i-t_1-1,j,0), 0 \le t_1 \le i/2$. Thus, $\alpha_3(i,j) = \alpha_4(i,j)$, for each $1 \le i \le n$, $\frac{1}{2}\log(i+1) \le j \le 2\log(i+1)$, and finally we have,

$$a(i,j,1) = \max\{\alpha_1(i,j-1), \alpha_2(i,j-1), \alpha_3(i,j-1)\} \tag{18}$$

The proof is complete.

3   The Improvement of Time Complexity

Some special pictures of the maximal red-black trees are listed in Fig. 2. It can be observed from these pictures of the maximal red-black trees that some properties of $r(n)$ are useful.

(1) The maximal red-black tree with $r(n)$ red nodes of n keys as shown above can be realized by a complete binary search tree.

(2) In the maximal red-black tree of n keys, the nodes along the left spine are colored red, black, $\cdots$, alternatively from the bottom to the top. In such a red-black tree, its black-height must be $\frac{1}{2}\log n$.

The dynamic programming formula in Theorem 1 we can be improved further from above observations. The second loop for j can be reduced to $j = \frac{1}{2}\log i$ to $1 + \frac{1}{2}\log i$, since the black-height of i keys must be $1 + \frac{1}{2}\log i$. The time complexity of the algorithm can thus be reduced immediately to $O(n^2)$.

It can be seen from observation (1) that the subtree of a T is a complete binary tree. If T has a size n, then its left subtree must have a size of

$$left(n) = 2^{\lfloor \log n \rfloor - 1} - 1 + \min\{2^{\lfloor \log n \rfloor - 1}, n - 2^{\lfloor \log n \rfloor} + 1\}$$

and its right subtree must have a size of

$$right(n) = n - left(n) - 1$$

It follows that the range $0 \le t \le i/2$ can be reduced to $t = left(i)$. The time complexity of the algorithm can thus be reduced further to $O(n)$.

Another efficient algorithm for $r(n)$ need only $O(\log n)$ space can be built as follows.

Theorem 2. *In a red-black tree T of n keys, let $r(n)$ be the maximal number of red nodes in T. The values of $d(1) = r(n)$ can be formulated as follows.*

$$d(m) = \begin{cases} h(m) & h(m) \le 1 \\ 1 + d(4m) + d(4m+1) + d(4m+2) + d(4m+3) & h(m) \mod 2 = 1 \\ d(2m) + d(2m+1) & h(m) \mod 2 = 0 \end{cases} \tag{19}$$

where

$$h(m) = \begin{cases} 1 + \lfloor \log n \rfloor - \lfloor \log m \rfloor & \frac{m}{2^{\lfloor \log n \rfloor - \lfloor \log m \rfloor}} \le n \\ \lfloor \log n \rfloor - \lfloor \log m \rfloor & \text{otherwise} \end{cases} \tag{20}$$

Proof. We can label the nodes of a maximal red-black tree like a heap. The root of the tree is labeled 1. The left child of a node i is labeled $2i$ and the right child is labeled $2i + 1$. Let $d(i)$ denote the maximal number of red nodes of T and $h(i)$, denote the height at node i. Then we have $r(n) = d(1)$. It is easy to verify that if $\frac{i}{2^{\lfloor \log n \rfloor - \lfloor \log i \rfloor}} > n$, then we have $h(i) = \lfloor \log n \rfloor - \lfloor \log i \rfloor$, otherwise, $h(i) = 1 + \lfloor \log n \rfloor - \lfloor \log i \rfloor$.

It is obvious that if $h(i) \leq 1$, then $d(i) = h(i)$.

Therefore, if $h(i)$ is even then the left subtree rooted at node $2i$ and the right subtree rooted at node $2i+1$ are both black. If $h(i)$ odd, the four nodes rooted at nodes $4i$, $4i + 1$, $4i + 2$ and $4i + 3$ can be all maximal red-black trees. Therefore, if $h(i) > 1$, we have

$$d(i) = \begin{cases} 1 + d(4i) + d(4i + 1) + d(4i + 2) + d(4i + 3) & h(i) \text{ odd} \\ d(2i) + d(2i + 1) & h(i) \text{ even} \end{cases}$$

The proof is complete.

A new recursive algorithm for $r(n)$ can be build as the following algorithm.

Algorithm 1. $t(i, j)$

Input: i, j, the row and the collum number
Output: $t(i, j)$

```
 1: if i < 2 then
 2:     return i
 3: else
 4:     if j = 1 then
 5:         return ⌈2/3(2^i − 1)⌉
 6:     else
 7:         if 2 ≤ j ≤ 2^{i-1} then
 8:             return t(i − 1, j) + ⌈2/3(2^{i-1} − 1)⌉
 9:         else
10:             if j = 2^{i-1} + 1 then
11:                 return 2^i − 1
12:             else
13:                 return t(i − 1, j − 2^{i-1}) + ⌊1/3(2^{i+1} + 1)⌋
14:             end if
15:         end if
16:     end if
17: end if
```

It can be seen that the time complexity of the algorithm is $O(n)$, since each node is visited at most once in the algorithm. The space complexity of the algorithm is the stack space used in recursive calls. The depth of recursive is at most $\log n$, and the space complexity of the algorithm is thus $O(\log n)$.

In order to find $r(n)$, the algorithm can be reformulated in a non-recursive form as follows.

Algorithm 2. $r(n)$

Input: n, the number of keys
Output: $r(n)$, the maximal number of red nodes
1: $r \leftarrow 1, j \leftarrow n$
2: **for** $i = 1$ to $\lfloor \log n \rfloor$ **do**
3:    **if** j mod $2 = 1$ **then**
4:       $r \leftarrow r + \eta(i)$
5:    **else**
6:       $r \leftarrow r + \xi(i - 1)$
7:    **end if**
8:    $j \leftarrow j/2$
9: **end for**
10: **return** r

By further improvement of the formula, we can reduce algorithm to a very simple algorithm as follows.

Algorithm 3. $r(n)$

Input: n, the number of keys
Output: $r(n)$, the maximal number of red nodes
1: $r \leftarrow 1, x \leftarrow 0, y \leftarrow 1, j \leftarrow n$
2: **for** $i = 1$ to $\lfloor \log n \rfloor$ **do**
3:    **if** j mod $2 = 1$ **then**
4:       $r \leftarrow r + y$
5:    **else**
6:       $r \leftarrow r + x$
7:    **end if**
8:    **if** i mod $2 = 1$ **then**
9:       $x \leftarrow 2x + 1, y \leftarrow 2y + 1$
10:    **else**
11:       $x \leftarrow 2x, y \leftarrow 2y - 1$
12:    **end if**
13:    $j \leftarrow j/2$
14: **end for**
15: **return** r

It is clear that the time complexities of above two algorithms are both $O \log n$.

If the number of n can fit into a computer word, then $a(n)$ and $o(n)$ can be computed in $O(1)$ time.

```
int a(int n)
{
    n = (n & (0x55555555)) + ((n >> 1) & (0x55555555));
    n = (n & (0x33333333)) + ((n >> 2) & (0x33333333));
    n = (n & (0x0f0f0f0f)) + ((n >> 4) & (0x0f0f0f0f));
    n = (n & (0x00ff00ff)) + ((n >> 8) & (0x00ff00ff));
    n = (n & (0x0000ffff)) + ((n >> 16) & (0x0000ffff));
    return n;
}
```

```
int o(int n)
{
    n = ((n >> 1) & (0x55555555));
    n = (n & (0x33333333)) + ((n >> 2) & (0x33333333));
    n = (n & (0x0f0f0f0f)) + ((n >> 4) & (0x0f0f0f0f));
    n = (n & (0x00ff00ff)) + ((n >> 8) & (0x00ff00ff));
    n = (n & (0x0000ffff)) + ((n >> 16) & (0x0000ffff));
    return n;
}
```

4   Concluding Remarks

We have presented a dynamic programming formula for computing $r(n)$, the maximal number of red nodes of a red-black tree with n keys. The time complexity of the new algorithm is finally reduced to $O(n)$ and the space is reduced to only $O(\log n)$.

Acknowledgement. This work was supported by Intelligent Computing and Information Processing of Fujian University Laboratory and Data-Intensive Computing of Fujian Provincial Key Laboratory.

References

1. Andersson, A.: Balanced search trees made simple. In: Dehne, F., Sack, J.-R., Santoro, N., Whitesides, S. (eds.) WADS 1993. LNCS, vol. 709, pp. 60–71. Springer, Heidelberg (1993). doi:10.1007/3-540-57155-8_236
2. Bayer, R.: Symmetric binary B-trees, Data structure and maintenance algorithms. Acta Informatica **1**(4), 290–306 (1972)
3. Goodrich, M.T., Tamassia, R.: Algorithm Design and Applications. Wiley, Hoboken (2015)
4. Guibas, L.J., Sedgewick, R.: A dichromatic framework for balanced trees. In: 19th FOCS, pp. 8–21 (1978)
5. Heejin, P., Kunsoo, P.: Parallel algorithms for redCblack trees. Theor. Comput. Sci. **262**(1–2), 415–435 (2001)
6. Sedgewick, R.: Left-leaning RedCBlack Trees. http://www.cs.princeton.edu/rs/talks/LLRB/LLRB.pdf
7. Warren, H.S.: Hackers Delight, 2nd edn. Addison-Wesley, New York (2002)
8. Weiss, M.A.: Data Structures and Problem Solving Using C++, 2nd edn. Addison-Wesley, New York (2000)

Author Index

Printed in the United States
By Bookmasters